APPLEWRITER™ II
MADE EASY

APPLEWRITER™ II
MADE EASY

Leah Freiwald

Osborne **McGraw-Hill**
Berkeley, California

Published by
Osborne **McGraw-Hill**
2600 Tenth Street
Berkeley, California 94710
U.S.A.

For information on translations and book distributors outside of the
U.S.A., please write to Osborne **McGraw-Hill** at the above address.

APPLEWRITER™ II MADE EASY

1234567890 DODO 898765

ISBN 0-07-881166-X

Cynthia Hudson, Acquisitions Editor
Denise Penrose, Technical Editor
Michael Fischer, Technical Reviewer
Ted Gartner, Copy Editor
Deborah Wilson, Bonnie Borzog, Composition
Pamela Webster, Text Design
Yashi Okita, Cover Design

CONTENTS

ACKNOWLEDGMENTS

I wish to thank several people who gave me technical support. Thank you, Paul Hoffman and Michael Fischer, for expert advice about different printers. Thank you, Eric Barkan, David Sklar, and Walter Prukschool, for helping to test modems. Brenda Wood and Kelly Stirn of Apple Computer also answered many questions.

I am grateful to Denise Penrose for her invaluable editorial contribution and to Cindy Hudson for her unflagging enthusiasm and encouragement.

INTRODUCTION

For anyone who spends time getting words onto paper, Apple Writer II is a marvelous help. Apple Writer II makes light work of memos and correspondence, reports, and even complicated tables. This word processing program for the Apple IIe and the Apple IIc is easy to learn, yet powerful and sophisticated.

INTRODUCING APPLE WRITER II

Apple Writer II has all the features you'd expect in a word processing program for typing and editing text. To type a table, for example, you quickly set tabs exactly where you want them. You can prepare a list of phrases you frequently type, and forget about typing them ever again. With one command Apple Writer II puts a phrase in your text where it should appear. While editing, you can delete and type over text, move entire paragraphs, and search for a particular word and change it instantly.

Apple Writer II also has an array of printing and formatting options to give text a polished look. Centered headings, double-spacing, and justified margins are but a few of the choices for printed documents. You can print an entire document, part of a document, or join several documents into one. Apple Writer II can accommodate extra-wide paper, up to 240 columns across.

In addition, Apple Writer II has a most unusual feature: its own programming language, called *WPL*. With WPL you can automate many Apple Writer II functions. Four WPL programs are provided for you; one of them lets you produce form letters automatically. It's also easy to learn enough WPL to write simple programs that streamline repetitive tasks.

The latest version, Apple Writer II ProDOS, uses the advanced operating system, ProDOS, for the Apple IIe and the Apple IIc. The ProDOS system commands you'll need most often while you work on text are conveniently included in Apple Writer II.

You can also use a modem with Apple Writer II. Modems (peripheral devices for sending and receiving electronic data over the telephone lines) let your computer communicate with other computers. Documents prepared with Apple Writer II can be sent to another computer near or far away. Information received via modem from another computer can be edited and printed out.

If you are new to word processing, the tutorial disk accompanying the Apple Writer II program offers an introduction. The tutorial chapter in the *Apple Writer II User's Manual* is a brief practice session on the fundamentals of the program. Try them both. This book is intended to take you farther — to genuine familiarity with Apple Writer II's powerful features.

USING THIS BOOK EFFICIENTLY

This book is a tutorial with exercises and explanations that teach you all of Apple Writer II's features, step by step. Technical terms are minimized; where they are necessary, they are clearly defined. In each chapter, simulations of the screen guide your progress at the keyboard.

The chapters are designed to demonstrate related groups of commands and to show you practical applications for typical word processing tasks. You should be able to complete the exercises in a chapter in one session. Succeeding chapters make use of sample documents you've already typed in earlier chapters, much as you'll do with your own work. Optional review exercises are at the end of each chapter.

Beginners will find it most efficient to go through the book one chapter at a time. Pull out the Command Reference Card at the back of the book and keep it nearby to refresh your memory. If time has elapsed between sessions, try the Review Exercises before going on to a new chapter.

If you have experience with word processing but are new to Apple Writer II, you can probably skim the early chapters to see how this program handles standard functions. If you are learning Apple Writer II DOS 3.3, read Appendix B first, which summarizes the differences between this version and Apple Writer II ProDOS.

This book is divided into four parts:

- Part I provides all the basic instruction you need to start using Apple Writer II.

- Part II teaches you Apple Writer II's more advanced features.

- Part III shows you how to use WPL.

- Part IV contains reference information organized into appendixes.

The emphasis in this book is on the many ways you can let Apple Writer II work for you. In Part I you'll type a short memo, edit it, and print it. By the end of Part I, you'll be able to produce similar documents. In Part II you'll create a table, an outline, and a report. You'll learn how to format pages, adding footnotes and page numbers. Then you'll print these documents with Apple Writer II's advanced formatting and printing options. In both Part I and Part II, there are tips and advice about how to avoid or overcome potential problems, especially if you have a printer other than one Apple manufactures. By the end of Part II, you'll be ready to enjoy the many advantages of word processing.

Part III is a thorough introduction to WPL. You'll learn how to produce form letters and how to write your own simple programs.

Throughout Parts I, II, and III, the sample documents map the development of an imaginary project, an auction for a non-profit organization. Beginning with a brief memo, the project expands, as such projects often do, to require a progress report and other documentation. In the process, you'll see how to recycle text in new documents and how to organize a growing body of documents efficiently.

Part IV has four appendixes. Appendix A clearly explains how to set up Apple Writer II for a serial printer and for a modem; it also explains how to type individual envelopes and labels. Appendix B is a concise comparison of the differences between

Apple Writer DOS 3.3 and Apple Writer II ProDOS. Appendix C explains modifications you can make to customize the program's print and tab settings. Appendix D summarizes commands for handy reference.

Throughout this book, certain conventions are used. The text you type is usually in boldface type; occasionally, it is a short inset paragraph of a few lines of text. When technical terms are introduced, they are printed in italics and then defined. The CONTROL key is represented by brackets ([]) surrounding another key. Many Apple Writer II commands are given by holding down the CONTROL key while you press another key. For example, [X] always means "hold down the CONTROL key while you press X."

It is assumed that you turn off the computer at the end of a chapter. You can, of course, continue on to the next chapter, if you like. "Getting Started," which follows, explains the steps to begin making the most of Apple Writer II.

GETTING STARTED

Before a spacecraft lifts off, the crew prepares months in advance to ensure a smooth, safe voyage. Luckily, preparing for the new world of word processing takes very little time. You simply set up your equipment and follow a few critical procedures to avoid unnecessary mishaps. In this chapter you will copy Apple Writer II's Master disk, format a disk for the practice exercises, and learn how to leave Apple Writer II.

In order to get started with Apple Writer II, you will need

- An Apple IIe or IIc
- A monitor or a television
- One disk drive
- A printer.

Although your system may have more than one disk drive and other optional equipment, you will need only the basic equipment listed here to carry out the exercises in this chapter and the following ones.

USING THE IIe OR THE IIc

Apple Writer II will work on both the IIe and the IIc. Although the IIe and the IIc look very different (see Figures GS-1 and GS-2), as far as the program is concerned, they are essentially the same.

There is, however, one difference between the two models that will occasionally show up when using Apple Writer II. The IIe has internal *slots* (locations inside the computer where parallel and serial interface cards for peripheral devices are placed). The IIc has external *ports* (outlets on the back of the computer for connecting cables to peripheral devices). If you have a IIc and the program asks for a slot number, do not be dismayed. The ports on the IIc correspond to the IIe slots, so the number to type in will be the same, even though the term "slot" does not apply to your computer.

The instructions in this book do not distinguish between the two models except where a difference in terminology affects the action you should take. For example, the placement of the disk drive (or drives) varies between the IIe and the IIc, because the IIc has one disk drive built into the computer. One or more disk drives for the IIe are in a separate device. Throughout this book the gen-

Courtesy of Apple Computer, Inc.

Figure GS-1.   *The Apple IIe*

eral terms "drive 1" and "drive 2" will be used. Drive 1 refers to the first (or only) disk drive on the IIe and to the built-in drive on the IIc. Drive 2 refers to a second disk drive on the IIe and to an external disk drive on the IIc. (See the next section for more information about disk drives.)

Some of the terminology on the disk containing the operating system utilities differs, and these differences are noted when they occur in instructions. For the IIe, the utilities are on the disk called the "ProDOS User's Disk." For the IIc, the disk is labeled "System Utilities." The System Utilities disk will only operate on the IIc, although the ProDOS User's Disk will work with both computers. You will ordinarily use the operating system utilities that are included on the Apple Writer II Master disk. On the few occasions when you need to use the separate operating system utilities, consult the *ProDOS User's Manual* or the *System Utilities Disk Manual* to review the correct procedure.

Courtesy of Apple Computer, Inc.

Figure GS-2.   *The Apple IIc*

USING ONE OR TWO DISK DRIVES

In order to produce finished documents with Apple Writer II, you will be saving early drafts, edited versions, and final versions on disks other than the Apple Writer II Master disk. You will use these disks, the *data disks,* to store the text you produce. Because the programs that make up Apple Writer II require most of the space on the Master disk, you should not save your text on this disk. Consequently, you will be using Apple Writer II with more than one disk, even if you have only one disk drive.

Apple Writer II can be used with one or two floppy disk drives. If you have only one disk drive, you can still use Apple Writer II successfully, but you will have to replace the Master disk with the data disk to *save* your work (that is, to make a copy on the data disk) and to use any previously saved work. Thus, most of the time, the data disk will be in use. Two disk drives are more convenient and faster than one for word processing because the Master disk can stay in drive 1 while the data disk is in drive 2.

Once Apple Writer II has been started up, much of the program remains in the computer's temporary memory until you turn off the computer. If you are using Apple Writer II with only one disk drive, you can remove the Master disk and insert the data disk. When you reach a point where you want to use a part of the program that is not in memory, for example, the Help menu (discussed in Chapter 1), reinsert the Master disk. Table GS-1 lists all the situations in which the Master disk must be in drive 1.

In addition to using Apple Writer II with floppy disks, you can also use it with Apple's ProFile hard disk. For installation procedures, see the appendix in the *Apple Writer II User's Manual.*

Required for	See
Starting up Apple Writer II	Getting Started
Using the Help menu	Chapter 1
Viewing the Master disk catalog	Chapter 3
Running WPL programs on Master disk	Chapter 10
Modifying files on Master disk	Appendix C

Table GS-1.   *Tasks Requiring the Master Disk in Drive 1*

USING ProDOS OR DOS 3.3

Apple Writer II exists in two versions that correspond to two operating systems available for both the IIe and the IIc: Apple Writer II version 2.0 ProDOS and Apple Writer II DOS 3.3. As the names of the two versions indicate, Apple Writer II ProDOS uses the ProDOS operating system, and Apple Writer II DOS 3.3 uses the DOS 3.3 operating system. Many of the features are the same or very similar in both versions.

Apple Writer II ProDOS contains some features that Apple Writer II DOS 3.3 does not. For example, the ability to operate a modem from within the program has been added to the ProDOS version. ProDOS is also a more recently developed operating system for the IIe and the IIc.

The exercises in this book illustrate Apple Writer II ProDOS. If you have already learned the earlier DOS 3.3 version, you will find it easy to adapt to the slight differences and to learn how to use the new features. You can convert any disks you may have prepared under the DOS 3.3 version for ProDOS, as will be explained in Appendix B, which summarizes the differences between the two versions.

If you have Apple Writer II DOS 3.3 only, the exercises in the next chapters will also be helpful. But you should read Appendix B first and consult your manual where procedures differ. Also be aware that the Apple Writer DOS 3.3 Master disk cannot be copied. A backup disk is included with the Master disk. Do *not* try to do the next exercise ("Copying the Apple Writer II ProDOS Master Disk"); it is written specifically for Apple Writer II ProDOS users who need to make a duplicate of the Master disk.

COPYING THE APPLE WRITER II ProDOS MASTER DISK

Whenever possible, you should always make a working copy of a program disk. If the copy is damaged, you can make another from the original Master disk. Accidents—a spilled cup of coffee, exposure to heat, or exposure to a powerful magnet in a piece of machinery—can ruin a disk. Or you might accidentally alter or erase part of the program. You will be cautioned how to avoid such mistakes when preserving your documents, and such drastic accidents probably will not occur. But if the Master disk has been duplicated and stored safely, you can relax, knowing that the software is still intact.

To make a working copy, you need

- The disk labeled "Apple Writer II Version 2.0 Master."
- A utilities disk (the Apple IIe ProDOS User's Disk or the Apple IIc System Utilities Disk).
- The *ProDOS User's Manual* or the *System Utilities Disk Manual.*
- A blank disk to receive the copy of Apple Writer II.

To make certain that nothing will be changed on the Apple Writer II Master disk, put a *write-protect tab* on it before copying it. Write-protect tabs are small silver squares that come in the boxes of new disks. Place one tab over the notch on the upper-right side of the Master disk.

Consult the manual for your utilities disk and follow the steps for making a duplicate of the contents of an entire disk. The *ProDOS User's Manual* explains this in Chapter 3 in the section on the "Copy a Volume" command. The *System Utilities Disk Manual* details the same operation with the "Duplicate a Volume" command. The main principle to keep in mind—especially when swapping disks in a one-drive system—is that the Apple Writer II Master disk is the *source* disk, and the disk that will become the working copy is the *destination* disk.

Insert your utilities disk and find the selection for copying or for duplicating a volume. Follow the instructions on the screen. Remove the utilities disk from drive 1 and insert the Apple Writer II disk. The screen will tell you when to insert the destination disk. If you have one disk drive, you must swap the source and destination disks during the copying whenever the screen tells you to do so.

When the copying or duplicating has been completed, a prompt will appear on the screen. Should the copying not be completely successful, go through the steps again carefully. If you still are not successful, try a new destination disk.

Once the Master disk has been copied, follow the instructions on the screen to exit from the utilities program. Remove the disks and turn off the computer and the monitor. Then take a moment to put the original Master disk away in a safe place and keep the working copy ready at hand.

USING APPLE WRITER II ProDOS COMMANDS

Any body of text you create on the screen with Apple Writer II is a *document*. When you create a document with Apple Writer II—a memo, a letter, a report, or even brief notes for a project—you will often want to save it on a data disk. A document that has been transferred onto a disk is called a *file*. Files can later be brought back onto the screen for such tasks as editing or printing by *loading* them from the data disk.

To prepare a data disk for receiving files, you must first *format* it. Formatting makes a disk compatible with ProDOS so that it can receive the documents written with Apple Writer II. A utilities program is used to format data disks. In fact, the operating system disk formatted the disk that now contains the working copy of Apple Writer II before it copied the Master disk onto it.

One of Apple Writer II's features is its ability to format data disks; however, Apple Writer II cannot copy the entire contents of one disk to another disk. (That is why you needed the operating system disk to copy the Master disk.)

So that you'll have a data disk ready for the exercises in the rest of this book, the next section outlines the step-by-step process of formatting a disk with Apple Writer II's Format Volume command, which is on the ProDOS Commands menu. You'll bring up the menu, issue the command, and name the disk.

Formatting a Data Disk

First insert your copy of the Master disk in drive 1. Then turn on the computer and the monitor. The *cursor* (the blinking rectangle) will appear on the title screen. Now press **RETURN**.

A new screen, the *editing display*, will appear. The editing display will be explained in Chapter 1. For now, you want to bring up the list of available ProDOS commands on the screen.

Hold down the **CONTROL** key and press **O**.

In this book such a *command sequence* will be represented by square brackets and the letter key to be pressed. For example, this command is represented by [O]. It is easier to type the letter O as lowercase, and that works fine, but do not type the number zero (which appears on the screen as 0) instead of the letter O.

As Figure GS-3 shows, the screen now lists the ProDOS commands that can be performed from within Apple Writer II. It is not necessary to stop working with Apple Writer II and insert the utilities disk for any of these operations.

The ProDOS Commands screen is a *menu* because it offers a number of choices. You indicate your choice by typing the letter (A to J) opposite the command you wish to select. The letter you type will appear where you now see the blinking cursor on the screen. The selection for formatting a disk is "I. Format Volume." In Apple Writer II, *volume* means a disk.

Type: I (either in uppercase or lowercase). The I will appear after the colon at the blinking cursor:

Enter your selection (A-J): I

The screen will display a new message, or *prompt,* asking you to type in a slot number, as shown in Figure GS-4.

The number you enter identifies the slot that has the disk controller card for the IIe. The correct number for the IIe and the IIc is 6. If you have a IIe with the disk controller card installed in another slot, enter that number instead.

At this point the program gives you the opportunity to return to the ProDOS Commands menu in case you made a mistake or do

```
    ProDOS COMMANDS

A.  Catalog
B.  Rename File
C.  Lock    File
D.  Unlock File
E.  Delete File
F.  List Volumes On-Line
G.  Create Subdirectory
H.  Set Prefix Volume
I.  Format Volume
J.  Set Printer/Modem Interface

    Press RETURN to Exit

    Enter Your Selection (A - J) :
```

Figure GS-3.   *ProDOS Commands menu*

not, after all, want to format a disk. To go back to the ProDOS Commands menu, you would press RETURN without typing a number.

Since you do want to format a disk, type **6** (or your slot number, if different).

Then press **RETURN** to go to the next prompt for formatting a disk. You will see

Enter Drive (1 or 2):

If you have only one disk drive, enter the number **1**. If you have two disk drives, enter the number **2**. Then press **RETURN**.

The next prompt asks for a name that will be the volume name. Every disk must be given a name before it can be formatted. Since this data disk will be used for the practice exercises in this book, name it PRACTICE.

Type: **PRACTICE** (lowercase is also acceptable), and then press **RETURN**.

Before formatting begins, a prompt asks you to double-check the information typed in so far. If you have designated drive 1 as the location for the disk to be formatted, the following prompt appears:

Okay to Format Slot 6, Drive 1 as
PRACTICE   (Y/N)?

When drive 2 has been designated, the prompt will say "Drive 2" instead.

If you have only one disk drive, you must now remove the Apple Writer II disk and insert the disk to be formatted.

If you have two disk drives, leave the Apple Writer II disk in drive 1, and insert the disk to be formatted in drive 2. Make sure

```
ProDOS Volume Formatter

Enter Location of Volume to be
Formatted, or no entry to quit

Enter Slot (1 through 7):
```

Figure GS-4.   *Format Volume prompt*

that the disk to be formatted is either blank or contains nothing worth keeping. Formatting a disk erases any files that were previously saved onto it.

Take the time to check that the designated drive contains the disk to be formatted, not the Apple Writer II disk. Otherwise, everything on the Apple Writer II copy will be erased, and you will have to make another copy.

When you have checked that the correct disk is in the correct disk drive, type **Y** for "yes"; then press **RETURN**.

The disk drive light will go on and you'll hear some clicking noises while the formatting is in progress. When the disk has been formatted, the screen will announce "Format Successful," as Figure GS-5 shows.

If the formatting has not been completed successfully, the screen will display a message, most likely "I/O Error." If this happens, check to see that the disk is inserted with the label side up and that the drive door is shut. If you should get the error message "Write Protect," it means that the write-protect notch has been covered. In this case, simply remove the tab from the data disk.

Usually, one of these problems prevents formatting. After correcting the problem, try to format again. If formatting is not successful this time, insert another blank disk and repeat the procedure.

```
ProDOS Volume Formatter

Enter Location of Volume to be
Formatted, or no entry to quit

Enter Slot (1 through 7):6

Enter Drive (1 or 2):2

Enter Volume Name :practice

Okay to Format Slot 6, Drive 2 as

PRACTICE        (Y/N)?y

Format Successful (Press RETURN):
```

Figure GS-5. *Volume formatted in drive 2*

Checking Volume Names

After a disk has been formatted with ProDOS, Apple Writer II can identify it by the volume name it has been given. Whenever a formatted disk has been placed in the disk drive, another ProDOS function, "List Volumes On-Line," can be selected to find the volume name.

Leave the newly formatted disk in the disk drive and press **RETURN**. A new prompt asks you to confirm that you do not wish to format another disk at this time:

Okay to Quit Formatter   (Y/N)?

Type **Y** and the ProDOS Commands menu is back on the screen. Now type **F** to see the volume name.

If you have one disk drive, the screen will show only the name of the disk (or volume) in slot 6, drive 1: "/PRACTICE". With two disk drives, the screen will show both the name of the Apple Writer II disk, "/AW2MASTER", and the name of the data disk in slot 6, drive 2, as in Figure GS-6. The slash (/) is a distinguishing sign Apple Writer II uses to identify the beginning of a volume name.

It is a good idea to write the volume name as well as the names of all files on the disk label so you know what each disk contains. Always write with a felt-tip pen, using gentle pressure. Of course, once the disk is in the drive, the label is not visible. Should you forget the exact spelling of a volume name after inserting the disk in the drive, you can check it by selecting **F** from the ProDOS Commands menu.

```
Volumes on-line :

Slot 6 Drive 1 /AW2MASTER
Slot 6 Drive 2 /PRACTICE

     (Press RETURN)
```

Figure GS-6.   *Two volumes on-line*

Naming Volumes

Frequently, an Apple Writer II prompt will ask for a volume name in order to perform some function. Although you can type either uppercase or lowercase characters, the name must be typed in exactly as it was given during formatting, and it must be preceded with a slash (/), as shown in Figure GS-6.

Apple Writer II will accept a volume name with any combination of letters, numbers, and periods. The name must begin with a letter and it must be no longer than 15 characters, not counting the slash. No other characters will be allowed; nor can spaces be included.

For example, the volume name for the Master disk, "AW2MASTER," combines letters with a number. A disk that will hold all of your correspondence for a month could be named "LETTERS.MAY" or "LETTERS.MARCH". However, the name "LETTERS.SEPTEMBER"—with 17 characters including the period—would be 2 characters too long. The abbreviated term "LETTERS.SEPT" works fine.

Finding disk files is easy if you invent volume names that describe the kinds of documents that will be stored on each disk. If the volume name is as short as possible, yet still reminds you of its intended contents, you can type it quickly and probably can recall it more easily.

QUITTING APPLE WRITER II

At the end of a word processing session, leave Apple Writer II by following the procedure for *quitting*. If you make a habit of quitting properly, it is unlikely that you will inadvertently lose any material that should have been saved.

To quit Apple Writer II, the editing display must be on the screen. To get the editing display on the screen from any of the menus in Apple Writer II, simply press RETURN. Depending on which part of the menu is currently on the screen, you may need press RETURN more than once.

The screen is showing the names of the volumes, so press **RETURN**. Now the main ProDOS menu appears.

Press **RETURN** once more, and the editing display appears.

Now press [**Q**] (the CONTROL key and the letter Q). You will see

```
ADDITIONAL FUNCTIONS MENU

A.  Load Tab File
B.  Save Tab File
C.  Load Print/Program Value File
D.  Save Print/Program Value File
E.  Load [G]lossary File
F.  Save [G]lossary File
G.  Toggle Carriage Return Display
H.  Toggle Data Line Display
I.  Connect Keyboard to Printer/Modem
J.  Quit Apple Writer

    Press RETURN to Exit

    Enter your selection (A - J) :
```

Figure GS-7. *Additional Functions menu*

a new menu, the Additional Functions menu, with choices from A-J on the screen. The last choice is "J. Quit Apple Writer" (see Figure GS-7).

Type: **J**

Before the program ends, there is one last chance to change your mind about quitting. The Quit prompt asks

(will lose memory contents)   (Yes/No)?

If you had meant to select one of the other choices on the Additional Functions menu and typed J by mistake, your probably would not be ready to quit. Or you might have thought you wanted to quit and then remembered that you did not save a document. Quitting would erase it. You could answer "no" here by typing N. This safety feature is very reassuring. It gives you a moment to check that you have really finished — for the present, at least — whatever work you started during the session.

It is time to quit Apple Writer II, and there is nothing in memory to be kept for future use, so type **Y** and press **RETURN**. Remove the disks from the disk drives and label the working copy "AW2MASTER" and the data disk "PRACTICE."

I

BASIC WORD PROCESSING: PRODUCING A FINISHED DOCUMENT

P art I covers the basics of word processing with Apple Writer II: how to insert and delete text, move it, and copy it from one place to another in the same document, and how to locate instantly a word or phrase anywhere in the text. Once you have typed a document and edited it, you save it on a disk. The final step is to print a copy of the finished document.

1

ENTERING TEXT

In this chapter you'll begin putting words on the screen and you'll see how easily Apple Writer II eliminates many of the tedious operations required on a typewriter. For the most part, you can forget pressing a carriage return, and, as a result, type faster. You can also increase your speed—and concentrate on what you want to say—by ignoring all typing errors until you have expressed your ideas. Then you can correct any errors painlessly and add new words or phrases so that they look as if you always meant them to be there.

For this chapter you will need only your copy of the Master disk. There's no need to save the exercises on another disk. You will learn how to preserve your editing efforts in Chapter 2.

First place the copy of the Master disk in drive 1 and turn on the computer to load the program. When the copyright screen appears, press **RETURN**.

The screen should now be blank except for a bright band with five labels across the top. The cursor is immediately beneath the line on the extreme left, as shown in Figure 1-1.

This screen is called the *editing display;* you will spend most of your time in this part of the program. The bright band is called the *data line;* it automatically appears at the top of the editing display unless you choose to turn it off. Since the data line is so

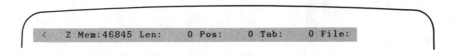

Figure 1-1.   *The editing display with data line*

informative, especially while you are becoming familiar with the program, we will keep it in view for now.

EXPLORING THE DATA LINE

The data line gives you valuable information about the text entered on the editing display. When you type in a document, the data line shows at a glance some vital statistics about your progress: how many characters have been typed so far, how much memory is still available, where the cursor is in relation to the beginning of the document and in relation to the last paragraph, and if you have previously created the document and have returned to work on it, what name you gave it.

Other information appears on the data line from time to time depending on the actions you have taken at the keyboard. An asterisk (*) appears when you type faster than Apple Writer II can put the characters on the screen. You can ignore the asterisk; or, if you prefer to see the text as soon as it is typed, just slow down.

These indicators are always present on the data line:

- *Mem:* is an abbreviation for memory; it shows how much space remains in memory for creating and editing a document. Knowing this helps you plan ahead so that you do not run out of space in memory while producing a document.
- *Len:* reports the length of the document in characters.
- *Pos:* reports, in characters, how far the cursor is from the beginning of the document.
- *Tab:* shows, in characters, how far the cursor is from the end of the last paragraph.
- *File:* reports the name of a document file loaded from a disk.

Since you haven't yet typed in any characters, only the amount of memory available when you start the program is now shown on the data line.

Checking the Cursor Position

Let's see how the data line constantly reports the cursor's position. Notice as you type in the following text that the numbers after Len:, Pos:, and Tab: change every time you type in a character, a space, or a punctuation mark. Type

Today is the first day of my word processing career.

If you made no mistakes, 52 now appears after Len:, because 52 is the length of the sentence you just typed — 52 characters, including the spaces and punctuation. The same number appears after Pos: because the cursor is now after the period at the end of the sentence, and 52 appears after Tab: also, because with only one sentence entered, that is the distance from the possible beginning of a paragraph. If the cursor were elsewhere, Pos: and Tab: would show different numbers. The cursor stops where you stop typing and indicates where the next character you type will be entered.

These indicators will become very useful when you are working on a longer document. You can easily determine how many pages have been entered by checking the length: one page of double-spaced text contains about 2500 characters. By comparing the position of the cursor to the length, you can tell whether the cursor is near the beginning, the middle, or the end of the document. Among other things, Tab: is useful for deciding how to break up large portions of text.

As you can see, Mem: has also changed to account for the 52 characters entered on a computer with 128K. If you have an Apple IIe with 64K, the number on the screen will be different; it reflects the amount you still have available, now decreased by 52 characters.

Changing Modes

In order to use some of Apple Writer II's helpful features, you change its functioning *mode*. A mode is a state in which the program is set up to interpret your instructions — different modes interpret your instructions in different ways. The data line tells you which mode is in effect.

When you first load Apple Writer II and bring up the editing display, you are automatically in Text Entry mode, but in the course of typing a document you may wish to change to some other mode.

For example, should you wish to turn the printer into a typewriter, so that what is typed at the keyboard will immediately print, you would switch from Text Entry mode to Terminal/Printer mode. You will learn how to do this in Chapter 4. Terminal/Printer mode is handy for typing an address on an envelope.

Apple Writer II has five modes: Text Entry, Terminal/Printer, Replace, Case Change, and Control-Character Insertion. Text Entry mode and Terminal/Printer mode do not show up on the data line. The three other modes do appear on the data line: when you change from Text Entry mode into Replace mode, Case Change mode, or Control-Character Insertion mode; the data line indicates which mode you are in.

Replace mode, which you use when it is easiest to correct some text by typing over it, is one of the modes that will appear on the data line as long as it is in use.

Press [**R**], which is the command to enter Replace mode. Notice that an R appears in the blank space to the left of Mem: on the data line.

Press [**R**] again. Now the R disappears. The key sequence for Replace mode is a *toggle*. Pressing [R] once turns on Replace mode and pressing it a second time turns off Replace mode. A more familiar toggle is the key on a typewriter that locks the SHIFT key for all capital letters. Once pressed, a toggle stays in effect until it is pressed again.

Let's type in some text that will demonstrate the effect of Replace mode. First press **RETURN** to start a new line. Then type

If I don't learn this program fast, I'm going to be upset.

In order to change the text, you have to put the cursor on the first word to be replaced. Use the ← (LEFT ARROW key) to move the cursor to the "t" in "this":

Press the **LEFT ARROW** key until the cursor is on the "t" in "this."

While you were moving the cursor you probably did not notice the data line change. But now the number after Pos: should be less than the number after Len:, because the cursor is no longer after the last character typed.

Press [**R**] to enter Replace mode.

Then type: **Apple Writer**. (Figure 1-2 shows "Apple Writer" replacing "this program.")

Since "this program" and "Apple Writer" both contain the same number of characters (counting the space), Replace mode offers an easy method for making this change. Replace mode is especially useful for changing numbers or characters in a table, where exact alignment is so important.

Had you wanted to put a shorter or longer phrase into the original sentence, Replace mode would not have been the best method; the new phrase would have either left some of the old characters on the screen or written over some correct characters.

You can, however, use Replace mode in some situations where the new characters are not identical in length to the ones that will be removed. For example, move the cursor to the "b" in "be":

Press → (the **RIGHT ARROW** key) until the cursor is on "b."

As soon as you press the RIGHT ARROW key once, R disappears from the data line. Pressing any ARROW key while in Replace mode will put you back in Text Entry mode.

Press [**R**] to return to Replace mode.

Then type: **scream!**

Since only seven characters have been replaced, two remain: the last "t" and the period, as Figure 1-3 shows.

Press the **SPACEBAR** twice. Because you are replacing characters at the end of the text, the last two letters can be covered with spaces (which are appropriate after an exclamation point anyway). If you wished, you could then go on entering new text in Replace mode until you needed to go back to Text Entry mode.

The data line also indicates when you have chosen Case Change mode. This mode allows you to alter the case of alphabeti-

```
 ‹ R Z Mem:46734 Len:  111 Pos:   78 Tab:   25 File:
Today is the first day of my word processing career.
If I don't learn Apple Wrgram fast, I'm going to be upset.
```

Figure 1-2.   *Replacing "this program" with "Apple Writer"*

```
< R Z Mem:46734 Len:  111 Pos:  109 Tab:   56 File:
Today is the first day of my word processing career.
If I don't learn Apple Writer fast, I'm going to scream!t.
```

Figure 1-3.   *Typing "scream" in Replace mode*

cal characters after entering them. You can change text from lowercase (abc) to uppercase (ABC) and vice versa.

Press [C] for Case Change mode. A U appears in the leftmost space on the data line, instead of the indicator (<) that had been in this space. (The < is the *direction arrow,* which is explained in Chapter 2.) Notice that the R has also vanished. When you switch to Case Change mode, you also turn off Replace mode without pressing [R].

The U in the data line stands for uppercase. As you move the cursor to the right or to the left over lowercase characters, they turn into uppercase. The cursor is now at the end of a line. It can't be moved to the right with the ARROW key because the cursor can only move over text, not over empty parts of the screen. Let's move the cursor backward.

Press the **LEFT ARROW** key until the cursor is on the "I" in "I'm." As you can see, nothing happened to the exclamation point or to the apostrophe. Only alphabetic characters are changed. But the "I" is also unchanged, because it is already an uppercase character (see Figure 1-4).

Case Change mode is useful when you have already entered some text and then decide to change the case. If you know you want uppercase before you type, you can simply press and lock the CAPS LOCK key; for example, to type a title all in uppercase. Or

```
U   Z Mem:46734 Len:  111 Pos:   89 Tab:   36 File:
Today is the first day of my word processing career.
If I don't learn Apple Writer fast, I'M GOING TO SCREAM!
```

Figure 1-4.   *Using Case Change mode for uppercase*

you can use the SHIFT key to enter an isolated uppercase character, as in the first letter of a name or at the beginning of a sentence. The CAPS LOCK and SHIFT keys operate just as they do on a standard typewriter.

The uppercase characters in the sentence on the screen certainly attract attention, but perhaps they shout too loudly. To turn them back to lowercase, move the cursor one space to the right (to keep the uppercase "I"). Then press [C].

The U on the data line has disappeared; L is there instead, to indicate that you can now change characters from uppercase to lowercase.

Move the cursor to the right until all the uppercase characters have changed back to lowercase. Your screen should now look like the one shown in Figure 1-5, with the cursor to the right of the exclamation point.

Press **RETURN** to leave Case Change mode. Press **RETURN** again to put the cursor on a new line.

Pressing [C] while you are in Text Entry mode turns Case Change mode on, displays U on the data line, and enables you to change lowercase characters to uppercase. Pressing this command again, however, does not turn Case Change mode off, as you have just seen. Pressing [C] again puts L on the data line to show that uppercase characters can now become lowercase. If you keep pressing [C], Case Change mode will continue to alternate between uppercase and lowercase. Try it and watch the data line. You must press **RETURN** to leave Case Change mode and return to Text Entry mode.

The data line signals one other mode. When you change to Control Character Insertion mode, a V will appear in the same location as the R does for Replace mode. This mode, which is necessary for advanced functions like sending certain signals to the

```
L   Z Mem:46734 Len:  111 Pos:  109 Tab:   56 File:
Today is the first day of my word processing career.
If I don't learn Apple Writer fast, I'm going to scream!
```

Figure 1-5.   *Using Case Change mode for lowercase*

Mode	Use
Text Entry	Type text onto editing display
Replace	Type over text
Case Change	Change characters to uppercase or lowercase
Control Character Insertion	Insert control commands in text
Terminal/Printer	Send and receive information via modem; type directly to printer

Table 1-1.   *Modes in Apple Writer II*

printer, will be explained in Chapter 7. Table 1-1 summarizes the five modes in Apple Writer II.

Wrapping Words

The Z just left of Mem: on the data line indicates that *word wraparound* is in effect. This means that when you type to the end of a line, Apple Writer II breaks the line and puts the next word on the following line. Word wraparound makes it easy to enter several lines of text at a time. There is no need to press a RETURN at the end of a line as you would on a typewriter. You don't have to pay attention to where a line ends, because the program takes care of the right margin automatically.

In previous exercises you pressed RETURN at the end of each line because the lines were not long enough to activate word wraparound. Normally the only times you will need to press RETURN are at the end of a paragraph, for headings, table entries or other short lines, and for inserting a blank line into your text.

To see how word wraparound frees you to concentrate on what you are typing, type the first sentence of Lincoln's Gettysburg Address without pressing RETURN. Press RETURN to put in a blank line, and use TAB to indent the first line. Remember, do not press RETURN at the end of a line:

Four score and seven years ago...

If you don't remember the rest, peek at Figure 1-6. As you can see, word wraparound has made three lines.

```
<    Z Mem:46548 Len:   297 Pos:   294 Tab:   183 File:
Today is the first day of my word processing career.
If I don't learn Apple Writer fast, I'm going to scream!

        Four score and seven years ago our fathers brought forth on this
continent a new nation, conceived in liberty and dedicated to the proposition
that all men are created equal.
```

Figure 1-6.   *First sentence of Gettysburg Address*

You now know each of the symbols that appear on the data line. Table 1-2 lists the symbols and their meanings.

TYPING ON THE EDITING DISPLAY

Most of the time, typing on the keyboard is just like pressing the keys of a typewriter. The alphabet keys operate the same way, and you use the SHIFT key to capitalize or to produce the upper symbol on a key cap. The SPACEBAR inserts a space and TAB moves the

Symbol	Meaning
< or >	Direction cursor will move through a document when searching, deleting, or retrieving
U	Uppercase in Case Change mode
L	Lowercase in Case Change mode
V	Control-Character Insertion mode
R	Replace mode
*	Typing faster than text can be displayed
Z	Word wraparound in effect
Mem:	Amount of available memory
Len:	Total number of characters in document
Pos:	Number of characters from beginning of document to cursor
Tab:	Number of characters from last RETURN to cursor
File:	Name of file in memory

Table 1-2.   *Information on the Data Line*

cursor several spaces. The number keys operate the same, except that you must not use a capital O (the letter "oh") for zero or the lowercase letter l (the letter "el") for the number 1 (one).

There are, however, keys on your Apple that are not found on a typewriter. You will use these special keys to enter text, to correct mistakes, to alter text, and to give instructions to Apple Writer II about how to treat your text.

Using Special Keys

Figure 1-7 shows the keyboard with all of the special keys. You have been using one of the special keys, RETURN, since you first loaded Apple Writer II. As you have seen, RETURN effectively ends a line by moving the cursor to the following line. RETURN also quickly makes a blank line—you need only one keystroke.

The RETURN key performs several other functions, including moving between screens. For example, you were prompted to press RETURN to move from the opening display to the editing display. The program provides similar prompts to press RETURN as needed; for example, when you are ready to return from screens, such as the ProDOS Commands menu, to the editing display. You also press RETURN to signal that a particular operation is finished, as when you turn off Case Change mode.

The LEFT and RIGHT ARROW keys function like the BACKSPACE key and SPACEBAR on a typewriter: the LEFT ARROW key moves the

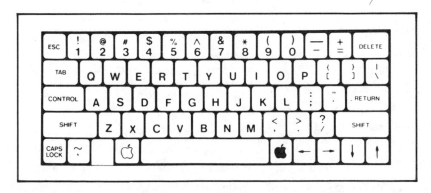

Courtesy of Apple Computer, Inc.

Figure 1-7.   *Apple IIe keyboard*

cursor back one space at a time, and the RIGHT ARROW key moves the cursor forward one space at a time over your text. While the SPACEBAR also moves the cursor to the right, it inserts an actual character—a space—in the text each time it is pressed. For this reason you cannot use SPACEBAR to move the cursor to the right over existing text.

Next to the LEFT and RIGHT ARROW keys on the keyboard are two more ARROW keys. The ↑ (UP ARROW) key moves the cursor up one line at a time (including blank lines); the ↓ (DOWN ARROW) key moves the cursor down to the next line of text already entered. To move the cursor down to an empty line, however, you press RETURN.

The ARROW keys simplify cursor movement. To move the cursor from its present position at the end of the three lines you just typed to the beginning of the second line, use the UP ARROW and LEFT ARROW keys:

Press the **UP ARROW** key once; then press the **LEFT ARROW** key until the cursor is on the beginning of the second line.

You can move the cursor more quickly by holding down one of the ARROW keys; all the keys, including the ARROW keys, repeat when held down. To move back to the end of the text:

Press the **RIGHT ARROW** key and hold it down until the cursor is close to the end of the line. Then press the **DOWN ARROW** key once.

Holding down an ARROW key moves the cursor very quickly. If you are only moving a few spaces left or right, or a few lines up or down, it is often better to press the key the correct number of times, or the cursor may move past the place where you want it.

The main reason for moving the cursor is to change text that has already been entered. You may make a typing or spelling mistake—everyone does. You may want to take out or add a word or phrase. And you may want to add some new text.

To practice moving the cursor and changing text, press **RETURN** twice to end the line and make a new blank line; then type

My favorite sandwich is a tunafish sandwich.

Removing text is very easy and quick. Simply move the cursor to the space immediately after the character you want to take out. Then you delete it with the DELETE key. We don't really need to say "sandwich" twice. Let's remove the second word.

Move the cursor until it is on the period; then press **DELETE** eight times.

The sentence now looks odd: "sandwich" is gone and the period moved over, but as Figure 1-8 shows, there is a space before the period. A space is a character in Apple Writer II. Press **DELETE** once more to remove the space.

The sentence is still peculiar. Let's take out the "a" and the space following it. Move the cursor to the space after the "a"; then press **DELETE** twice.

The sentence on your screen now reads: "My favorite sandwich is tunafish." But someone might rightly object that "tunafish" is redundant. So delete "fish" from "tunafish."

Often, once some characters have been deleted, new ones need to be added. Suppose, for example, you misspell "irrelevant" as "irrevelant." In order to correct it you would have to delete the "v" and put an "l" in its place; then you would have to delete the next "l" and put in a "v." To insert a character, you move the cursor to the space where you want the new character to be and type it in. Insertions appear on the screen to the left of the cursor.

Our sentence is now pretty skimpy. Let's amplify it a little. Type: **with a pickle**

Since the cursor was on the period, all the new characters were inserted in front of it. But there is no space between "tuna" and "with." So move the cursor to the "w" in "with"; then press the **SPACEBAR**. Usually you can anticipate the need for such a space before inserting characters and thereby avoid having to go back.

Before inserting new text, be sure to check that your cursor is in

```
<   Z Mem:46510 Len:   335 Pos:  331 Tab:    35 File:
Today is the first day of my word processing career.
If I don't learn Apple Writer fast, I'm going to scream!

        Four score and seven years ago our fathers brought forth on this
continent a new nation, conceived in liberty and dedicated to the proposition
that all men are created equal.

My favorite sandwich is a tunafish .
```

Figure 1-8.   *Second "sandwich" deleted*

the desired location. For instance, to add more sentences here, you would move the cursor to the space after the period and resume typing.

You have now seen one of the three major differences between changing text with Replace mode and changing it with the delete and insert technique in Text Entry mode. In Replace mode, the remaining text stays in place on the screen. When you delete, the text to the right of the cursor moves over to fill up the deleted spaces. When you insert, the text to the right of the cursor moves to make room for the insertion.

You can see that if you are entering text in the middle of a paragraph that is different in length from the original, deleting and inserting is better. On the other hand, if you are changing a table in which the columns must remain aligned, Replace mode is better. When you are adding new text at the end of a document, you can use either Text Entry mode or Replace mode.

You now know how to go back and correct any typing errors you made in the earlier exercises: move the cursor to the error, delete, and insert where necessary. Or use Replace mode if it is the better option.

Table 1-3 explains what each special key does. The other special keys will be explained later in this chapter and in the following chapters as you need to use them. A most important key, CONTROL, is explained next.

Typing In Commands

Word processing can do much more than put text on the screen and let you correct it. Apple Writer II is a powerful tool that you control: you command it to perform various deeds. To issue commands, you type them in.

The CONTROL key is used to tell Apple Writer II that you are sending it a command from the keyboard. When you press CONTROL, no character appears on the screen.

Press **CONTROL**.

As you can see, pressing CONTROL alone doesn't do anything; the result is like pressing the SHIFT key without also pressing a character. In fact, one of the most common typing errors an inexperienced person makes is to press CONTROL instead of the SHIFT key just below it on the keyboard. If you press CONTROL instead of

Key	Name	Use
CONTROL	Control	Give a command with another key
DELETE	Delete	Remove character to left of cursor
ESC	Escape	Go back to another part of program
RESET	Reset	Restart computer (with CONTROL and OPEN APPLE keys)
RETURN	Return	Complete a command; move to different part of program; start new line or insert blank line
←	LEFT ARROW	Move cursor left
→	RIGHT ARROW	Move cursor right
↑	UP ARROW	Move cursor up
↓	DOWN ARROW	Move cursor down
⌂	OPEN APPLE	Display Help menu (with ?); restart computer (with CONTROL and RESET keys); delete and retrieve a character
⬤	SOLID APPLE	Move ARROW keys quickly; copy text (with other keys)

Table 1-3.   *Special Keys*

SHIFT when trying to type an uppercase letter, you may give a command instead.

When you press CONTROL with one or more other keys to give a command, neither CONTROL nor the other characters appear on the screen as text. Appendix D lists all of the CONTROL commands. You learned [C] and [R] in this chapter. You'll learn more CONTROL commands in the following chapters. Essentially, pressing CONTROL says, "Here comes a command, not a text character." The key pressed while holding down CONTROL identifies the particular command. Most of the CONTROL commands are easy to remember because the key pressed with CONTROL is usually the initial character of the name of the command, as in [R] for Replace mode and [C] for Case Change mode.

Here is a command that you will probably use frequently: it clears the screen of everything you have typed and provides a clean area for entering new text. It is [N], the New Screen command. There won't be any further need for the text you've typed in so far, and the screen is getting cluttered, so now is a good time to make it all disappear.

Press [N].

Another step is necessary before everything in memory is erased. You will see the prompt shown in Figure 1-9 at the bottom of the screen.

Type **Y** for "Yes" and then press **RETURN**.

Apple Writer II clears your screen and resets the indicators of the data line. The zeroes after Len:, Pos:, and Tab: confirm that the text has been removed from memory. It's gone forever. That's all right; we wanted to erase it.

When you are creating documents and want to get rid of what is on the screen, do not use [N] until you have saved your work on a disk (saving text is covered in Chapter 2) or until you are certain you won't regret erasing. Should you press [N] by mistake, the prompt allows you to recover. By typing N in response to the prompt you are saying, "No, I really want to keep the text."

A few commands do not use the CONTROL key. One of these is the Help command. (For those with only one disk drive, this is one of the times when the Apple Writer II disk must be in drive 1 because the help information is on the Master disk.) To ask for help, you press the key to the left of the SPACEBAR that has the

```
<   Z Mem:46503 Len:   342 Pos:   325 Tab:    29 File:
Today is the first day of my word processing career.
If I don't learn Apple Writer fast, I'm going to scream!

        Four score and seven years ago our fathers brought forth on this
continent a new nation, conceived in liberty and dedicated to the proposition
that all men are created equal.

My favorite sandwich is tuna with a pickle.







[N]ew (Erase Memory) Yes/No ?  ▌
```

Figure 1-9.   *The New Screen prompt*

outline of an apple, called the OPEN APPLE key. This key and the key to the right of the SPACEBAR that has a solid figure of an apple (the SOLID APPLE key) are used in some Apple Writer II commands.

You can ask for help from Apple Writer II at any time from the editing display. To get help on the screen while working on a document, you hold down the OPEN APPLE key and type a question mark at the same time. You can also type a slash instead of a question mark for the Help command, which is slightly easier.

Press **OPEN APPLE-?**

The data line and the rest of the editing display disappear and you see the list of choices on the Help menu, as in Figure 1-10.

There are ten choices on the Help menu. As the prompt at the bottom of the screen indicates, you can either press RETURN to go back to the editing display—in case you suddenly remembered what you wanted to find out—or type one letter, A through J, to select a help category.

Type **A** to select the Command Summary; then press **RETURN**.

Now an alphabetical listing of the first ten CONTROL commands appears on the screen, as shown in Figure 1-11. Take a moment to read this list.

The prompt at the bottom of the screen asks you to choose between viewing the rest of the Command Summary and exiting to the editing display. You must press RETURN after making your choice. Let's look at the rest of the commands.

```
    HELP SCREEN MENU

A.  Command Summary
B.  Cursor Movement
C.  Upper/Lower Case Change
D.  Delete/Retrieve Text
E.  Tabs
F.  Glossary
G.  Saving Files
H.  Loading Files
I.  Find/Replace Text
J.  Print Format Commands

    Press RETURN to Exit
    Enter Your Selection (A - J) :
```

Figure 1-10.   *The Help screen menu*

Type **C** and press **RETURN**.

After you have looked at the second screen, press **RETURN** again. The Help screen menu reappears. You can select another category or go back to the editing display. When you are ready, press **RETURN** and go back to the editing display.

You have now learned the commands to bring up three of the menu screens in Apple Writer II: OPEN APPLE-? for the Help screen menu, [O] for the ProDOS Commands screen menu, and [Q] for the Additional Functions screen menu. There are four menus in Apple Writer II. The command to see the fourth menu, the Print/Program Commands menu, will be introduced in Chapter 4.

CHANGING TEXT AFTER TYPING

Since your screen is now clear and Apple Writer II is waiting for some commands, let's type in a few lines of text and make Apple Writer II do a little work while you conserve your energy. Use

```
                    APPLE WRITER // COMMAND SUMMARY              PAGE 1A
      -------------------------------------------------------------------
                          CONTROL [ ] COMMANDS

      COMMAND/KEYSTROKE                       ACTION
      ------------------              -----------------------------------

           [A]                   Adjust display margins
           [B]                   Moves Cursor to BEGINNING of file and sets Data
                                 Line Arrow to >
           [C]                   Enables CASE CHANGE Mode
           [D]                   Sets DIRECTION of Data Line Arrow
           [E]                   Moves Cursor to END of file and sets Data Line
                                 Arrow to <
           [F]                   FINDS and REPLACES text segments
           [G]                   Enables GLOSSARY creation or access
           [L]                   LOADS text file from disk
           [N]                   CLEARS screen and memory of present file
           [O]                   Displays PRODOS Commands Menu

         Press "C" to continue, or "E" to Exit, and then press RETURN
```

Figure 1-11.   *First screen in Command Summary*

RETURN to end each short line and use TAB to indent the third and fourth lines:

There once was a struggling writer
Whose workload was so much lighter
He deleted with glee
Inserted text happily
And said, "How did I manage before Apple Writer?"

Once you get your own documents on the screen in rough form, you will no doubt want to make changes. Soon you'll be able to estimate quickly whether Replace mode or deleting and inserting in Text Entry mode is the better way to change some text. The following exercise illustrates alternative methods for revising the lines you have typed. If you forget how to give a command, go to the Help menu. When you return to the editing display, the text will still be there.

This verse could certainly stand some improvement. That second line is clunky. Perhaps it should say, "Whose world grew suddenly brighter."

Move the cursor to the "k" in "workload". Then give the command for Replace mode. Replace by typing in the new characters until you reach the "i" in "lighter".

The third line could also be changed, if we wanted to say that the writer is female. Let's change "He" to "She". To do so, we can't easily replace the "H" with "Sh" because the "h" in "She" would replace the "e" in "He", and so on. Besides, moving the cursor would turn off Replace mode, and we would have to give the command again to reenter it. In this instance, deleting and inserting is easiest:

Delete the "H"; then insert "**Sh**".

```
<   Z Mem:46659 Len:  186 Pos:  158 Tab:   26 File:
There once was a struggling writer
Whose world grew suddenly brighter
        She deleted with glee
        Inserted text happily
And said, "How did I ever manage before Apple Writer?"
```

Figure 1-12.   *Revised limerick*

The last line seems a little flat. Insert **ever** before "manage".

Having made all these changes (as shown in Figure 1-12), you may still judge the result to be hopeless.

No one would blame you if you erased it, so give the command to clear the screen.

REVIEW EXERCISES

1. Type:

    The quick brown fox jumps over the lazy dog

    Change "fox" to "dog" and "dog" to "fox".

2. Clear memory; then type:

    A rose is a rose is a rose

    Find the easiest way to change the last "rose" to "nasturtium".

3. Type:

    Every day, in every way, I'm getting better at word processing

    Change the sentence to all capital letters.

2

CREATING A MEMO

O ne of the most common uses for word processing is writing memos. Whether you write two or twenty memos a week, getting one off your desk and on its way is faster and easier with Apple Writer II. Never again will crumpled papers pile up in the wastebasket because a crucial phrase was left out, a name was misspelled, or other mistakes were made that, if corrected on a typewriter, would detract from the memo's appearance.

In this chapter you will enter a short memo and correct some typical mistakes. When the document is presentable—after just a few simple alterations—you'll save it on a data disk.

ENTERING THE MEMO

Often a brief document can be typed with only a few commands to remember or adjustments to make. Although Apple Writer II has sophisticated features for formatting text and page layouts that you will learn in Part II of this book, you won't need them to create a memo.

Word processing lets you correct errors on the screen before they ever appear on paper. This is a great advantage, even when a document is only a few paragraphs long. You can type in a portion of text without stopping and later make all the corrections. It may seem odd at first to ignore a misspelling, but you'll find this method is faster. There is really no mistake someone can make in typing that can't be fixed afterwards, and the time saved by not stopping until the end can add up.

Typing the Memo's Heading

The heading of a memo usually contains a series of lines too short to activate word wraparound. You will use the RETURN key to end each line in the heading and to put the cursor at the beginning of a new line. You will also use RETURN to enter a blank line between the date and the next item, and so on.

Start up Apple Writer II. Then press **RETURN** to move from the title screen to the editing display.

When you see the editing display, type the entire heading of the memo as shown in Figure 2-1. Type without stopping to correct errors. Press **RETURN** twice at the end of each line: once to indicate the end of the line and again to insert a blank line.

Now look at the screen to spot any typing errors. Check carefully the name of the person to whom the memo is addressed; a misspelling here would be embarrassing. To correct any errors, move the cursor and delete, insert, or replace characters as needed.

Typing the Body of the Memo

The simplest form for paragraphs in the body of a memo is single spacing, no indentation of the first line, and a blank line between paragraphs. Apple Writer II is already set for single spacing and

```
<   Z Mem:46743 Len:   102 Pos:   102 Tab:    31 File:
Date:   October 15, 1985

To:   Dr. Tracy Fontenrose

From:   Lee Herman

Subject:   Fund Raising Projects
```

Figure 2-1.   *Memo heading*

```
<   Z Mem:46561 Len:  284 Pos:  284 Tab:  180 File:
Date:   October 15, 1985

To:  Dr. Tracy Fontenrose

From:  Lee Herman

Subject:  Fund Raising Projects

This year the Young Executives Association is considering several projects to
raise money for Las Madres School.  It is my privilege to serve as head of the
fund raising committee.
```

Figure 2-2.   *The first paragraph of the memo*

for automatic word wraparound. Therefore, the only place you press RETURN is at the end of a paragraph.

Type the first paragraph as shown in Figure 2-2. (Remember to press **RETURN** twice after "committee.")

Type the second and third paragraphs as shown in Figure 2-3,

```
>   Z Mem:45985 Len:  860 Pos:    0 Tab:    0 File:
Date:   October 15, 1985

To:  Dr. Tracy Fontenrose

From:  Lee Herman

Subject:  Fund Raising Projects

This year the Young Executives Association is considering several projects to
raise money for Las Madres School.  It is my privilege to serve as head of the
fund raising committee.

You outlined the main areas where the school could use our help in fund
raising at our last meeting.  My committee has decided to focus its energies
on obtaining funds to purchase three more computers.  We hope you and your
staff agree with this decision.

We are now beginning to plan an auction to be held in the early Spring, and we
will shortly start contacting local merchants and others in the community for
donations.  We are also thinking of a project that will involve the students.
If you have any suggestions, please feel free to call me at home or at my
office.
```

Figure 2-3.   *The entire memo*

but do not stop to correct typing errors. In the next section you will learn how to go back to make any changes.

Notice that as you begin typing the second paragraph, the text on the screen moves up a line and the first line that was typed disappears. Whenever the screen is half full of text, this movement will begin; each new line causes the top line to *scroll* off the top of the screen. The text that is no longer displayed is, however, still in the computer's temporary memory. Incidentally, deleting a line causes the text to scroll down a line.

Since this is the longest document you have typed so far, now is a good time to look at the data line. No matter how much memory your computer has, Mem: will show that there is plenty more. Len: and Pos: will both read 860 (assuming your memo is correct). Remember, Len: records the total number of characters entered and Pos: records the number of characters from the beginning of the document to the cursor. Tab: will show the number 317, the number of characters in the last paragraph after the last RETURN, unless you pressed RETURN at the end.

MOVING THROUGH TEXT

The text has been scrolling up one line at a time while you were entering the memo; now only the last line of the first paragraph is at the top of the screen. To see the rest of the memo, you could press the UP ARROW key, and one more line would reappear at the top each time you pressed it.

Similarly, to see text that has scrolled off the bottom of the screen, you can press the DOWN ARROW key. There are, however, faster ways to scroll up and down through a document and to move the cursor to the right or left over text.

Moving the Cursor Quickly

Six commands will move the cursor through text more quickly. The cursor can be moved to the beginning of the document (to the first character), to the end of the document (after the last character), up or down 22 lines, and left or right one word at a time. With these commands you can move the cursor to and from any place in a document without pressing the ARROW keys so many times.

To move the cursor to the end of a document with one command, press [E] (for End) and the cursor immediately appears after the last character of typed text.

Moving the cursor to the first character of the document is equally fast and simple: press [B] (for Beginning) and the cursor jumps to the "D" in "Date:". A full screen of text is displayed.

You can use these commands at any time while you are entering text. Any time you wish to see the part of a document no longer displayed because you have typed more than half a screen, press [B]. After viewing it, press [E] to return the cursor to the last line entered.

To move the cursor 22 lines up or 22 lines down also requires only one command. The SOLID APPLE key together with the UP ARROW key moves the cursor up 22 lines at a time; the SOLID APPLE key together with the DOWN ARROW key moves the cursor down 22 lines.

Hold down the **SOLID APPLE** key and press the **DOWN ARROW** key. The text scrolls up and the cursor appears after the period on the last line of the memo.

Now hold down the **SOLID APPLE** key and press the **UP ARROW** key. The cursor is now back on the "D" in "Date:". This document happens to be 22 lines in length. Therefore, pressing SOLID APPLE-UP ARROW produces the same result as pressing [B] when the cursor is at the end of this document.

Rarely will the documents you create turn out to be exactly 22 lines long. You will then use the SOLID APPLE-UP ARROW and SOLID APPLE-DOWN ARROW commands for cursor movements other than those [B] and [E] would produce. If, for example, a document is much longer than 22 lines, [B] and [E] will move the cursor farther with one command. However, moving 22 lines at once is convenient in a long document, since 22 lines is approximately one screen of text. So these two commands allow you to move easily backward or forward one screen at a time.

Once the cursor has been moved up or down to the line you want to correct, you can move it left or right more than one character at a time. You press the SOLID APPLE key together with either the LEFT ARROW or the RIGHT ARROW key.

Since the cursor is now on the "D" in "Date:", press the **DOWN ARROW** key eight times to move to the first line of the first paragraph in the body of the memo. You may have noticed that the cursor does not move down to the same position on each line, but zigzags through the lines of text and the blank lines.

Hold down the **SOLID APPLE** key and press the **RIGHT ARROW** key once. The cursor moves to the right to the first character in the next word.

Now press **SOLID APPLE-RIGHT ARROW** again and the cursor skips to the next word.

Continue pressing **SOLID APPLE-RIGHT ARROW** until the cursor is on the first letter of the last word of the line. The cursor jumps to the initial letter of each word each time you press SOLID APPLE-RIGHT ARROW.

Press **SOLID APPLE-LEFT ARROW** and the cursor moves to the space between "projects" and "to". Keep pressing **SOLID APPLE-LEFT ARROW** and the cursor jumps left one word at a time.

Table 2-1 summarizes how to move the cursor through text.

Observing the Direction Arrow

So far you've had no need to pay attention to the direction arrow on the data line. This indicator becomes important when you give

	Press		To Move Cursor
↑		UP ARROW	Up one line
↓		DOWN ARROW	Down one line
←		LEFT ARROW	Left one character
→		RIGHT ARROW	Right one character
- ↑		SOLID APPLE-UP ARROW	Up 22 lines
- ↓		SOLID APPLE-DOWN ARROW	Down 22 lines
- ←		SOLID APPLE-LEFT ARROW	Left one word
- →		SOLID APPLE-RIGHT ARROW	Right one word
[B]		CONTROL-B	Beginning of document
[E]		CONTROL-E	End of document

Table 2-1.   *Moving the Cursor*

several commands in Apple Writer II that move the cursor rapidly through text. Before giving such a command, you must check that the arrow points in the appropriate direction.

When you first start Apple Writer II and bring up the editing display, the direction arrow points left (<). Neither entering text nor moving the cursor with the ARROW keys changes its direction. Deleting and inserting individual characters does not affect the direction arrow.

The direction arrow continues to point left until you give a command that reverses it. Certain commands do reverse the direction of the arrow. The command to go to the beginning of the document, [B], changes the direction arrow so that it points to the right (>). If you type [E], the command to go to the end of the document, the direction arrow points left again.

The other cursor movements do not change the direction arrow. After [B] has been pressed, the direction arrow will remain pointing right even if the cursor moves up or down one line or 22 lines, left or right one character, or a word at a time.

Press [B] and notice that the direction arrow now points right (>). When the direction arrow points right it is said to point *forward,* and when it points left it is said to point *backward.*

Try some of the cursor movements you've just learned and watch the direction arrow. Move the cursor down and right or left while the direction arrow points forward; then move to the end of the document and watch the direction arrow while the cursor moves up and right or left.

The commands that require the direction arrow to point either forward or backward will be detailed in this chapter and the next. When you need to reverse the direction arrow, you press [D].

Press [D] now and watch the direction arrow on the data line. Press [D] again; as you can see, it is a toggle.

DELETING AND RETRIEVING TEXT

You have been using the DELETE key to remove characters from text. Often this will be the most convenient method for deleting a single character in order to insert a different one. Replace mode also removes a character when a new one is typed over it.

Sometimes it is not immediately clear whether some text should be removed. Using either the DELETE key or Replace mode could make unnecessary work, because both remove the selected characters permanently. Apple Writer II offers a more efficient method. If you might change your mind about a deletion, you can remove characters to see how the text reads without them and then retrieve the deletion if you decide to keep it. This kind of deleting — where you retain the option to restore the text — is especially handy when several characters in a series are deleted.

Deleting to the Character Buffer

To delete and retrieve characters, you put them in the Character buffer, a place in memory reserved just for this purpose. Let's delete some characters from the memo to see whether they should be removed permanently or brought back from the Character buffer.

The word "the" in the first line of the third paragraph is not strictly necessary. But it is not an error, either. Perhaps it should be taken out.

Move the cursor to the space between "the" and "early." The word "the" and the extra space can be deleted temporarily.

Press the **OPEN APPLE** key together with the **LEFT ARROW** key four times. This deletes four characters from the screen and puts them in the Character buffer.

Now press the **OPEN APPLE** key together with the **RIGHT ARROW** key four times. The deleted space and the word reappear exactly where they were before; they can be retrieved because they were not permanently deleted.

You can also delete some characters temporarily to try new changes in the text, and then retrieve the deletion. Move the cursor to the space between "shortly" and "start" in the third paragraph. Remove all the letters of the word "shortly" except the "s":

Press **OPEN APPLE-LEFT ARROW** six times. The characters "hortly" have been deleted and the cursor is to the right of the remaining "s".

Now type: **oon**

The word "soon" is now on the screen instead of the word "shortly." You could retrieve the deleted characters by pressing OPEN APPLE-RIGHT ARROW. But leave it as "soon" for now.

Move the cursor to the space between "call" and "me" in the next-to-last line. We'll change "call" to "contact."

Press **OPEN APPLE-LEFT ARROW** three times.

Then type: **ontact**

Let's get "call" back. To do so, first delete "ontact" permanently with the **DELETE** key, since we've decided to retain "call." Then press **OPEN APPLE-RIGHT ARROW** three times, and the deleted characters "all" are retrieved.

Move the cursor up to the space between "soon" and "start." Even though the characters deleted from "shortly" were not retrieved right away, they can still be retrieved. But first use the **DELETE** key to remove "oon" permanently.

Then press **OPEN APPLE-RIGHT ARROW** until the word "shortly" has been restored on the screen. Figure 2-4 shows "shortly" being retrieved character by character.

The Character buffer can hold 128 characters (including spaces and other punctuation). When characters are retrieved from the Character buffer with the OPEN APPLE and RIGHT ARROW keys, they reappear in the opposite order: the last character deleted is the first retrieved.

As the previous exercises demonstrate, you can perform such actions as moving the cursor, inserting new characters, and permanently deleting them while characters are being held in the Character buffer. The characters removed with DELETE do not go into the Character buffer.

Since the Character buffer holds 128 characters, the characters

---

```
  <    Z Mem:45988 Len:   857 Pos:   631 Tab:    88 File:
This year the Young Executives Association is considering several projects to
raise money for Las Madres School.  It is my privilege to serve as head of the
fund raising committee.

You outlined the main areas where the school could use our help in fund
raising at our last meeting.  My committee has decided to focus its energies
on obtaining funds to purchase three more computers.  We hope you and your
staff agree with this decision.

We are now beginning to plan an auction to be held in the early Spring, and we
will shor start contacting local merchants and others in the community for
donations.  We are also thinking of a project that will involve the students.
If you have any suggestions, please feel free to call me at home or at my
office.
```

Figure 2-4. *Retrieving "shortly" character by character*

deleted from "shortly" were still in the buffer after you deleted the three characters from "call." But since the last deleted characters are the first to be retrieved, the characters needed to put "shortly" back in the text could only be retrieved after "call" had been restored on the screen.

Characters deleted to the buffer can be retrieved at any point until the end of a session. Quitting Apple Writer II empties the Character buffer. If more than 128 characters are deleted to the Character buffer, the first characters deleted will be emptied to make room for the last ones deleted. If 128 more characters had been deleted to the Character buffer before "hortly" had been retrieved, "hortly" would no longer have been in the buffer.

Deleting to the Character buffer and to the Word and Paragraph buffer (explained next) are very useful features of Apple Writer II. As you become more familiar with these methods, you will discover how to delete and retrieve efficiently in a variety of situations.

Deleting to the Word and Paragraph Buffer

The Word and Paragraph buffer holds 1028 characters and can be used to delete temporarily a word or a paragraph at a time. The Word and Paragraph buffer is most convenient when you want to remove larger amounts of text with the option of retrieving them.

As with the Character buffer, the last characters deleted to the Word and Paragraph buffer will be the first to reappear when the Retrieve command is given. If you delete more than 1028 characters, the first characters deleted to this buffer will be erased in order to make room for the last characters deleted to it. However, so long as you do not exceed the 1028 character capacity of the buffer, you can retrieve any of the contents, even after other changes have been made on the screen or other deletions have been put into the buffer.

To delete words or paragraphs so that you can retrieve them, you use a CONTROL command. The command to delete a word to the Word and Paragraph buffer is [W]; for a paragraph, it is [X].

You must pay attention to the direction arrow when you use the Word and Paragraph buffer. The direction arrow must point left before you delete to this buffer and it must point right before you retrieve words or paragraphs.

Move the cursor to the space after "energies" in the second line of the second paragraph. Look at the data line and see in which direction the arrow is pointing. You can remember the rule if you keep in mind that the cursor moves to the left when deleting and to the right when retrieving.

With the direction arrow pointing left, press [W] and "energies" is deleted with one command, as in Figure 2-5.

Press [W] again, and "its" is deleted.

To retrieve a word from the the Word and Paragraph buffer, you must first change the direction arrow to point forward.

Press [D]. Then press [W] twice and the two deleted words reappear where they were before.

Suppose that you want to delete a word or two permanently. Even if the text probably won't be retrieved, the Word and Paragraph buffer is useful since you can make such a deletion more quickly with [W] than with the DELETE key.

Move the cursor to the space between "with" and "this" on the last line of the second paragraph. Let's change "agree with" to "approve" by using the Word and Paragraph buffer.

```
<   Z Mem:45994 Len:   851 Pos:   425 Tab:   139 File:
To:  Dr. Tracy Fontenrose

From:  Lee Herman

Subject:  Fund Raising Projects

This year the Young Executives Association is considering several projects to
raise money for Las Madres School.  It is my privilege to serve as head of the
fund raising committee.

You outlined the main areas where the school could use our help in fund
raising at our last meeting.  My committee has decided to focus its on
obtaining funds to purchase three more computers.  We hope you and your staff
agree with this decision.

We are now beginning to plan an auction to be held in the early Spring, and we
will shortly start contacting local merchants and others in the community for
donations.  We are also thinking of a project that will involve the students.
If you have any suggestions, please feel free to call me at home or at my
office.
```

Figure 2-5.   *Word "energies" deleted to buffer*

First change the direction arrow to point backward. For the previous retrieval it was set forward and it still points forward.

Then delete "agree with" by pressing [W] twice. That was faster than pressing the DELETE key ten times.

Now press the **SPACEBAR**. Type **approve** and the change is complete.

You can delete an entire paragraph to the Word and Paragraph buffer with one command and then retrieve it. This also saves a good deal of time and energy when you want to delete a paragraph permanently.

Move the cursor to the space after the "s" in "Fund Raising Projects" in the memo's heading. The easiest way is to press [B] to move to the beginning of the document, and then move the cursor down to the line that begins "Subject:". However, pressing [B] also changes the direction arrow so that it is now pointing forward.

With the cursor on the space after the "s" in "Projects," check the direction arrow and make certain it is pointing backward.

Now press [X] and the entire line is deleted to the Word and Paragraph buffer. The screen should now look like Figure 2-6.

```
<   Z Mem:46020 Len:   825 Pos:    70 Tab:    0 File:
Date:  October 15, 1985

To:  Dr. Tracy Fontenrose

From:  Lee Herman


This year the Young Executives Association is considering several projects to
raise money for Las Madres School.  It is my privilege to serve as head of the
fund raising committee.

You outlined the main areas where the school could use our help in fund
raising at our last meeting.  My committee has decided to focus its energies
on obtaining funds to purchase three more computers.  We hope you and your
staff approve this decision.

We are now beginning to plan an auction to be held in the early Spring, and we
will shortly start contacting local merchants and others in the community for
donations.  We are also thinking of a project that will involve the students.
If you have any suggestions, please feel free to call me at home or at my
office.
```

Figure 2-6.   *Line deleted to buffer*

Apple Writer II considers any group of text that ends with RETURN to be a paragraph, so it recognized this line as a paragraph.

What if you wanted to put "Subject:" back and then type something different? Try to retrieve "Subject:" as a word:

Press [D] and then [W].

The screen should now look like Figure 2-7.

That worked nicely because "Subject:" was the last word deleted into this buffer, even though it was deleted as part of a paragraph.

Now press [X] and the rest of the paragraph remaining in the buffer is retrieved.

Table 2-2 summarizes how to delete and retrieve text.

SAVING THE MEMO

You can now go back and correct any typing errors using the various methods to move the cursor quickly and delete or change text. With the errors corrected, the memo is a document that ought to be preserved.

```
>    Z Mem:46011 Len:   834 Pos:    79 Tab:     8 File:
Date:   October 15, 1985

To:  Dr. Tracy Fontenrose

From:  Lee Herman

Subject:

This year the Young Executives Association is considering several projects to
raise money for Las Madres School.  It is my privilege to serve as head of the
fund raising committee.

You outlined the main areas where the school could use our help in fund
raising at our last meeting.  My committee has decided to focus its energies
on obtaining funds to purchase three more computers.  We hope you and your
staff approve this decision.

We are now beginning to plan an auction to be held in the early Spring, and we
will shortly start contacting local merchants and others in the community for
donations.  We are also thinking of a project that will involve the students.
If you have any suggestions, please feel free to call me at home or at my
office.
```

Figure 2-7.　　*"Subject:" retrieved*

Keys		Function
DELETE		Deletes a character permanently
⌂ - ←	OPEN APPLE-LEFT ARROW	Deletes a character temporarily
⌂ - →	OPEN APPLE-RIGHT ARROW	Retrieves a character
[W] (<)	CONTROL-W	Deletes a word temporarily
[W] (>)	CONTROL-W	Retrieves a word
[X] (<)	CONTROL-X	Deletes a paragraph temporarily
[X] (>)	CONTROL-X	Retrieves a paragraph

Table 2-2.   *Deleting and Retrieving Text*

Saving the memo as a file on the data disk will make it possible to leave Apple Writer II and turn off the computer. Whenever you like, you can bring the saved document back onto the screen, revise it further, and print it.

Giving the Save Command

A document you want to save must be on the screen before you give the Save command. When you give the command, [S], the Save prompt will appear at the bottom of the screen.

Press [S] for "Save." The bottom of the screen should now look like Figure 2-8.

The next step in saving is to type in a file name for the memo. In order to put the memo in a file on your data disk, you must enter two names: the name of the volume first and then the name of the file. Both the volume name and the file name must be preceded by a slash (/) as in /PRACTICE/MEMO.

If you were to omit the name of the volume, Apple Writer II would save the file onto the disk in drive 1; and if you have two disk drives, drive 1 contains the Master disk. Even if you have only one disk drive and the data disk is in it now, you should learn how to enter the volume and file name in this exercise.

The data disk already has a volume name, PRACTICE, given

```
>    Z Mem:45988 Len:  857 Pos:  102 Tab:   31 File:
Date:  October 15, 1985

To:  Dr. Tracy Fontenrose

From:  Lee Herman

Subject:  Fund Raising Projects

This year the Young Executives Association is considering several projects to
raise money for Las Madres School.  It is my privilege to serve as head of the
fund raising committee.

You outlined the main areas where the school could use our help in fund
raising at our last meeting.  My committee has decided to focus its energies
on obtaining funds to purchase three more computers.  We hope you and your
staff approve this decision.

We are now beginning to plan an auction to be held in the early Spring, and we
will shortly start contacting local merchants and others in the community for
donations.  We are also thinking of a project that will involve the students.

[S]ave :
```

Figure 2-8.   *The Save prompt*

to it when it was formatted. We will name this file MEMO. The same rules for naming a volume apply to naming a file. The name must begin with a letter of the alphabet; it can contain letters, numbers, and periods; and it can be 15 characters long. The name cannot contain spaces or any other characters. File names, like volume names, should be simple, short, descriptive, and easy to remember.

Type: **/PRACTICE/MEMO**

The screen should look exactly like Figure 2-9. Before doing anything more, check whether you have typed the volume name and the file name correctly. If you have made an error, the next section will explain how to correct it.

Correcting Errors in Command Entries

If there are typing errors in the names entered for the Save command (or for any other command that requires typing), you cannot correct them the same way you correct text on the editing display.

```
>   Z Mem:45988 Len:   857 Pos:   102 Tab:    31 File:
Date:   October 15, 1985

To:  Dr. Tracy Fontenrose

From:  Lee Herman

Subject:  Fund Raising Projects

This year the Young Executives Association is considering several projects to
raise money for Las Madres School.  It is my privilege to serve as head of the
fund raising committee.

You outlined the main areas where the school could use our help in fund
raising at our last meeting.  My committee has decided to focus its energies
on obtaining funds to purchase three more computers.  We hope you and your
staff approve this decision.

We are now beginning to plan an auction to be held in the early Spring, and we
will shortly start contacting local merchants and others in the community for
donations.  We are also thinking of a project that will involve the students.

[S]ave :/practice/memo
```

Figure 2-9.   *The Save prompt with volume and file names*

The DELETE key will not remove the character to the left of the cursor, but will simply move the cursor one space left to the next character. The LEFT ARROW and RIGHT ARROW keys also move the cursor to the next character. It is, however, possible to correct an error in most cases by typing over it or to cancel the command by pressing RETURN when the cursor is over the first character in the entry.

Suppose that instead of /PRACTICE/MEMO you typed /PRACTICE/MEMS. In this instance, correcting is simple. You would move the cursor until it is on top of the "S" (if it were not there already) and type an "O" over the "S."

Try recovering from such an error. Move the cursor to the second "M".

Type **N**

Now move the cursor left one space until it is on the "N" again.

Type **M**

If you fail to correct this kind of error in a file name, when you give the Save command, the file will be saved with the misspelled name, such as MENO or MEMS. Some errors, however, can prevent the command from executing. Making an error in the volume name or omitting a slash will prevent the command's action.

Move the cursor to the "E" in PRACTICE.

Type **F**

Press **RETURN**. You will hear a two-tone beep and see an error message on your screen:

ProDOS Error: Volume Not Found

Press **RETURN** and the message disappears from the screen.

Whenever this message appears, press RETURN. If you detect an error ahead of time that will cause this message, press RETURN while the cursor is on the first character of the entry to cancel the command. Similarly, should you happen to press [S] when you intended a different command, press RETURN; do not type in any characters after the Save prompt. This will cancel the command.

Press **RETURN** when the spelling of the entry is correct. The file

```
< Z Mem:45988 Len:  857 Pos:  102 Tab:   31 File:/practice/memo
Date:  October 15, 1985

To:  Dr. Tracy Fontenrose

From:  Lee Herman

Subject:  Fund Raising Projects

This year the Young Executives Association is considering several projects to
raise money for Las Madres School.  It is my privilege to serve as head of the
fund raising committee.

You outlined the main areas where the school could use our help in fund
raising at our last meeting.  My committee has decided to focus its energies
on obtaining funds to purchase three more computers.  We hope you and your
staff approve this decision.

We are now beginning to plan an auction to be held in the early Spring, and we
will shortly start contacting local merchants and others in the community for
donations.  We are also thinking of a project that will involve the students.
If you have any suggestions, please feel free to call me at home or at my
office.
```

Figure 2-10.   *File name appears on data line*

has been saved and the name you gave it appears on the data line after File:, as in Figure 2-10.

Now when you quit Apple Writer II, you can answer "yes" to the prompt that asks if you are ready to lose what is in memory. The memo will be lost from the editing display's memory and any text in the Character buffer or the Word and Paragraph buffer will be lost. But the memo is saved on the data disk.

REVIEW EXERCISES

1. Type:

   6+7=42

   What is the second fastest method to change this into a true statement?

2. Type:

   Madam, I'm Adam

   Delete this to the Character buffer; then retrieve it.

3. Type:

   Tra la la la la la la

   There are too many "la's". Find the easiest method to remove the fourth and fifth "la."

4. Type:

   Blood is thicker than water

   Find the method that will allow you to
   a. delete "water" so that it can be retrieved;
   b. insert "mud";
   c. delete "mud" so that it can also be retrieved after "water" is retrieved.

3

EDITING A MEMO

Often you'll use Apple Writer II just to enter a short document, correct typing errors, and then print it. At other times you may need to revise a document extensively. One of the strengths of word processing is the ability to rearrange and alter a document in order to make major revisions. You might wish to reorder words or paragraphs or to take a long paragraph out of one page and cause it to reappear two pages later. In this chapter we will use the memo created in Chapter 2 to demonstrate some simple yet remarkable editing features that are in Apple Writer II.

With a single command you can move a word or an entire paragraph to another position or switch the order of two paragraphs. A word that occurs many times throughout a document can be instantly changed. You can, of course, make these changes before saving the document. However, if you have already saved your work and then have second thoughts, you can bring the document back on the screen and edit it further.

LOADING THE MEMO FILE

To bring a document back to the editing display after saving it, you *load* the file. Loading does not remove the document from the file on the disk; rather, loading brings a copy of the document onto

55

the editing display. You can change the text on the screen without making any changes to the original file on the disk until you are ready to do so.

The Load command is similar to the Save command; the volume name and the file name must be typed in accurately. Otherwise the computer will not be able to find the file on the disk and Apple Writer II will break the bad news with the error message "File Not Found." Should this happen, check the spelling and retype the correct volume name and file name.

Start the Apple Writer II program and go to the editing display. Insert the data disk in drive 2; or if you have only one disk drive, remove the Master disk after the program is started and insert the data disk.

Checking the Catalog

In order to load a file, the computer must know both the name of the volume and the name of the file. If you labeled the data disk with the volume and file name, you probably noted the names before inserting the disk. If you don't remember the exact name of a file, you can always view the *catalog,* Apple Writer II's internal directory of a disk. You select the catalog from the ProDOS Commands menu.

Give the command to see the ProDOS Commands menu, [O]. The first choice on the menu is "Catalog."

Type **A** and the prompt asks for the volume name, as shown in Figure 3-1.

Type /**PRACTICE** and check the spelling. Then press **RETURN**.

The catalog for the volume PRACTICE is displayed (as in Figure 3-2) and the one file on the PRACTICE disk, MEMO, is listed under "Name." When other files are saved to this disk, their names will also be added to the directory.

The catalog provides more information than just the names of files. Notice that the file's length is given in two ways: 857 characters in length and 3 blocks. There are 270 of the 280 blocks remaining on the disk because formatting the disk takes up some space. The ProDOS manual explains what a block is and what the other terms mean in the catalog.

Sometimes it is important to know that a disk has room for a large file when you want to add it. Since MEMO is a short docu-

```
ProDOS COMMANDS

A. Catalog
B. Rename File
C. Lock    File
D. Unlock File
E. Delete File
F. List Volumes On-Line
G. Create Subdirectory
H. Set Prefix Volume
I. Format Volume
J. Set Printer/Modem Interface

   Press RETURN to Exit

   Enter Your Selection (A - J) :a

Enter Volume Name :
```

Figure 3-1.   *ProDOS Commands menu, with "A" selected*

ment and it was saved to a disk that contained no other files, we assumed that it ould fit. Before attempting to save a long document on a disk that already has files on it, you should check the catalog to determine how much space is available. That way, you can avoid receiving the "Disk Full" error message while saving the document.

```
PRACTICE (00/00/00 00:00) V001

Type   Blocks Name            Created  Time  Modified Time  Length
Text      3   MEMO            00/00/00 00:00 00/00/00 00:00    857

   270 Blocks Available of   280 Total (Press RETURN)
```

Figure 3-2.   *Volume catalog for "PRACTICE"*

Now press **RETURN** to go back to the ProDOS Commands main menu.

To see what happens when you do not enter the volume name, type **A**. (If you have only one disk drive, insert the Master disk.) Then press **RETURN**.

The screen should now look like Figure 3-3. This is the first of several full screens that list all the files on the Master disk. When you fail to enter a specific volume name, Apple Writer II assumes you want to see the catalog on the Master disk.

The Master disk is the *default* volume; that is, unless you specify another volume, Apple Writer II looks for the Master disk, even if the Master disk has been removed. When you want to view the AW2MASTER catalog, the Master disk must be in one of the disk drives.

Press **RETURN** until the last screen of the AW2MASTER catalog is shown. The last line reads

8 Blocks Available   280 Total

This confirms that very little space remains on the Master disk. It is therefore not advisable to attempt saving any more files on it.

Press **RETURN** again and look at the menu of ProDOS commands. You now know how to use several of them: Catalog, List Volumes On-Line, and Format Volume. In the next section you will use Set Prefix Volume, and the other commands will be covered in later chapters.

Setting the Prefix

Because many prompts require the volume name, you can eliminate some typing by *setting the prefix* (that is, specifying a default volume of your choice). Setting the prefix to the volume name of your data disk designates the data disk as the default volume. Then, whenever a prompt asks for the volume name, you can just press RETURN. And when a prompt requires both the volume and file name, only the file name need be entered.

Type **H** and the prompt appears (as in Figure 3-4), requesting that you type in the volume name to be set as the default.

Type: /**PRACTICE**

Press **RETURN** twice to go back now to the editing display.

```
 AW2MASTER (05/10/84 16:01) V000

 Type     Blocks Name         Created  Time  Modified Time  Length
 *System    30   PRODOS       09/28/83 00:00 09/18/84 00:00 14848
 *System     1   AW.SYSTEM    05/15/84 12:28 01/11/84 17:51   461
  Binary     1   SYS.PRT      05/15/84 12:28 05/15/84 12:14   368
  Binary     1   SYS.TAB      05/15/84 12:28 04/20/84 14:08   128
 *System    33   AWC.SYS      12/12/84 00:00 12/12/84 00:00 16009
 *System    34   AWD.SYS      12/12/84 00:00 12/12/84 00:00 16395
 *System    33   AWB.SYS      12/12/84 00:00 12/12/84 00:00 15967
 *Binary     9   FORMATTER    05/15/84 12:29 03/15/84 15:13  4096
 *Text       1   ADDRESSES    05/15/84 12:29 04/20/84 14:11   159
 *Text       3   FORMLET      05/15/84 12:29 04/20/84 14:11   590
 *Text       3   CLAUSES      05/15/84 12:30 04/20/84 14:11   651
 *Text       1   ADDRS        05/15/84 12:30 04/20/84 14:11   263
 *Text       1   CONTRACTEND  05/15/84 12:30 04/20/84 14:12   508
 *Text       1   CONTPRINT    05/15/84 12:30 04/20/84 14:12   420
 *Text       1   FORMLETTER   05/15/84 12:30 04/20/84 14:13   453
```

Figure 3-3.   *First screen of "AW2MASTER" catalog*

```
 *Text       3   HELP40       05/15/84 12:36 04/20/84 14:23   986
 *Pasdta     1   QUARK.INSTALL 05/15/84 12:36 05/03/84 11:38   448
 *Direct     2   HS4          05/15/84 12:45 05/15/84 12:50  1024

       8 Blocks Available of   280 Total (Press RETURN)

     ProDOS COMMANDS

 A. Catalog
 B. Rename File
 C. Lock   File
 D. Unlock File
 E. Delete File
 F. List Volumes On-Line
 G. Create Subdirectory
 H. Set Prefix Volume
 I. Format Volume
 J. Set Printer/Modem Interface

     Press RETURN to Exit

     Enter Your Selection (A - J) :h

 Enter Volume Name :
```

Figure 3-4.   *ProDOS Commands menu, with "H" selected*

Once set, the prefix will remain in effect until you reset it or turn off the program. Setting the prefix to the data disk makes loading and saving files easier. If you finish using one data disk and begin to work on another one, you can reset the prefix for the new volume name.

Giving the Load Command

The command to load a file is [L].

Type [L]. Now type **MEMO** (no slash) and press **RETURN**. The name of the file appears on the data line, and the file loads with the cursor at the end (see Figure 3-5).

The Load command gives you another method for viewing the catalog faster than going through the ProDOS Commands menu; it can be used if the prefix has already been set.

Type [L]. MEMO appears in the prompt, because this is the file that is currently loaded. Do not move the cursor, and type ?.

After you press **RETURN**, you'll see

Enter Volume Name

However, since you have set the prefix, just press **RETURN** and the catalog appears.

```
<    Z Mem:45988 Len:   857 Pos:   857 Tab:   317 File:memo
fund raising committee.

You outlined the main areas where the school could use our help in fund
raising at our last meeting.  My committee has decided to focus its energies
on obtaining funds to purchase three more computers.  We hope you and your
staff approve this decision.

We are now beginning to plan an auction to be held in the early Spring, and we
will shortly start contacting local merchants and others in the community for
donations.  We are also thinking of a project that will involve the students.
If you have any suggestions, please feel free to call me at home or at my
office.
```

Figure 3-5.   *MEMO loaded on editing display*

Press **RETURN** again and the same Load prompt reappears at the bottom of the screen, as in Figure 3-6.

You might type [L]? as a shortcut to the catalog when you do not actually want to load a file. For example, in the middle of working on a document, you might want to check the space remaining on a disk and then return to the document already on the editing display. In such a situation, pressing RETURN instead of entering a file name would bring back the editing display with whatever was on it before you gave the Load command.

Press **RETURN** now (without moving the cursor) to go back to the editing display.

MOVING TEXT

If you have ever had to take a paragraph out of its original position in a document prepared on a typewriter and insert it else-

```
PRACTICE (00/00/00 00:00) V001

Type    Blocks Name             Created  Time  Modified Time  Length
Text       3   MEMO             00/00/00 00:00 00/00/00 00:00    857

   270 Blocks Available of   280 Total (Press RETURN)

[L]oad :memo
```

Figure 3-6.   *Load command prompt on Catalog screen*

where, you probably had to resort to cutting out the paragraph with scissors and then pasting or taping it in the new position. Retyping several pages was often the only way to make this kind of change. With Apple Writer II, once text has been entered on the editing display, words and entire paragraphs can be moved.

Moving a Word

To move a word, you first delete it to the Word and Paragraph buffer; next, you move the cursor to the new location for the word; finally, you retrieve the word from the buffer. Let's move the word "shortly" in the last paragraph of the memo to the end of the same sentence.

Put the cursor on the space between "shortly" and "start". The direction arrow is already pointing backward when a file is loaded, so it need not be changed for deleting to the Word and Paragraph buffer.

Press [W] and "shortly" is deleted temporarily from the screen.

Put the cursor on the period after "donations" in the next line, as in Figure 3-7.

Now change the direction arrow to point forward for retrieving

```
<   Z Mem:45996 Len:   849 Pos:   699 Tab:   159 File:memo
This year the Young Executives Association is considering several projects to
raise money for Las Madres School.  It is my privilege to serve as head of the
fund raising committee.

You outlined the main areas where the school could use our help in fund
raising at our last meeting.  My committee has decided to focus its energies
on obtaining funds to purchase three more computers.  We hope you and your
staff approve this decision.

We are now beginning to plan an auction to be held in the early Spring, and we
will start contacting local merchants and others in the community for
donations.  We are also thinking of a project that will involve the students.
If you have any suggestions, please feel free to call me at home or at my
office.
```

Figure 3-7.   *Cursor at end of sentence, with "shortly" deleted to buffer.*

and press [W] again.

You'll see the word moved to its new position. Figure 3-8 shows how the rearranged sentence now looks.

Often it is just as easy to delete a single word and retype it in another place as it is to move it. But for a long word or several words, moving is faster. Suppose you want to move "at our last meeting" from the end of the sentence (in the second paragraph of the memo) to the beginning of that sentence. You could move it with [W], [D], and [W]. Then you could make the necessary adjustments of uppercase and lowercase characters with the DELETE key.

Moving a Paragraph

Moving an entire paragraph to a new location is delightfully easy. To demonstrate the power of this feature, we will move the longest paragraph in the memo—the last one—so that it precedes the second paragraph.

Put the cursor at the end of the document, after "office." Check that the direction arrow is set for deleting to the Word and Paragraph buffer (<).

Press [X]. If the paragraph disappeared, you did it right.

```
>   Z Mem:45988 Len:  857 Pos:  706 Tab:  166 File:memo
This year the Young Executives Association is considering several projects to
raise money for Las Madres School.  It is my privilege to serve as head of the
fund raising committee.

You outlined the main areas where the school could use our help in fund
raising at our last meeting.  My committee has decided to focus its energies
on obtaining funds to purchase three more computers.  We hope you and your
staff approve this decision.

We are now beginning to plan an auction to be held in the early Spring, and we
will start contacting local merchants and others in the community for
donations shortly.  We are also thinking of a project that will involve the
students.  If you have any suggestions, please feel free to call me at home or
at my office.
```

Figure 3-8.   *Word "shortly" moved to end of sentence*

Now put the cursor on the blank line above the second paragraph. Set the direction arrow for retrieving from the Word and Paragraph buffer (>). Press [X] again and the third paragraph reappears, having switched places with the second paragraph, as shown in Figure 3-9.

Since a blank line created with RETURN is treated as a paragraph in Apple Writer II, you could have moved the blank line also, by pressing [X] twice instead of once. However, a new blank line can be inserted now between the two paragraphs by pressing **RETURN**.

COPYING TEXT

Consider how often you repeat certain words and phrases in the same document—for instance, a list of names, an important reminder, the chorus of a song. You can copy any recurring text rather than typing it in again. You can also copy some text you are considering moving to see how it will actually appear in each place.

```
>   Z Mem:45988 Len:   857 Pos:   603 Tab:   317 File:memo

Subject:   Fund Raising Projects

This year the Young Executives Association is considering several projects to
raise money for Las Madres School.  It is my privilege to serve as head of the
fund raising committee.

We are now beginning to plan an auction to be held in the early Spring, and we
will start contacting local merchants and others in the community for
donations shortly.  We are also thinking of a project that will involve the
students.  If you have any suggestions, please feel free to call me at home or
at my office.
You outlined the main areas where the school could use our help in fund
raising at our last meeting.  My committee has decided to focus its energies
on obtaining funds to purchase three more computers.  We hope you and your
staff approve this decision.
```

Figure 3-9. *Second and third paragraphs switched*

Copying text, unlike moving it, keeps the original on the screen. Apple Writer II can copy words and paragraphs to the Word and Paragraph buffer without deleting the text. As always when the Word and Paragraph buffer is used, the direction arrow must be set correctly.

Copying a Word

Copying can be a useful editing tool for adding text that includes a word or phrase already entered. If the word is especially liable to be misspelled or has unusual combinations of characters (for instance, ProDOS), copying eliminates the potential for error.

Move the cursor to the end of the document and add the text in Figure 3-10 to the memo as the beginning of a new paragraph.

Then move the cursor to the first paragraph, to the space after "Las Madres School." Make sure the direction arrow is set to delete (◄).

Hold down the **SOLID APPLE** key while you press [W] three times (until the cursor is between "for and "Las"). The words "Las Madres School" and the period remain on the screen as they were, because you have given the Copy command for a word at a time

```
<   Z Mem:45915 Len:   930 Pos:   930 Tab:    71 File:memo
We are now beginning to plan an auction to be held in the early Spring, and we
will start contacting local merchants and others in the community for
donations shortly.  We are also thinking of a project that will involve the
students.  If you have any suggestions, please feel free to call me at home or
at my office.

You outlined the main areas where the school could use our help in fund
raising at our last meeting.  My committee has decided to focus its energies
on obtaining funds to purchase three more computers.  We hope you and your
staff approve this decision.

The other committee members and I look forward to meeting our goals for
```

Figure 3-10. *Start of new paragraph in memo*

(SOLID APPLE-[W]), not the Delete command. The words are nevertheless in the Word and Paragraph buffer, as the next exercise will prove.

Now put the cursor at the end of the document and leave a space after "for". Change the direction arrow for retrieving (>) and hold down the **SOLID APPLE** key while you press [W] three times. The sentence is completed by the words and the period, as shown in Figure 3-11.

Copying a Paragraph

In memos or other short documents, it's unusual to copy an entire paragraph to include it in the same text twice. However, copying a paragraph can be effective when you would like to see a paragraph on the screen in two places at once and then choose where it should remain.

Copy the text that has just been typed in so that it can be added to the end of the first paragraph.

Reset the direction arrow (<). Then hold down the **SOLID APPLE** key while you press [X] once. The text is not deleted, but it

```
>   Z Mem:45896 Len:   949 Pos:   949 Tab:    90 File:memo
will start contacting local merchants and others in the community for
donations shortly.  We are also thinking of a project that will involve the
students.  If you have any suggestions, please feel free to call me at home or
at my office.

You outlined the main areas where the school could use our help in fund
raising at our last meeting.  My committee has decided to focus its energies
on obtaining funds to purchase three more computers.  We hope you and your
staff approve this decision.

The other committee members and I look forward to meeting our goals for Las
Madres School.
```

Figure 3-11.   *Copied text added to end of paragraph*

has been copied to the Word and Paragraph buffer.

Now move the cursor to the end of the first paragraph, one space past the period after "committee." Set the direction arrow forward (>).

Hold down the **SOLID APPLE** key while you press [**X**]. The paragraph is copied as a new paragraph on the line below the first one.

You can easily combine the first paragraph with the one just copied. Move the cursor to the first character of the copied text, the "T" in "This". Press the **DELETE** key once to delete the carriage return that is separating the two paragraphs. Then insert two spaces. The screen should now look like Figure 3-12.

Although it could stay in this position, the copied text seems more appropriate as a closing. So delete it from the first paragraph and leave it at the end of the memo.

```
>   Z Mem:45804 Len:  1041 Pos:   286 Tab:   182 File:memo
Date:   October 15, 1985

To:  Dr. Tracy Fontenrose

From:  Lee Herman

Subject:  Fund Raising Projects

This year the Young Executives Association is considering several projects to
raise money for Las Madres School.  It is my privilege to serve as head of the
fund raising committee.  The other committee members and I look forward to
meeting our goals for Las Madres School.

We are now beginning to plan an auction to be held in the early Spring, and we
will start contacting local merchants and others in the community for
donations shortly.  We are also thinking of a project that will involve the
students.  If you have any suggestions, please feel free to call me at home or
at my office.

You outlined the main areas where the school could use our help in fund
raising at our last meeting.  My committee has decided to focus its energies
on obtaining funds to purchase three more computers.  We hope you and your
staff approve this decision.
```

Figure 3-12.   *Copied paragraph combined with first paragraph*

FINDING AND REPLACING TEXT

Apple Writer II can search through a document to locate a word or group of words you ask it to find. It can search text from beginning to end and from any point in between, forward or backward. You give the Find command by typing [F]. Then, in response to the prompt, you indicate whether you wish to locate some text, change it, or change it every time it occurs in the document.

The Find command has many uses. For example, if you suspect that a word has been repeated more often than is stylistically elegant, you can substitute some other word or words to avoid monotony. Or if you habitually misspell a particular word (for instance, "occasion"), or use two spellings (like "catalog/catalogue"), you can type without worrying about consistency, knowing that later you can make one correction all at once.

Another handy use of the Find command is to move the cursor quickly to another section of the document, perhaps several pages away, by specifying a distinctive word from that section.

Finding a Word

When the Find command is given, the cursor stops on the initial letter of the first occurrence of the word in the text, as determined by the direction arrow's setting. If the direction arrow is pointing forward, the cursor moves forward through the text from its current position; it searches until it reaches the first word that matches the entry in the Find command prompt. In the same way, if the direction arrow is pointing backward, the cursor moves backward through the document until it reaches the first match.

Therefore, the direction arrow must be set before giving the Find command. Table 3-1 lists all the direction arrow settings.

The most efficient way to search through the whole document from the beginning is to use [B]. This command puts the cursor on the first character in the document and sets the direction arrow forward at the same time. Similarly, to search from the end of the document, use [E], which also moves the cursor and sets the direction arrow simultaneously.

Type [E].

Now type [F] to give the Find command. The prompt appears on the screen as in Figure 3-13.

Direction Arrow	When	Use [D]
<	Editing display first appears	No
<	File is loaded	No
>	[B]	No
<	[E]	No
<	Deleting, moving, or copying to Word and Paragraph buffer	Yes
>	Retrieving, moving, or copying to Word and Paragraph buffer	Yes
>	Searching forward through text with [F]	Yes
<	Searching backward through text with [F]	Yes

Table 3-1.   *Direction Arrow Settings*

```
<   Z Mem:45895 Len:  950 Pos:  950 Tab:   90 File:memo
will start contacting local merchants and others in the community for
donations shortly.  We are also thinking of a project that will involve the
students.  If you have any suggestions, please feel free to call me at home or
at my office.

You outlined the main areas where the school could use our help in fund
raising at our last meeting.  My committee has decided to focus its energies
on obtaining funds to purchase three more computers.  We hope you and your
staff approve this decision.

The other committee members and I look forward to meeting our goals for Las
Madres School.




[F]ind :
```

Figure 3-13.   *The Find command prompt*

You enter the word or phrase to be located, preceded and followed by a slash (/).

Type: **/committee/**

Then press **RETURN**.

The cursor instantly moves to the "c" in "committee" in the first line of the last paragraph. The cursor found the occurrence of this word closest to the end of the document.

A new prompt appears, as in Figure 3-14. The prompt indicates that you can now either ask for the next occurrence of "committee" or you can discontinue the search at this point. To stop finding this word, you press any key other than RETURN. The SPACEBAR is a convenient key for this purpose.

Press **SPACEBAR** and the prompt disappears.

Let's search for a word from the beginning of the document to the end. Press [B] and both the cursor and the direction arrow are set.

Press [F] and you will notice that the previous word entered, "committee," reappears. (This allows you to continue searching

```
<    Z Mem:45895 Len:   950 Pos:   870 Tab:    10 File:memo
We are now beginning to plan an auction to be held in the early Spring, and we
will start contacting local merchants and others in the community for
donations shortly.  We are also thinking of a project that will involve the
students.  If you have any suggestions, please feel free to call me at home or
at my office.

You outlined the main areas where the school could use our help in fund
raising at our last meeting.  My committee has decided to focus its energies
on obtaining funds to purchase three more computers.  We hope you and your
staff approve this decision.

The other committee members and I look forward to meeting our goals for Las
Madres School.




[F]ind:RETURN=Proceed
```

Figure 3-14.   *The Find command prompt after finding first word*

for it, if you so choose). Move the cursor past the slash and type **fund/** (as shown in Figure 3-15).

Press **RETURN** and the cursor stops on "fund" in the third line of the first paragraph. Yet it skipped "Fund Raising", which occurs first in the text. The Find command only locates words that match exactly the characters entered. Since "fund" was typed with a lowercase letter, Apple Writer II ignores the uppercase "F."

Press **RETURN** and the cursor moves to "fund raising" in the first line of the third paragraph.

Press **RETURN** again and the cursor stops on "funds" in the third line of that paragraph. Because "funds" contains the characters in "fund", the cursor locates this word, too.

You may sometimes wish to find all of the words that contain the characters entered in the Find command prompt, as we just did. But when you want to find the exact word and nothing else, you can do so by inserting a space before and after the word inside the slashes.

```
>    Z Mem:45895 Len:  950 Pos:    0 Tab:     0 File:memo
Date:  October 15, 1985

To:  Dr. Tracy Fontenrose

From:  Lee Herman

Subject:  Fund Raising Projects

This year the Young Executives Association is considering several projects to
raise money for Las Madres School.  It is my privilege to serve as head of the
fund raising committee.

We are now beginning to plan an auction to be held in the early Spring, and we
will start contacting local merchants and others in the community for
donations shortly.  We are also thinking of a project that will involve the
students.  If you have any suggestions, please feel free to call me at home or
at my office.

You outlined the main areas where the school could use our help in fund
raising at our last meeting.  My committee has decided to focus its energies

[F]ind :/fund/ttee/
```

Figure 3-15. *Word "fund" replacing "committee" in Find command prompt*

To try this, press **SPACEBAR** and set the direction arrow to search backward through the text.

Type [F] again. When the prompt and "/fund/" appear, insert a space after the first slash.

Type **are**, press **SPACEBAR**, and type another slash as in Figure 3-16.

Press **RETURN**.

Apple Writer II found the word "are" in the third line of the second paragraph, but it ignored "areas." Since a space is a character, the spaces before and after "are" effectively limit the Find command to that word alone. If you pressed RETURN again, the cursor would move to the next occurrence of "are", two lines up.

Replacing a Word

The Find command can also be used to locate a word or phrase that you may wish to change. Instead of finding the text and then

```
<   Z Mem:45895 Len:   950 Pos:   768 Tab:   162 File:memo
raise money for Las Madres School.  It is my privilege to serve as head of the
fund raising committee.

We are now beginning to plan an auction to be held in the early Spring, and we
will start contacting local merchants and others in the community for
donations shortly.  We are also thinking of a project that will involve the
students.  If you have any suggestions, please feel free to call me at home or
at my office.

You outlined the main areas where the school could use our help in fund
raising at our last meeting.  My committee has decided to focus its energies
on obtaining funds to purchase three more computers.  We hope you and your
staff approve this decision.

The other committee members and I look forward to meeting our goals for Las
Madres School.




[F]ind :/ are /
```

Figure 3-16.   *Word "are" with spaces in Find prompt*

deleting or replacing it in two separate operations, you can find
and replace it all at once. You do this by entering the change to be
made in the Find command prompt.

Since the phrase "fund raising" occurs so often in the memo,
we can replace it in one instance.

Press **SPACEBAR** and then [F]. Type over the word "are" in the
prompt and then complete the entry as follows:

/fund raising/projects/

Press **RETURN** and the cursor moves to "fund raising" in the
third line of the first paragraph, and a new prompt appears, as in
Figure 3-17.

Type **Y** and "projects" replaces "fund raising", as in Figure 3-
18. Pressing RETURN at this point would have put thc cursor on the
next occurrence of "fund raising" without making the replacement.

The Find command also provides a shortcut for finding and

```
<    Z Mem:45895 Len:   950 Pos:   261 Tab:   157 File:memo
Date:  October 15, 1985

To:  Dr. Tracy Fontenrose

From:  Lee Herman

Subject:  Fund Raising Projects

This year the Young Executives Association is considering several projects to
raise money for Las Madres School.  It is my privilege to serve as head of the
fund raising committee.

We are now beginning to plan an auction to be held in the early Spring, and we
will start contacting local merchants and others in the community for
donations shortly.  We are also thinking of a project that will involve the
students.  If you have any suggestions, please feel free to call me at home or
at my office.

You outlined the main areas where the school could use our help in fund
raising at our last meeting.  My committee has decided to focus its energies

[F]ind:RETURN=Proceed / Y=Replace
```

Figure 3-17.   *Find and Replace prompt*

```
< Z Mem:45899 Len:  946 Pos:  260 Tab:  156 File:memo
Date:  October 15, 1985

To:  Dr. Tracy Fontenrose

From:  Lee Herman

Subject:  Fund Raising Projects

This year the Young Executives Association is considering several projects to
raise money for Las Madres School.  It is my privilege to serve as head of the
projects committee.

We are now beginning to plan an auction to be held in the early Spring, and we
will start contacting local merchants and others in the community for
donations shortly.  We are also thinking of a project that will involve the
students.  If you have any suggestions, please feel free to call me at home or
at my office.

You outlined the main areas where the school could use our help in fund
raising at our last meeting.  My committee has decided to focus its energies

[F]ind:RETURN=Proceed
```

Figure 3-18. *Phrase "fund raising" replaced by word "projects"*

replacing a word or phrase throughout a document. After typing the text to be found and the text to replace it between slashes, you type **A** for "all." When you press RETURN, the program immediately replaces all matches. The cursor does not stop at each one and wait for your response to the prompt. For example, to replace all instances of "fund raising" with "projects," the entry would be "/fund raising/projects/a".

The slashes that must precede and follow the entries for the Find command are called *delimiters*; they mark off or delimit the text to be located, so that Apple Writer II can distinguish it from the rest of the text in a document.

The delimiter can only mark off text that does not already contain the same mark. Suppose, for instance, that you wanted to replace "their" with "his/her". In order to use the Find command to make this substitution, you would have to enter some other set of delimiters. The exclamation point can also delimit text in the Find command prompt. So the entry in this situation could be "!their!his/her!"; the exclamation point separates "their" from "his/her".

Press **SPACEBAR** now to cancel the Find command. Having revised the memo, we'll save it in the next section.

SAVING AN EDITED MEMO

None of the editing changes made to the memo in this chapter has had any effect on the version that was saved on the data disk. If you cleared the screen now, MEMO on the data disk would be just as it was before it was loaded. Therefore, to preserve the changes, you must save the revised memo.

Give the Save command and notice that the prompt already says "MEMO." The prefix is still set to PRACTICE, the volume name of the data disk. You need not type in anything. Simply move the cursor past the "O" with the **RIGHT ARROW** key and press **RETURN**.

A new prompt appears:

Delete old MEMO (Yes/No) ?

This prompt is a safety feature. In case you started to give the Save command accidentally, when a new version was not complete, you could cancel the command by typing N.

You can also give the Save command for an edited file by typing [S]=. When you give the Save command this way, you do not see a prompt asking you to confirm that you do intend to delete the earlier version of the file.

Type **Y** and press **RETURN**.

The light goes on, the disk whirrs, and the edited memo is saved while the earlier version is deleted. The memo is ready to be prepared for printing, which you will do in the next chapter.

REVIEW EXERCISES

1. In the following sentence, switch the order of the two actions:

   In the event of a fire, first notify the fire department, then vacate the building.

2. Type the following and copy as much as you can:

> My bonny lies over the ocean
> My bonny lies over the sea
> My bonny lies over the ocean
> O bring back my bonny to me.

3. Type:

> Hamlet is a successful army commander who falls in love with the beautiful Desdemona. Hamlet marries Desdemone, but Iago makes him jealous and, after killing Desdemoana, Hamlet kills himself.

> Find and replace all instances of "Hamlet" with "Othello." Then use the Find command to correct any misspellings of "Desdemona."

4

PRINTING A MEMO

Watching a perfect copy of a document emerge from the printer is an exciting, satisfying moment. The paper copy, called a *hard copy* or *printout,* to distinguish it from the electronic copy on the data disk, is for most people the goal of word processing. We produce a document on paper so that it can be sent in this familiar, tangible form to someone else. Although alternative means of transmitting documents are available, such as sending the disk itself or sending the document via a modem to another computer, printing a hard copy is still the most common way to distribute a word processed document.

In this chapter you'll learn how to print the memo and how to specify the document's appearance on the printed page, using Apple Writer II's *printing* and *formatting* commands. Printing commands tell the printer whether you are using single sheets or fanfold paper, for example. Formatting commands determine how and where the text will be placed on the page—the size of margins, number of spaces between lines, and such special formats as page numbers and footnotes.

This chapter introduces only the basic printing functions. Apple Writer II's more advanced printing capabilities are covered in later chapters. In Chapters 7 through 9 you will produce a variety of printed documents, and in Chapters 10 and 11 you will streamline and customize printing with WPL programs. But by the end of this chapter you'll be able to print your own memos, letters, and other similar documents.

Before continuing, you may need to make some preliminary adjustments to your printer. If you have a serial printer, read "Setting the Printer/Modem Interface" in Appendix A; it explains how to inform Apple Writer II about the printer's specifications. To find out whether your printer is serial or parallel, check your printer manual.

If you have a parallel printer and you get unusual results, such as extra blank lines on the page, consult your dealer. Apple Writer II sometimes communicates less effectively with printers not manufactured by Apple. Apple has been fixing this problem, and your dealer should be aware of ways to make different parallel printers fully compatible with Apple Writer II.

No matter what kind of printer you have, the printer interface card should be installed in slot 1 on the Apple IIe. If the printer interface card cannot occupy slot 1, you will have to tell Apple Writer II which slot it is in, by setting the print destination (as explained in the next section). The printer port for the Apple IIc is port 1.

Finally, check that the printer is properly connected and plugged in. Before giving the Print command, turn on the printer and see that the paper is in place.

CHOOSING FROM THE PRINT/PROGRAM COMMANDS MENU

With Apple Writer II a document can be entered in its entirety and then made ready for printing in one operation. To print the memo, you need only select a few simple printing and formatting commands from Apple Writer II's fourth menu, the Print/Program Commands menu.

Load the MEMO file. The file to be printed must always be loaded into the computer's memory before the Print command is given. With MEMO on the editing display, you can begin to select options from the Print/Program Commands menu.

Press [P] and then type ?. Typing the question mark from the editing display requests this menu. The screen should look like Figure 4-1.

Press **RETURN** and the Print/Program Commands menu

appears, as in Figure 4-2. The sixteen items on the menu offer considerable flexibility in determining the finished appearance of a document.

The last column of the menu contains a default value; that is, Apple Writer II is already set to make these choices. For example, the default value for "Line Interval" (LI) is zero. The zero value for this item tells the printer to single space each line. (A value of 1 indicates double spacing; 2 indicates triple spacing).

You can change any value on the menu, and the menu will display the new value. Once changed, the command keeps that value until you reset it or turn off the computer.

Printing Commands

There are three printing commands on the Print/Program Commands menu: SP indicates the type of paper; PD identifies the slot

```
<   Z Mem:45899 Len:   946 Pos:   946 Tab:    90 File:memo
will start contacting local merchants and others in the community for
donations shortly.  We are also thinking of a project that will involve the
students.  If you have any suggestions, please feel free to call me at home or
at my office.

You outlined the main areas where the school could use our help in fund
raising at our last meeting.  My committee has decided to focus its energies
on obtaining funds to purchase three more computers.  We hope you and your
staff approve this decision.

The other committee members and I look forward to meeting our goals for Las
Madres School.




[P]rint/Program :?
```

Figure 4-1.   *Giving the [P]? command*

```
Print/Program Commands:

Left        Margin    (LM) = 0
Paragraph Margin      (PM) = 0
Right       Margin    (RM) = 78
Top         Margin    (TM) = 1
Bottom      Margin    (BM) = 1
Page Number           (PN) = 1
Printed Lines         (PL) = 58
Page Interval         (PI) = 66
Line Interval         (LI) = 0
Single Page           (SP) = 0
Print Destination     (PD) = 1
Carriage Return       (CR) = 1
Underline Token       (UT) = \
Print Mode (LJ,FJ,CJ,RJ) = LJ
Top Line              (TL) :

Bottom Line           (BL) :

Press RETURN to Exit

[P]rint/Program :
```

Figure 4-2.   *The Print/Program Commands menu*

or port to which the printer is connected; and CR coordinates carriage returns between Apple Writer II and the printer. It is most important for smooth printing that these be set properly.

To change a particular value, you type the two-letter command, the new value, and press RETURN. Apple Writer II immediately updates the menu to reflect the change. The prompt then reappears so that another value can be changed. When all the changes have been entered, pressing RETURN brings back the editing display with the loaded document on the screen. We'll set SP, PD, and CR now, before printing the memo.

The SP (Single Page) command is already set for continuous fanfold paper. If you wish to print separate sheets of paper, you must change the value. Leave SP set to zero if you have fanfold paper in your printer.

To print with separate sheets, type SP 1 and press RETURN. Once this value has been set, the printer stops after each page so that you can insert the next sheet of paper. It resumes printing when you press RETURN.

The PD (Print Destination) command identifies the computer slot or port through which Apple Writer II will communicate with the printer. If your printer interface card is in slot 1 or if you are using an Apple IIc, you can leave the default setting at 1. If the printer interface card is in a different slot, change the value for PD to the number of that slot: type PD, the number of the slot, and press RETURN.

There are two other possible print destinations. Apple Writer II can print to the screen and to a modem. Printing to the screen enables you to see on the screen how formatted text will look when printed on paper. This feature is demonstrated in Chapter 7. Printing to a modem sends your documents electronically to another computer. Appendix A explains how to use a modem with Apple Writer II.

A carriage return on a printer accomplishes the same result as it does on a typewriter: the printhead is repositioned on the first space of a new line. On a typewriter, pressing the carriage return key triggers a mechanical operation; in Apple Writer II, CR (Carriage Return) is a command to issue a line feed that will reposition the printhead at the end of each line automatically.

Apple Writer II needs to know which device should handle the line feed: the computer or the printer (or in some cases, the interface card). Your printer may be set up to issue a line feed. Check the manual for the printer to find out how it handles the end of a line. Many printers can be adjusted so that the printer does or does not issue a line feed with a carriage return.

The default value for CR (Carriage Return) is 1; this means that Apple Writer II issues a line feed for each carriage return. If your printer issues its own line feed command, change the value to 0. If not, leave the default value as it is.

Table 4-1 summarizes the printing commands on the Print/Program Commands menu.

Formatting Commands

The remaining choices on the Print/Program Commands menu allow you to design the appearance of text on the printed page by changing the default values. Some default values are set exactly as you will want them to be for most printouts.

For example, the PI command (Page Interval) specifies how

Keys	Command	Default	Function
SP	Single Page	0	Set printer for fan-fold or continuous paper
PD	Print Destination	1	Send output to printer connected to card in slot 1 or to port 1
CR	Carriage Return	1	Insert a carriage return/linefeed at end of line

Table 4-1.   *Printing Commands on the Print/Program Commands Menu*

many lines to the page. It is set to 66; this figure includes the number of blank lines for the top and bottom margins, the headings and footnotes, and the body of the text. A standard page is 11 inches long and a printer typically prints six lines of text per inch. This value would be changed to use paper of a different length or, if your printer can produce condensed type, to increase the number of lines of text per inch.

Similarly, the default value for "Page Number" (PN) will probably not need changing often. Apple Writer II counts the number of pages in a document. When the value is 1, the counting begins with the number 1 for the first page of the document. Setting the page number does not, however, cause the number to be printed on the page.

While the various formatting commands are all useful and convenient for printing different kinds of documents, you can print a short document that requires only minimal formatting, such as the memo we've been working on, leaving most of the default values unchanged. Single spacing is appropriate for the memo, as is the default for "Print Mode" (LJ), which lines up or *justifies* the text along the left margin.

There is no underlined text in the memo, so "Underline Token" (UT) can be ignored for now. Nor is there any text to be printed at the top or the bottom of the page; therefore, the values for TL ("Top Line") and BL ("Bottom Line") are of no concern at this point. While these have default settings, they are not in effect unless you use them in a document.

The default values for the left and right margins need to be changed. Apple Writer II is set to put 78 characters on a line, beginning at the left edge of the paper. The 78-character line allows you to see as much text as possible on the screen while entering a document. However, most printouts will be more attractive and more readable with adjusted side margins.

The values for the left and right margin refer to number of characters, not to inches. Thus, a value of 5 for the left margin will start the line of text five spaces from the left. To leave space in the right margin, you decide how many characters you want in a line of text and count from the left. Subtracting the left margin value from the right margin value will give you the maximum number of characters per line. For example, setting LM to 10 and RM to 75 allows for a maximum of 65 characters per line.

Because of differences in the size of type in different printers, you may have to experiment a bit in order to establish which left and right margin settings you prefer. But after printing a few times, the results will soon show which values provide the desired margins.

Let's set the left and right margins to print the memo with a 65-character line.

Type **LM 10** and press **RETURN**.

When the new value has appeared on the menu, type **RM 75** and press **RETURN**.

We won't set the value for PM (Paragraph Margin) to print the memo. The PM command indents the first line of a paragraph a specified number of spaces beyond the left margin. But the memo will look better without indenting the paragraphs. Moreover, since the paragraph margin value takes effect after each RETURN (normally the end of a paragraph), the short lines of the heading that were broken with RETURN would also be indented as paragraphs. In a brief document, it is easy enough to indent the first line of each paragraph with the TAB key. You'll learn how to indent selected paragraphs in Chapter 7.

Two other choices on the Print/Program Commands menu could also be set: "Top Margin" (TM) and "Bottom Margin" (BM). The text of the memo will not reach the bottom of the page, so there is no need to change the bottom margin value. The top margin is presently set to begin printing on the second line of the page and the printout would be more attractive if the text started lower on the page. Therefore, change the top margin to make

```
Print/Program Commands:

Left        Margin    (LM)  =  10
Paragraph Margin      (PM)  =  0
Right       Margin    (RM)  =  75
Top         Margin    (TM)  =  4
Bottom      Margin    (BM)  =  1
Page Number           (PN)  =  1
Printed Lines         (PL)  =  58
Page Interval         (PI)  =  66
Line Interval         (LI)  =  0
Single Page           (SP)  =  0
Print Destination     (PD)  =  1
Carriage Return       (CR)  =  0
Underline Token       (UT)  =  \
Print Mode (LJ,FJ,CJ,RJ)  =  LJ
Top Line              (TL)  :

Bottom Line           (BL)  :

Press RETURN to Exit

[P]rint/Program :
```

Figure 4-3.   *The Print/Program Commands menu with values changed*

some room at the top of the memo.

Type **TM** 4 and press **RETURN**.

The Print/Program Commands menu now reflects all the changed values. Figure 4-3 shows the menu set for a printer connected to slot 1 that issues its own line feed and prints on fanfold paper. The left margin is set at 10, the right margin at 75, and the top margin at 4. The other commands still reflect the default values. Table 4-2 summarizes the formatting commands on the Print/Program Commands menu.

Adjusting Screen Margins

Now that you have specified the various printing and formatting values, return to the editing display. Notice that the memo on the screen has not been affected by the changes made to the Print/Program Commands menu. In particular, the number of characters

Keys	Command	Default	Function
LM	Left Margin	0	Set left margin.
PM	Paragraph Margin	0	Indents first line of paragraph
RM	Right Margin	78	Sets right margin
TM	Top Margin	1	Sets blank line(s) between header and first line of text
BM	Bottom Margin	1	Sets blank line(s) between last line of page text and footer
PN	Page Number	1	Sets number of first page for counting
PL	Printed Lines	58	Sets total number of printed lines on a page
PI	Page Interval	66	Sets number of lines per page from top to bottom edge of paper
LI	Line Interval	0	Sets line spacing
UT	Underline Token	\	Marks text to be underlined
LJ FJ CJ RJ	Print Mode	LJ	Sets how text is distributed between left and right margin
TL	Top Line	(blank)	Formats a header or page number
BL	Bottom Line	(blank)	Formats a footer or page number

Table 4-2.   *Formatting Commands on the Print/Program Commands Menu*

per line of text on the screen is still 78, not 65 (as the first line of the third paragraph, with 77 characters, illustrates).

Once the left and right margin values have been set for printing, the line of text on the screen can be adjusted to match the side margins, which will appear on the printed page. You use the Adjust Screen Display command, which is [A], to change the length of the line on the screen to reflect the values you have set on the Print/Program Commands menu.

Type [A] and the prompt appears, as in Figure 4-4.

Type **Y** to indicate that the side margins on the screen should match the new values and press **RETURN**.

Word wraparound reforms all the lines instantly, so that now the longest line is the first one in the first paragraph, with 65 characters. (See Figure 4-5.)

Adjusting the margins on the screen gives you a better idea of how the memo will look when printed. Once you have given the command to adjust the screen margins, the current values for the left and right margins stay in effect for text displayed on the screen until the computer is turned off. If you create new text or load another file, the text will be displayed on the screen with 65 char-

```
<   Z Mem:45899 Len:   946 Pos:   946 Tab:    90 File:memo
will start contacting local merchants and others in the community for
donations shortly.  We are also thinking of a project that will involve the
students.  If you have any suggestions, please feel free to call me at home or
at my office.

You outlined the main areas where the school could use our help in fund
raising at our last meeting.  My committee has decided to focus its energies
on obtaining funds to purchase three more computers.  We hope you and your
staff approve this decision.

The other committee members and I look forward to meeting our goals for Las
Madres School.




[A]djust display margins (Yes/No) ?
```

Figure 4-4. *Giving the Adjust Screen Display command*

```
<   Z Mem:45899 Len:  946 Pos:  946 Tab:   90 File:memo
Spring, and we will start contacting local merchants and others
in the community for donations shortly.  We are also thinking of
a project that will involve the students.  If you have any
suggestions, please feel free to call me at home or at my office.

You outlined the main areas where the school could use our help
in fund raising at our last meeting.  My committee has decided to
focus its energies on obtaining funds to purchase three more
computers.  We hope you and your staff approve this decision.

The other committee members and I look forward to meeting our
goals for Las Madres School.
```

Figure 4-5. *Left and right screen margins adjusted*

acters per line, unless you reset the Print/Program Commands menu and then give the Adjust Screen Display command again.

GIVING THE PRINT COMMAND

You give the Print command by typing [P] and then NP from the editing display when a file has been loaded into memory. The MEMO file is loaded and you have made all the preparations for printing, except for the final one: turn your printer on now.

Type [P] and **NP**.

Then press **RETURN**. Figure 4-6 shows a printout of the memo.

But what if you want to use letterhead stationery? The current top margin does not leave enough space. You can, however, change the top margin—and any of the other values for the printing and formatting values—without going back to the Print/Program Commands menu. Especially when you are going to make just one change, use this shortcut:

Type [P]. Then, instead of the question mark, type **TM 6**. Press **RETURN**.

The new value for the top margin has been entered on the Print/Program Commands menu. If you were to bring the menu on the screen now, it would show a 6 for the top margin. That is, however, an unnecessary step.

```
Date:  October 15, 1985

To:  Dr. Tracy Fontenrose

From:  Lee Herman

Subject:  Fund Raising Projects

This year the Young Executives Association is considering several
projects to raise money for Las Madres School.  It is my
privilege to serve as head of the projects committee.

We are now beginning to plan an auction to be held in the early
Spring, and we will start contacting local merchants and others
in the community for donations shortly.  We are also thinking of
a project that will involve the students.  If you have any
suggestions, please feel free to call me at home or at my office.

You outlined the main areas where the school could use our help
in fund raising at our last meeting.  My committee has decided to
focus its energies on obtaining funds to purchase three more
computers.  We hope you and your staff approve this decision.

The other committee members and I look forward to meeting our
goals for Las Madres School.
```

Figure 4-6.   *Printout of MEMO*

Check that the paper is positioned in the printer. Fanfold paper will probably need adjusting manually to bring the perforation to the correct spot, since the memo was less than a page long. Then give the Print command again. The text will begin farther down the page, as in Figure 4-7.

This method of changing the top margin will work for individual sheets of letterhead paper or for centering short one-page documents. To choose a top margin that accommodates your letterhead, experiment with different values until you arrive at a suitable one.

Should you wish to interrupt printing before a file is finished, press ESC. The printer stops in a moment. To start printing the same document again, you give the [P] NP command again. The printing will start from the beginning of the document.

SAVING PRINT VALUES

Although the printout conforms to the changed printing and formatting commands, the MEMO file on the data disk has not been altered. Should you turn off the computer now, the next time you

```
Date:  October 15, 1985

To:  Dr. Tracy Fontenrose

From:  Lee Herman

Subject:  Fund Raising Projects

This year the Young Executives Association is considering several
projects to raise money for Las Madres School.  It is my
privilege to serve as head of the projects committee.

We are now beginning to plan an auction to be held in the early
Spring, and we will start contacting local merchants and others
in the community for donations shortly.  We are also thinking of
a project that will involve the students.  If you have any
suggestions, please feel free to call me at home or at my office.

You outlined the main areas where the school could use our help
in fund raising at our last meeting.  My committee has decided to
focus its energies on obtaining funds to purchase three more
computers.  We hope you and your staff approve this decision.

The other committee members and I look forward to meeting our
goals for Las Madres School.
```

Figure 4-7.   *Printout of MEMO with top margin increased*

loaded MEMO to print it, you would have to prepare it for the printer again. Saving the memo now would not preserve these values in the MEMO file.

If a file might be printed more than once, the print values should be saved in a separate file on the same data disk. Then the print value file can be loaded along with the text file to reproduce exactly the same printout any number of times. Also, if you establish a standard set of values, for all memos or all letters, for example, you can save those values once and use them with any such document files. Saving the print values is similar to saving a document in a file, except that, instead of giving the Save command, you put the Additional Functions menu on the screen.

The fourth selection on the Additional Functions menu is "Save Print/Program Value File". Select **D** to save the current values on the Print/Program Commands menu.

When the prompt asks for the file name, type in the same name as the document file name. If you have set the prefix, type only **MEMO**, as in Figure 4-8. If the prefix is not set, the volume name must also be entered. Then press **RETURN**.

Apple Writer II saves the print values and the editing display

```
        ADDITIONAL FUNCTIONS MENU

   A.  Load Tab File
   B.  Save Tab File
   C.  Load Print/Program Value File
   D.  Save Print/Program Value File
   E.  Load [G]lossary File
   F.  Save [G]lossary File
   G.  Toggle Carriage Return Display
   H.  Toggle Data Line Display
   I.  Connect Keyboard to Printer/Modem
   J.  Quit Apple Writer

        Press RETURN to Exit

        Enter your selection (A - J) :d

   Enter File Name :memo
```

Figure 4-8.   *Additional Functions menu, with "D" selected*

reappears. The catalog now lists a new file, named MEMO.PRT. See Figure 4-9. The ".PRT" ending indicates that this is a print values file, not the document file.

Loading the print values file automatically resets the values on the Print/Program Commands menu. Should you wish to print MEMO again with the same values for the printing and format-

```
   PRACTICE (00/00/00 00:00) V001

   Type    Blocks Name            Created  Time  Modified Time  Length
    Text      3   MEMO            00/00/00 00:00 00/00/00 00:00    946
    Binary    1   MEMO.PRT        00/00/00 00:00 00/00/00 00:00    368

    269 Blocks Available of   280 Total (Press RETURN)
```

Figure 4-9.   *Print values files listed in PRACTICE catalog*

```
ADDITIONAL FUNCTIONS MENU

A.  Load Tab File
B.  Save Tab File
C.  Load Print/Program Value File
D.  Save Print/Program Value File
E.  Load [G]lossary File
F.  Save [G]lossary File
G.  Toggle Carriage Return Display
H.  Toggle Data Line Display
I.  Connect Keyboard to Printer/Modem
J.  Quit Apple Writer

    Press RETURN to Exit

    Enter your selection (A - J) :c

Enter File Name :memo
```

Figure 4-10. *Loading a print values file*

ting commands, you would load the print values file by selecting C on the Additional Functions menu and then entering the name of the print values file, as in Figure 4-10. You would not enter ".PRT", just the name of the file. Then you would load the MEMO document file to print it.

It is possible to change the default values on the Print/Program Commands menu so that whenever you start Apple Writer II, your values will be loaded as the defaults. This will be covered in Appendix C.

REVIEW EXERCISES

1. Check the catalog to see the MEMO.PRT file.

2. Find the most efficient way to load the MEMO print values

file and the MEMO document file when the computer has been turned off.

3. Change one of the values on the Print/Program Commands menu so that MEMO will print double-spaced, and then print it.

II

POWERFUL WORD PROCESSING: PRODUCING VARIED DOCUMENTS

Part II demonstrates the power of Apple Writer II when you work with different kinds of documents that require sophisticated formatting and printing. You can organize related files in a subdirectory to find them quickly, and you can prepare a glossary to eliminate typing frequently used text. Reports, tables, and outlines can be formatted to your specifications; then you can print them individually or in various combined forms.

5

MAKING A
SUBDIRECTORY

So far we have been working with only one file, MEMO, on the data disk; but normally a disk contains numerous files. When you are working with quite a few files from the same disk, keeping them organized becomes important. Imagine trying to find the right document from among 30 or 40 file names in the catalog. Fortunately, this is easily accomplished with Apple Writer II. You can arrange groups of related files into subdirectories for easier identification.

The volume catalog on a disk is the main directory; as you know, each time you save a file on a disk, it is listed in the volume catalog. The volume catalog is a list of the entire contents of a disk (which ProDOS calls a volume). When you create a subdirectory and assign files to it, the volume catalog lists the name of the subdirectory, and a new catalog lists the subdirectory files. If you give related files the same subdirectory name, you can locate these file names quickly by viewing the subdirectory catalog.

In addition, a subdirectory increases the number of files a disk can contain. The ProDOS operating system allows 51 file names to be listed in the volume catalog. That number may be more than you'll ever need. If your files are long, a disk won't be able to store

51 files. However, if you want to store more than 51 files on a disk, subdirectories allow you to do so. Each subdirectory can list its own files, while the subdirectory name counts as only one name on the volume catalog.

Most people do not require such a large number of files because the amount of storage space on floppy disks is limited. Nevertheless, subdirectories offer practical benefits, even if some subdirectories list only a few files at first. An excellent reason for creating subdirectories is to develop a plan for the efficient use of a disk's storage space by organizing the files. In this chapter you will create a subdirectory, put a file in it, and also move the MEMO file into the subdirectory.

ORGANIZING GROUPS OF FILES

After a while, a jumble of files on a disk can become confusing. A little foresight can simplify word processing tasks that will involve several files. Planning how documents will be saved on the disk can also help you avoid eyestrain once the volume catalog has grown to fill several screens of file names.

You already began organizing the disk when you gave it a volume name that described the overall contents (**PRACTICE**). A file name (such as **MEMO**) provides the most specific description of a particular document. Subdirectory names can provide intermediate descriptions. Although you could actually list all kinds of files — related or not — in a subdirectory, it makes sense that they be similar in some way and that the subdirectory name describe the group.

For example, suppose you devote a disk to correspondence. Individual files might include business letters and letters to friends and family. The volume name for such a disk could be **CORRESPONDENCE**, and subdirectories could be named **BUS.LETS.MAY**, **FRIEND.LETS**, and **FAM.LETS**. As long as sufficient room remains on the disk in June, a new subdirectory, **BUS.LETS.-JUNE**, could be added. Or if the correspondence with one person is sufficient to warrant its own grouping, a subdirectory could be created just for those letters: **MOM.LETS**. Figure 5-1 shows the organization of a disk with these subdirectories.

Naming a subdirectory is like naming volumes and files. The same rules apply: the subdirectory name must begin with a letter

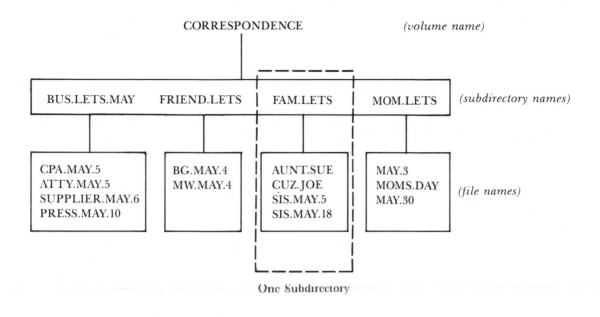

CORRESPONDENCE   *(volume name)*

BUS.LETS.MAY   FRIEND.LETS   FAM.LETS   MOM.LETS   *(subdirectory names)*

CPA.MAY.5
ATTY.MAY.5
SUPPLIER.MAY.6
PRESS.MAY.10

BG.MAY.4
MW.MAY.4

AUNT.SUE
CUZ.JOE
SIS.MAY.5
SIS.MAY.18

MAY.3
MOMS.DAY
MAY.30   *(file names)*

One Subdirectory

Figure 5-1.   *A volume organized into subdirectories*

of the alphabet; it can contain letters, numbers, and periods, but no spaces or other characters; and it can be up to 15 characters long. For speed and clarity, choose subdirectory names that identify the contents of the group of files.

A subdirectory can be created within a subdirectory as well. See the ProDOS manual if you would like to find out how to do this.

CREATING A SUBDIRECTORY

The fund-raising project for Las Madres School, the topic of MEMO, has been getting underway. Because planning the auction will call for several documents to track its progress, a subdirectory will help organize the various files.

Let's reserve one file for notes about deadlines, meetings, and other random jottings. Start up Apple Writer II and enter the fol-

```
        ProDOS COMMANDS

    A.  Catalog
    B.  Rename File
    C.  Lock    File
    D.  Unlock File
    E.  Delete File
    F.  List Volumes On-Line
    G.  Create Subdirectory
    H.  Set Prefix Volume
    I.  Format Volume
    J.  Set Printer/Modem Interface

        Press RETURN to Exit

        Enter Your Selection (A - J) :g

    Enter File Name :
```

Figure 5-2.   *Creating a subdirectory*

lowing text. It will become a file in the subdirectory we'll create for the auction project:

10/15/85 Sent memo to T.F.
Finance committee meets 10/23/85.
Assign someone to handle publicity.
Also, someone in charge of volunteers.
I'll prepare a letter for donors.
What indoor facilities if it rains?

If a subdirectory for this file already existed, the file could be saved on the disk in the subdirectory at this point. However, there are no subdirectories yet on the PRACTICE volume, so we will first create one.

Go to the ProDOS Commands menu and select "Create Subdirectory." The prompt appears as in Figure 5-2.

Type: **/PRACTICE/AUCTION** and press **RETURN**.

The disk light goes on and in a moment the subdirectory has been created. To see AUCTION listed as a subdirectory on the volume catalog, as in Figure 5-3, select "Catalog" and enter the volume name. Auction is labeled "Direct" to indicate it is a subdirectory, not a text file like MEMO.

```
PRACTICE (00/00/00 00:00) V001

Type   Blocks Name          Created  Time  Modified Time  Length
 Text    3    MEMO          00/00/00 00:00 00/00/00 00:00    946
 Binary  1    MEMO.PRT      00/00/00 00:00 00/00/00 00:00    368
 Direct  1    AUCTION       00/00/00 00:00 00/00/00 00:00    512

 268 Blocks Available of   280 Total (Press RETURN)
```

Figure 5-3.   *AUCTION subdirectory listed on PRACTICE volume catalog*

Had the prefix been set, the subdirectory could have been created without typing in the volume name. AUCTION (with no slash) would have been sufficient. Set the prefix now, before returning to the editing display, since the ProDOS commands menu is still on the screen.

Type **H** and then **/PRACTICE/AUCTION** and press **RETURN**.

Once a subdirectory has been created, the volume name and the subdirectory name can become the prefix. Using this feature eliminates typing the subdirectory name when saving or loading files that are in it. So when you will be spending some time working on files that are in the same subdirectory, set the prefix, as you just did.

Now if you ask to see the catalog from the ProDOS Commands menu, you will see a different one: because the subdirectory has been set as part of the prefix, selecting A and pressing RETURN shows you the subdirectory catalog.

Type **A**, and instead of typing a volume name, press **RETURN**. The screen should look like Figure 5-4.

The catalog for the subdirectory, AUCTION, is ready for files to be listed on it. Return to the editing display so that the new document, NOTES, can be saved as a file in the subdirectory.

SAVING A SUBDIRECTORY FILE

Saving a file in a subdirectory is just like saving a file in the main directory (to be listed on the volume catalog), except that the computer must be informed of your intention. In order to list the file

```
AUCTION (00/00/00 00:00) V000

Type    Blocks Name              Created   Time   Modified Time   Length

(Press RETURN)
```

Figure 5-4.   *AUCTION subdirectory catalog*

correctly, the computer needs the volume name, the subdirectory name, and the file name. Otherwise, the computer will list the file on the volume catalog only. Since the prefix has been set, only the file name need be entered.

Give the Save command and type **NOTES**, as in Figure 5-5. Then press **RETURN**.

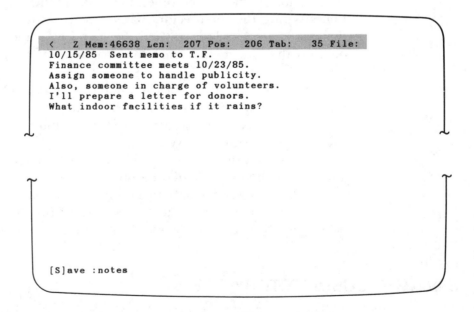

```
<    Z Mem:46638 Len:   207 Pos:   206 Tab:     35 File:
10/15/85   Sent memo to T.F.
Finance committee meets 10/23/85.
Assign someone to handle publicity.
Also, someone in charge of volunteers.
I'll prepare a letter for donors.
What indoor facilities if it rains?
```

```
[S]ave :notes
```

Figure 5-5.   *File name entered when volume and subdirectory names are set as prefix*

If the prefix had not been set for the volume and subdirectory name, you would have had to type in the volume name, the subdirectory name, and the file name. The entry to save the NOTES file would then be "/PRACTICE/AUCTION/NOTES."

The name on the data line confirms that the file has been saved. You can, however, check the AUCTION catalog from the editing display, either with the [L]? command or with [S]?.

Give the Save command, and when the prompt appears, type a question mark where the cursor is, on the "N" of NOTES.

Then press **RETURN**. The prompt for the volume name will appear, as in Figure 5-6.

Just press **RETURN** and the AUCTION catalog will show the file listed, as in Figure 5-7.

It may happen that after creating a subdirectory you realize that some files in the main directory really belong in the subdirectory. In this case, put such files into the new subdirectory to maintain the system of organization you have established. Otherwise you

```
Finance committee meets 10/23/85.
Assign someone to handle publicity.
Also, someone in charge of volunteers.
I'll prepare a letter for donors.
What indoor facilities if it rains?




[S]ave :?

Enter Volume Name :
```

Figure 5-6.   *Prompt after pressing [S]?*

```
AUCTION (00/00/00 00:00) V000

Type    Blocks Name              Created  Time  Modified Time  Length
 Text        1 NOTES             00/00/00 00:00 00/00/00 00:00    207

(Press RETURN)
```

Figure 5-7.   *NOTES file listed in AUCTION subdirectory catalog*

might assume that all the files related to a subject are in one catalog, when they are not.

You can use the ProDOS utilities disk to copy an existing file on a disk into a newly created subdirectory. You would use the "Copy Files" command on the ProDOS utilities disk to copy the file under a new name on the same disk and then delete the first file. The ProDOS manual covers the steps required.

However, you can achieve the same results with Apple Writer II by saving the document to the subdirectory. This method is more convenient while you are working with Apple Writer II. First you must load the file on the editing display.

Let's put the MEMO file into the subdirectory for all the documents relating to the fund-raising project. Clear the screen and give the Load command.

When the Load prompt appears, type **/PRACTICE/MEMO**. Then press **RETURN**.

The prefix has been set for the volume name and the subdirectory name, but MEMO is not yet in the subdirectory. Therefore, to prevent the computer from searching the AUCTION subdirectory — and not finding MEMO — the full volume and file name must be typed. Whenever you want to use a file or another subdirectory — or even another volume — and the prefix is set, typing in the full name at the prompt is necessary. If you will be doing extensive work with the new volume or subdirectory, make that the prefix.

To save MEMO in the subdirectory, you need enter only the file name. With the prefix for the volume name and the subdirectory name set, any file saved with only a file name goes into the subdirectory.

```
<   Z Mem:45899 Len:  946 Pos:  946 Tab:   90 File:/practice/memo
will start contacting local merchants and others in the community for
donations shortly.  We are also thinking of a project that will involve the
students.  If you have any suggestions, please feel free to call me at home or
at my office.

You outlined the main areas where the school could use our help in fund
raising at our last meeting.  My committee has decided to focus its energies
on obtaining funds to purchase three more computers.  We hope you and your
staff approve this decision.

The other committee members and I look forward to meeting our goals for Las
Madres School.




[S]ave :memoctice/memo
```

Figure 5-8.   *MEMO typed over /PRACTICE/MEMO in Save prompt*

Type **MEMO** over the slash and first three characters of
/PRACTICE/MEMO, as shown in Figure 5-8.

Then press **RETURN**.

The file MEMO has now been saved to the subdirectory AUC-
TION and it will be listed in the subdirectory catalog, as shown in
Figure 5-9. This file has the same text but a different name

```
AUCTION (00/00/00 00:00) V000

Type    Blocks Name           Created    Time  Modified Time  Length
Text       1   NOTES          00/00/00 00:00 00/00/00 00:00    207
Text       3   MEMO           00/00/00 00:00 00/00/00 00:00    946

(Press RETURN)
```

Figure 5-9.   *MEMO listed in AUCTION subdirectory catalog*

```
PRACTICE (00/00/00 00:00) V001

Type    Blocks  Name            Created  Time  Modified Time  Length
Text    3       MEMO            00/00/00 00:00 00/00/00 00:00    946
Binary  1       MEMO.PRT        00/00/00 00:00 00/00/00 00:00    368
Direct  1       AUCTION         00/00/00 00:00 00/00/00 00:00    512

   264 Blocks Available of   280 Total (Press RETURN)
```

Figure 5-10. *MEMO still listed in PRACTICE volume catalog*

(/PRACTICE/AUCTION/MEMO) from the original /PRACTICE /MEMO file. Therefore you can save both files on the same disk.

The original /PRACTICE/MEMO file is still in the main catalog, as Figure 5-10 illustrates.

MANAGING FILES AND SUBDIRECTORIES

As you accumulate files on a disk, you'll see ways to organize them into subdirectories. You can rename existing files to relate them more accurately to new or anticipated future files. If you want to make sure a file won't be inadvertently altered, you can lock it. You can also remove unnecessary files from the main directory or from a subdirectory by deleting them. The rest of this chapter illustrates these Apple Writer II features.

Renaming a File

Since the subdirectory AUCTION might ultimately contain more memos, it's a good idea to change the name of the first memo. Then if other memos are added to the subdirectory, they can be clearly distinguished.

To give a file a different name, you go to the ProDOS Commands menu. Select "Rename File" and the prompt asks for the present file name.

```
     ProDOS COMMANDS

A. Catalog
B. Rename File
C. Lock    File
D. Unlock File
E. Delete File
F. List Volumes On-Line
G. Create Subdirectory
H. Set Prefix Volume
I. Format Volume
J. Set Printer/Modem Interface

   Press RETURN to Exit

   Enter Your Selection (A - J) :b

Present Name :memo
```

Figure 5-11.   *Selecting "Rename File"*

Type **MEMO**, as in Figure 5-11. This is all you have to type because the prefix contains the rest of the information needed to rename the subdirectory file.

Then press **RETURN**.

In response to the prompt for the new name, type: **MEMO1.TF** (as in Figure 5-12).

Press **RETURN**.

Check the subdirectory catalog quickly from the ProDOS Commands menu; it will show the new name, MEMO1.TF, as in Figure 5-13.

Table 5-1 shows which part of a file name you enter, according to the current prefix.

Locking and Unlocking a File

Tracy Fontenrose has already received a printout of the memo and the file is merely a record. While the document will not undergo any further editing, it is desirable to preserve it in its present state — to lock the file. Locking a file means that it can be loaded

```
        Enter Your Selection (A - J) :b

   Present Name :

        ProDOS COMMANDS

   A. Catalog
   B. Rename File
   C. Lock    File
   D. Unlock File
   E. Delete File
   F. List Volumes On-Line
   G. Create Subdirectory
   H. Set Prefix Volume
   I. Format Volume
   J. Set Printer/Modem Interface

        Press RETURN to Exit

        Enter Your Selection (A - J) :b

   Present Name :memo

   New Name :memo1.tf
```

Figure 5-12. *New name entered to "Rename File"*

and read on the editing display, but the version on the disk cannot be changed.

Locking protects against unintentional changes to a file, including accidental deletions. It is not, however, as permanent as it sounds. Locking and unlocking a file are both simple proce-

```
AUCTION (00/00/00 00:00) V000

Type    Blocks Name               Created   Time  Modified Time  Length
Text      1    NOTES              00/00/00 00:00 00/00/00 00:00     207
Text      3    MEMO1.TF           00/00/00 00:00 00/00/00 00:00     946

(Press RETURN)
```

Figure 5-13. *Renamed MEMO1.TF file in AUCTION subdirectory catalog*

Prefix Set	File Name Entered
/AW2MASTER	/PRACTICE/MEMO
/AW2MASTER	/PRACTICE/AUCTION/MEMO1.TF
/PRACTICE	/AUCTION/MEMO1.TF
/PRACTICE	MEMO1.TF
/AUCTION	

Table 5-1.   *Prefix and File Name Entries*

dures. The advantage of locking a file is that since you must deliberately unlock it, you may remember why it was locked in the first place and possibly reconsider.

Return to the ProDOS Commands menu and select "Lock File". At the prompt, enter the file name.

Type: **MEMO1.TF** (as in Figure 5-14).

Press **RETURN**.

That's all there is to it. If you wished to unlock the file, you would simply select "Unlock File" from the same menu and enter

```
Type      Blocks  Name            Created   Time   Modified Time   Length
  Text      1     NOTES           00/00/00  00:00  00/00/00 00:00     207
  Text      3     MEMO1.TF        00/00/00  00:00  00/00/00 00:00     946

(Press RETURN)

   ProDOS COMMANDS

A. Catalog
B. Rename File
C. Lock    File
D. Unlock File
E. Delete File
F. List Volumes On-Line
G. Create Subdirectory
H. Set Prefix Volume
I. Format Volume
J. Set Printer/Modem Interface

   Press RETURN to Exit

   Enter Your Selection (A - J) :c

Enter File Name :memo1.tf
```

Figure 5-14.   *Locking a file*

the file name at the prompt.

Mistakes can occur, and locking the file of a final draft can prevent some of them. For instance, if two files have similar names and you inadvertently give the command to delete the wrong one, the deletion will not be carried out. Instead, you'll see the error message "File Access Error" and have time to undo the mistake.

Deleting a File

There are, however, occasions when deleting a file is precisely what you intend to do. If a file is no longer needed, there's no point in taking up room on a disk for it. But always be certain that a file is excess baggage before discarding it. Once deleted, it cannot be retrieved.

You can also delete a subdirectory. But you must first delete all the files in the subdirectory. Then you delete the subdirectory the same way you delete any file in the main directory.

```
       Press RETURN to Exit

       Enter Your Selection (A - J) :c

   Enter File Name :memol.tf

       ProDOS COMMANDS

   A. Catalog
   B. Rename File
   C. Lock    File
   D. Unlock File
   E. Delete File
   F. List Volumes On-Line
   G. Create Subdirectory
   H. Set Prefix Volume
   I. Format Volume
   J. Set Printer/Modem Interface

       Press RETURN to Exit

       Enter Your Selection (A - J) :e

   Enter File Name :/practice/memo
```

Figure 5-15.   *Deleting old MEMO file*

```
PRACTICE (00/00/00 00:00) V001

Type     Blocks  Name            Created  Time   Modified Time   Length
  Binary    1    MEMO.PRT        00/00/00 00:00  00/00/00 00:00    368
  Direct    1    AUCTION         00/00/00 00:00  00/00/00 00:00    512

  267 Blocks Available of    280 Total (Press RETURN)
```

Figure 5-16.   *Old MEMO file deleted from PRACTICE volume catalog*

Since the memo has been copied into the subdirectory, the version that is still in the main directory is superfluous. So select "Delete File" on the ProDOS Commands menu and in response to the prompt, type **/PRACTICE/MEMO** as in Figure 5-15, and press **RETURN**.

If you had typed the new file name by mistake, an error message would have appeared on the screen, because that file is locked. The correct file has been deleted, and it has been removed from the list of files on the PRACTICE volume catalog (see Figure 5-16).

REVIEW EXERCISES

1. Following the rules for naming, invent two subdirectory names to organize these files:

   MEMO.1.CJ
   NEW.YR.RES
   GRT.IDEAS
   RESTRNT.REVS
   SUMRY.MEETING
   NOVEL.NOTES
   MEMO.2.CJ
   MEMO.3.CJ

2. Delete from the volume catalog the print values file for the now defunct MEMO file.

6

USING GLOSSARIES

This chapter demonstrates the glossary, a feature of Apple Writer II that eliminates retyping text that occurs frequently in a document. A *glossary* is a list of words, phrases, stock sentences, and even paragraphs. Once you have created a glossary, you give the Glossary command, identify the text, and Apple Writer II instantly inserts it in the document where you want it.

You'll find many opportunities for taking advantage of glossaries. The name of a company, the title of a book, someone's name and address—these are all candidates for glossary entries. For instance, in a book report on *The Selected Short Stories of Ernest Hemingway*, the title and the author's name would never have to be typed in; they could be inserted each time from a glossary.

Your own name can go in a glossary, since you probably type it at least once in many of your documents. Some of the entries in the glossary used to write this book are "Apple Writer II," "Word and Paragraph buffer," and "Print/Program Commands menu"; they come up frequently and would otherwise have to be typed in full each time.

Apple Writer II reserves an area of memory called the *Glossary buffer* for the contents of a glossary. The Glossary buffer can hold 2048 characters. You put a glossary into the Glossary buffer by loading an existing glossary file and by making entries directly into the Glossary buffer. In this chapter you'll learn both methods

111

and you'll see how to create a variety of useful glossary entries. You'll also learn how key sequences for Apple Writer II commands you frequently use can be put in a glossary.

CREATING A GLOSSARY FILE

It is often convenient to have a glossary ready to use when you start typing a document. Glossary entries can be typed all at one time on the editing display and then saved as a file to be loaded into the Glossary buffer. Like document files, glossary files can be edited to add, delete, or change the wording of entries. A glossary file can also be printed, just like a document file.

The maximum number of characters in a glossary file is 2048, the size of the Glossary buffer. You can, however, create an unlimited number of glossary files. Two kinds of glossary files are convenient time-savers: general glossaries, such as a glossary file for business letters containing items commonly recurring in similar documents; and glossaries for individual documents, such as a long report, or for a series of documents on the same subject.

Making Glossary Entries
On the Editing Display

To build a glossary file that will speed up typing documents in this chapter and the following ones, we'll create some glossary entries on the editing display. Start up Apple Writer II and set the prefix to /PRACTICE/AUCTION. Then go to the editing display.

As our imaginary auction project progresses, it calls for additional correspondence—memos, letters, and a report. Since certain phrases will be used repeatedly in various documents, we can start a glossary now and add entries to it as needed. Obviously, "Young Executives Association" and "Las Madres School" are key phrases that belong in the glossary.

You make an entry for a glossary by typing a character to represent the text to be retrieved and a *definition*, that is, the text itself. Only one character can represent a definition, and it cannot represent more than one definition in the same glossary. When you create your own glossaries, try to pick a letter of the alphabet that reminds you of the text or use some other simple shorthand. For the definition "Young Executives Association", the character representing it will be "y".

Type: **yYoung Executives Association**

Then press **RETURN**.

Each glossary entry must start on the first space of a line and end with RETURN. It is important to enter capital letters and spaces in the definition exactly as they should appear when retrieved.

If you put a space between the definition and the character representing it, the retrieved text begins with a space. You'll need some system for distinguishing between which entries begin with spaces and which do not. Words and phrases that almost always occur in the middle of sentences can begin with a space. Leave a space in the next entry.

Type: **l Las Madres School**

Press **RETURN**.

There are now two separate glossary entries, each of which can be retrieved independently and inserted into a document wherever appropriate. Since Lee Herman's name will probably be typed at the end of letters and at the top of memos, let's add one more entry.

Type: **LLee Herman**

Press **RETURN**.

The editing display should look like Figure 6-1, with three glossary entries.

Although no character can be used twice in the same glossary, Apple Writer II recognizes the lowercase "l" for "Las Madres School" as a different character from the uppercase "L" for "Lee Herman". But if you put both an uppercase and a lowercase letter in a glossary to represent two different definitions, be careful to keep track of which character stands for which definition.

```
<    Z Mem:46782 Len:    63 Pos:    63 Tab:    0 File:gloss
yYoung Executives Association
l Las Madres School
LLee Herman
```

Figure 6-1.   *Three glossary entries on the editing display*

A glossary can contain 99 entries, as long as the total number of characters, including the characters that represent the definitions, does not exceed 2048. An extensive glossary will, of course, require uppercase and lowercase letters of the alphabet and perhaps other characters as well in order to represent all the definitions. Numbers, some punctuation marks, and CONTROL characters can also represent definitions. The following characters cannot be used: (*), ?, [A], [G], [H], [L], [M], [U], [W], [X]. Nor can the LEFT or RIGHT ARROW keys, ESCAPE, or TAB be pressed as characters to represent definitions.

It's a good idea to print a glossary file and keep it at hand. Then you needn't memorize all the characters that represent the glossary definitions.

Many of the entries you'll want to put in a glossary will probably be brief words and phrases, similar to the previous examples. You can, however, make an entry of any length on the editing display, providing the Glossary buffer can hold it. In fact, a glossary can be created with one entry that is 2048 characters long.

For entries made on the editing display, check the data line to see if the Glossary buffer has room for more. According to the data line now, the three entries add up to 61 characters.

Saving and Loading a Glossary File

A glossary created on the editing display is saved the same way you save a document file. Give the Save command and the familiar Save prompt appears. Because the prefix is set, you need type only the new file name.

Type **GLOSS** and press **RETURN**.

The glossary file is now listed on the AUCTION subdirectory as a text file named GLOSS with 61 characters. If you are going to add items to an existing glossary file, you can check the catalog to see how many characters are already in the glossary. If more than one glossary file will be listed in a catalog, you should distinguish them by naming them more precisely. The catalog does not add an identifying extension, such as the .PRT for print value files. You can name a glossary file to describe its contents and use your own extension, such as LETTER.GL.

Whenever you wish to edit a glossary file, you load it on the editing display the same way you load a document file, not into the Glossary buffer. After making any changes, save the file again with

[S]=. When a glossary file has been loaded on the editing display, it can be printed out. If you merely want to view a glossary in the Glossary buffer, you needn't load it on the editing display. You'll learn later in this chapter how to do this.

Once a glossary file has been saved, it can be loaded into the Glossary buffer so that the entries can be retrieved in a document you're typing on the editing display. The GLOSS file you created has been saved on the data disk, and it can now be put in the Glossary buffer.

Go to the Additional Functions menu and select "Load Glossary File".

Enter the file name **GLOSS**, as in Figure 6-2.

Press **RETURN**.

INSERTING GLOSSARY ENTRIES
INTO A DOCUMENT

The rewards for following the simple steps to create a glossary file are quite dramatic. To see how convenient a glossary can be, let's type a letter that uses the glossary entries now stored in the buffer.

```
ADDITIONAL FUNCTIONS MENU

A. Load Tab File
B. Save Tab File
C. Load Print/Program Value File
D. Save Print/Program Value File
E. Load [G]lossary File
F. Save [G]lossary File
G. Toggle Carriage Return Display
H. Toggle Data Line Display
I. Connect Keyboard to Printer/Modem
J. Quit Apple Writer

    Press RETURN to Exit

    Enter your selection (A - J) :e

Enter File Name :gloss
```

Figure 6-2.   *Loading a glossary file*

Clear the screen and enter the date and the greeting of the letter shown in Figure 6-3. The left and right margins have been adjusted to LM10 and RM75. You can adjust your screen display if you wish. If not, the lines will be broken slightly differently.

In the body of the letter, "Young Executives Association," "Las Madres School," and "Lee Herman" will be inserted from the glossary. To retrieve a glossary definition, you hold down the OPEN APPLE key and press the character that represents it. As an alternative, [G] can be used with the character. However, usually it is easier to press the OPEN APPLE key.

In the first line of the first paragraph, type **The** and press the **SPACEBAR**.

Next, hold down **OPEN APPLE** and type a lowercase **y**. As you can see, Apple Writer II inserts the corresponding definition in the text on the editing display.

Then type: **is raising funds to benefit**

(Do not press SPACEBAR after "benefit" because the glossary entry will be retrieved with a space.)

```
<   Z Mem:46228 Len:   617 Pos:      0 Tab:     0 File:letter1
November 4, 1985

Dear Local Merchant:

The Young Executives Association is raising funds to benefit Las
Madres School.  We have undertaken to provide three computers for
the use of the students and faculty.

Our main fundraising event will be an auction to be held on
Saturday, March 22 and we are asking businesses in the community
to support this worthwhile project.  Any goods or services you
can donate for the auction will be most appreciated.

A member of the Young Executives Association will contact you
personally in the next few weeks.  Please join us in helping Las
Madres School.

Sincerely,


Lee Herman
```

Figure 6-3.   *Text of letter*

Now hold down **OPEN APPLE** and type the lowercase character "l". Apple Writer II retrieves "Las Madres School" from the Glossary buffer. Continue entering the letter and insert glossary definitions wherever possible.

The entries in a glossary file can be loaded into the Glossary buffer any time they are useful for typing a document. Glossary entries can also be put directly into the Glossary buffer temporarily while you are typing a document on the editing display, as explained in the next section.

ADDING NEW ENTRIES TO THE GLOSSARY BUFFER

Sometimes while entering a document you'll type some text that you realize will be handy to have in a glossary. In such a case, you can make a glossary entry directly into the Glossary buffer without clearing the document in progress from the editing display. An entire glossary can be created with this method; but in order to use the entries again with another document, you must save them from the Glossary buffer to a glossary file.

If you have already loaded a glossary file into the Glossary buffer, any new entries put directly into the buffer will be added to the file. You can use the combined file entries and the additions while you type the document. Then you can make the additions a permanent part of the file by saving them in it.

However, before making a large number of additions to a glossary file in the buffer, you should determine whether the buffer has room for them all. One way to do this is to view the catalog; it shows the length of the glossary file the last time it was saved.

In creating your own glossaries, you would probably enter the new definitions in the course of entering the document, especially if the text for an entry will be repeated in that document. But you can also review a completed document and identify text you'll use in related documents. You can then make several glossary entries at one time, putting each one directly into the Glossary buffer and then saving them from the buffer. The next exercise illustrates how to make temporary entries directly into the Glossary buffer.

The letter just entered has some text that might be used again in future documents. Since we know the file GLOSS is only 61 characters long, we can put more entries directly into the Glossary buffer.

You press [G] to give the command to put text directly into the Glossary buffer.

Press [G]. The prompt appears as in Figure 6-4.

You now have a choice: either to enter a new definition after the character that will represent it or to *purge* the contents of the Glossary buffer—that is, to empty out any entries already in it. Suppose you had reached a point in a document when the contents of the Glossary buffer were no longer needed for the rest of the document, but a new entry or series of entries you do need won't fit in the buffer. You could purge the buffer and thereby make room for more entries. Since there is plenty of room in the Glossary buffer, we won't purge it now.

Instead, type a question mark and the prompt appears for creating a new entry. The entries from the loaded GLOSS file also appear on the screen. Should you decide, after all, not to make an entry, pressing RETURN cancels the Glossary command. And, should you forget the character that represents a particular defini-

```
>   Z Mem:46228 Len:   617 Pos:    0 Tab:     0 File:letter1
November 4, 1985

Dear Local Merchant:

The Young Executives Association is raising funds to benefit Las
Madres School.  We have undertaken to provide three computers for
the use of the students and faculty.

Our main fundraising event will be an auction to be held on
Saturday, March 22 and we are asking businesses in the community
to support this worthwhile project.  Any goods or services you
can donate for the auction will be most appreciated.

A member of the Young Executives Association will contact you
personally in the next few weeks.  Please join us in helping Las
Madres School.

Sincerely,


[G]lossary(?=Define/*=Purge) :
```

Figure 6-4.   *Glossary command prompt on the editing display*

tion, pressing [G] ? shows you the contents of the Glossary buffer without disturbing the document being entered.

Type: **t to support this worthwhile project**

If you make a typing error, you cannot use the DELETE key to correct it. You can move the cursor with the LEFT ARROW and RIGHT ARROW keys and type over the error with characters or blank it out with the SPACEBAR. If an error is too complicated to correct, move the cursor back to the first character and press RETURN to cancel the command. Then try the procedure again.

A space between the character "t" and the definition is convenient here, since this phrase will be inserted in the middle of a sentence when it is retrieved. Some entries, however, might be inserted at the beginning of a sentence, in which case an initial space would be inappropriate. For example, if the definition "Lee Herman" began with a space, you would have had to delete the space after it was inserted in this document.

When the entry is correctly typed, as in Figure 6-5, press RETURN.

You would follow the same steps to put more glossary definitions in the Glossary buffer, one by one. For example, the date of the auction, March 22, could be entered next, as well as any other potentially useful entries.

New entries can be put into the Glossary buffer with the [G] ? command when a file has already been loaded into the buffer, as you've just done. But if you put some new entries directly into the Glossary buffer and then load a glossary file, the new entries are

```
yYoung Executives Association
1 Las Madres School
LLee Herman


Enter new definition :t to support this worthwhile project
```

Figure 6-5.   *New entry added to the Glossary buffer*

lost. Loading a glossary file in effect purges the Glossary buffer; anything in the buffer is written over by the file.

There is, however, a limit on the number of characters an individual glossary entry can contain if put directly into the Glossary buffer. An entry made this way cannot contain more than 128 characters. Thus, if you want to put a very large definition in a glossary, you should enter it on the editing display and save it. Entries made this way, you'll recall, can be up to 2048 characters in length.

Nesting Glossary Entries

The 128 character limit on entries put directly into the Glossary buffer can also be overcome by breaking up a large entry into smaller segments. You put segments in the Glossary buffer as separate entries and then create a definition that combines them. This method is called *nesting*. Apple Writer II can combine as many as eight segments. In other words, glossary entries can be nested eight deep.

For example, the last paragraph of the letter might be used again, perhaps in an appeal to school parents or to members of other organizations. But if you put the cursor at the end of the paragraph, Tab: on the data line indicates that the entire paragraph is 141 characters — too long for a single entry into the Glossary buffer. However, breaking it into two segments will allow it to be inserted in future documents as one glossary entry. Let's do that now. We'll make one long segment first.

Press [**G**]? and type

AA member of the Young Executives Association will contact you personally in the next few weeks. Please join us in helping

Press **RETURN**.

Then press [**G**]? and the screen should look like Figure 6-6.

Since "Las Madres School" is already an entry in this glossary, it need not be entered again in order to combine it with the rest of the paragraph. If it were not already entered, then you would have to enter it now.

To nest two (or more) entries, you tell Apple Writer II to insert

```
yYoung Executives Association
l Las Madres School
LLee Herman


t to support this worthwhile project
AA member of the Young Executives Association will contact you personally in the
 next few weeks.  Please join us in helping


Enter new definition :
```

Figure 6-6.   *Most of the final paragraph entered into the Glossary buffer*

one segment first and then the other. The definition for a nested entry consists of the [G] command, the character that represents the first definition segment, the [G] command again, the character that represents the second definition segment, and so on. Another character, one not used to represent any of the nested definition segments, stands for the entire definition.

You enter a CONTROL character like [G] in a glossary definition just as you do when giving a command: hold down CONTROL and press the key for the character. But as a composite character in a glossary definition, it appears on the screen as a dark highlighted letter, the inverse of a normal character.

Type: **p[G]A[G]l**

Press **RETURN**.

This glossary entry uses the character "p" to represent the entire nested definition. The two segments are the definition represented by "A" (most of the paragraph) and "l" (Las Madres School). The two [G] characters give the command to retrieve each of the nested definitions, one after the other.

There are now three entries added to the glossary buffer. If you press [G]?, the contents of the glossary will appear, as in Figure 6-7.

To see how nesting works, move the cursor to the line below "Lee Herman" at the end of the letter.

Now hold down **OPEN APPLE** and type the lowercase character **p**.

With one command the whole paragraph is retrieved from the Glossary buffer.

```
yYoung Executives Association
l Las Madres School
LLee Herman

t to support this worthwhile project
AA member of the Young Executives Association will contact you personally
 next few weeks.  Please join us in helping
pGAG1


Enter new definition :
```

Figure 6-7.   *Contents of Glossary buffer after all entries made*

Saving the Glossary Buffer's Contents

You must save glossary entries you've put directly into the Glossary buffer if you want to keep them for future use. But they cannot be saved with the [S] command, the way you save text typed on the editing display. Instead, they must be saved from the Additional Functions menu.

Let's add the new entries we've put directly into the buffer to the GLOSS file. Go to the Additional Functions menu and select "Save Glossary File". Give the file the same name.

Type **GLOSS**, press **RETURN**, and type **Y** in response to the prompt that asks if you want to delete the old GLOSS file. You do because the new GLOSS file will have all the entries, old and new. A glossary composed of all entries put directly into the Glossary buffer would be saved the same way, except that there would be no old file to delete.

Now go to the editing display, delete the extra paragraph, and save the letter as LETTER1 in the usual way with [S]. Then clear the screen.

USING CARRIAGE RETURNS IN A DEFINITION

An entry in a glossary can consist of a series of short, separate lines. But to make such an entry, you need to use carriage return

```
 < 　Z Mem:46802 Len:　　43 Pos:　　43 Tab:　　　0 File:memo.gloss
hDate:]]To:]]From:　Lee Herman]]Subject:]]
```

Figure 6-8.　　*Glossary entry for memo heading*

characters, not the RETURN key. Pressing RETURN, as you know, signals the end of a definition.

The right bracket (]) stands for RETURN in a glossary definition. When it is part of a definition, the text will be inserted with the lines broken wherever the right bracket character has been entered. Therefore, you should not use the right bracket as the character that represents a definition.

By using carriage returns (right brackets), you can create a glossary definition that inserts, for example, the name and address in the heading of a letter to someone with whom you correspond regularly. Similarly, a list of people who typically receive copies of memos or reports could be inserted as a glossary definition. The following exercise demonstrates how to put carriage returns in a glossary definition so that it can serve as a ready-made form for a memo heading.

Such a glossary file can be created either on the editing display or with the [G]? command. We'll use the editing display. But the Glossary buffer still contains the previous entries. Since they have been saved, it is safe to purge the buffer.

Press [G] and then an asterisk (*) to purge the buffer. Now the old entries will not be part of the new file to be created.

On the editing display type (as in Figure 6-8)

hDate:]]To:]]From: Lee Herman]]Subject:]]

The double carriage returns will break each line and insert a blank line between them. There will be two spaces after "From:".

Save this glossary entry as a text file, giving it the name MEMO.GLOSS. Then load the MEMO.GLOSS file into the Glossary buffer.

Clear the screen. Then hold down **OPEN APPLE** and type the lowercase character **h**. The memo's heading should appear, as in Figure 6-9.

```
<   Z Mem:46804 Len:     41 Pos:     41 Tab:      0 File:
Date:

To:

From:   Lee Herman

Subject:
```

Figure 6-9.   *Memo heading retrieved from glossary buffer*

USING COMMANDS IN A GLOSSARY

The [G] and the right bracket for a carriage return are examples of characters that, as part of glossary definitions, are not inserted into the text of a document but rather give instructions to the computer. Other CONTROL characters can also be used in glossary definitions to speed up commands you might give while entering a document.

For example, instead of pressing several keys in succession to bring the catalog on the screen, you can enter this sequence in the glossary and then just give the Glossary command. You create such an entry as you would any other — with a character to represent the definition and then the definition.

If "c" is used to represent the command to see the catalog, the entire entry would look like this: "c[O]a]". The [O] tells Apple Writer II to display the ProDOS Commands menu, the "a" selects "Catalog", and the carriage return ends the command. That is all you need to go to the catalog, since the prefix has been set.

Press G?

Then type c[O]a] and press RETURN.

Now hold down OPEN APPLE and type the lowercase character c. The AUCTION catalog will appear on the screen.

If the prefix were not set, Apple Writer II would look for the catalog on the AW2Master disk. However, if you want to use this shortcut without setting the prefix, omit the carriage return from the definition. Then the command will put the ProDOS Commands menu on the screen with "Catalog" selected and the prompt asking for the volume name.

REVIEW EXERCISES

1. Create glossary entries for the following in the Glossary buffer:

   The check is in the mail.
   antidisestablishmentarianism

2. Create a standard closing for a letter similar to the following and save it in a file. Then load it into the Glossary buffer and retrieve it on the editing display.

   I look forward to hearing from you soon.

   Sincerely,

   (Your Name)

7

EMBEDDING PRINTER COMMANDS

As you saw in Chapter 4, the default values on the Print/ Program Commands menu can easily be changed. In addition to specifying new values that affect the printing of an entire document, you can *embed* printer commands that affect only a portion of text. Embedded commands enable you to produce versatile formats such as centered headings, inset paragraphs, and underlined text.

An embedded command is entered on the editing display at the precise point where it is to be executed. It tells the printer that the text that follows is to be treated differently from the rest of the document. In this chapter you'll learn how to embed commands and then you'll print a document using some of Apple Writer II's special printing features.

CHANGING SET MARGINS

Every time you change a value on the Print/Program Commands menu, the new value becomes the current default until you change it again or turn the computer off. This occurs whether several values are changed directly on the Print/Program Commands menu, a new value is entered from the editing display with the [P] command, or a print values file is loaded. Commands that will remain the same throughout a printing, such as specific values for your printer (PD, CR, SP) or double-spacing, need not be embedded. Once you have decided what these values should be, you can

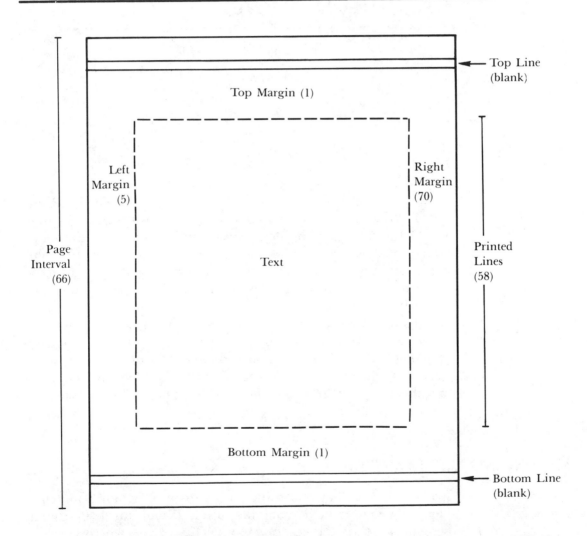

Figure 7-1.   *Page layout for report*

change the defaults, if necessary, either before or after creating a document.

It is simpler to determine the general layout of the pages and to set the Print/Program Commands menu accordingly before entering the document on the editing display. But often some of the specifications will not apply to a particular part of a document. If one paragraph requires a left margin greater than the preceding one, an embedded command can accomplish this change and then another embedded command can restore the margin for succeeding paragraphs. Embedded commands override the corresponding values on the Print/Program Commands menu.

The document you are going to create in this chapter—the first page of a report—has a title, subheadings, indented paragraphs, and a list that requires its own paragraph formatting. The left and right margins can be set from the menu for most of the text; exceptions and other formatting specifications will be embedded as needed.

The page layout is 58 lines of single-spaced text on a standard page of 66 lines; these are all default values on the Print/Program Commands menu. The page layout is illustrated in Figure 7-1.

Start up Apple Writer II and set the prefix for the volume and subdirectory names of the data disk. Then put the Print/Program Commands menu on the screen. If necessary, adjust Print Destination (PD), Carriage Return (CR), and Single Page (SP) for your particular printer. Leave Top Line and Bottom Line blank and retain the default values for Paragraph Margin, Top Margin, Bottom Margin, Printed Lines, Page Interval, Line Interval, Print Mode, Page Number, and Underline Token.

Enter these new values: **LM5** and **RM70**. The menu should look like Figure 7-2, except where your printer requires different printing commands for PD, CR, and SP.

Justifying Text

The default setting for Print Mode—left justified—is the most common choice for printing many kinds of documents: a letter, a business summary, or a book report. Left justified means that text lines up against the left margin, while the right margin is uneven.

There are three other choices for Print Mode: Fill Justify (FJ), Center Justify (CJ), and Right Justify (RJ). These, like Left Justify

```
Print/Program Commands:

Left        Margin     (LM) = 5
Paragraph Margin       (PM) = 0
Right       Margin     (RM) = 70
Top         Margin     (TM) = 1
Bottom      Margin     (BM) = 1
Page Number            (PN) = 1
Printed Lines          (PL) = 58
Page Interval          (PI) = 66
Line Interval          (LI) = 0
Single Page            (SP) = 0
Print Destination      (PD) = 1
Carriage Return        (CR) = 0
Underline Token        (UT) = \
Print Mode (LJ,FJ,CJ,RJ) = LJ
Top Line               (TL) :

Bottom Line            (BL) :

Press RETURN to Exit

[P]rint/Program :
```

Figure 7-2.   *Print/Program Commands menu set for report*

(LJ), can be set on the Print/Program Commands menu or embedded in a document.

Fill justified text appears in Figure 7-3. The text is spread out between the left and right margins so that both margins are absolutely even. The effect is similar to the typeset text in a book or magazine, and it can be used for a newsletter or a document that

```
Fill  justified text looks more like a page in a book or magazine.
But there may be gaps between the words.

When  text  is center justified, each line extends the same number
of  characters to the left and to the right from the center of the
page.

Right  justified  text  lines up against the right margin, but the
left margin is uneven.
```

Figure 7-3.   *Fill justified text*

```
    Fill justified text looks more like a page in a book or magazine.
          But there may be gaps between the words.

    When text is center justified, each line extends the same number
    of characters to the left and to the right from the center of the
                              page.

    Right justified text lines up against the right margin, but the
                      left margin is uneven.
```

Figure 7-4.   *Center justified text*

you want to look rather formal.

However, in order to spread out the text between the margins, extra spaces are often inserted between words. While professional typesetting can create unobtrusive proportional spacing, most computers cannot reproduce this sophisticated look. Consequently, fill justified text can look spotty on the page because some lines will have large gaps between words.

Center justified text distributes characters and spaces equally across a line from the midpoint. Each line is centered on the page and both left and right margins are uneven. Center justified text appears in Figure 7-4. Although you certainly don't want an entire document to look like this, you can center titles and headings with this command.

Right justified text lines up against the right margin, while the left margin is uneven — just the opposite of left justified text. Figure 7-5 shows how right justified text looks. It produces a startling, unusual effect.

The text for most of the report will be left justified, but the title should be centered. Therefore, the command to center the title will have to be embedded.

You type an embedded command on the line above the text it affects. The command must begin with a period in the extreme left space and must end with RETURN. More than one command can be embedded, each on a separate line, if a portion of text requires more than one formatting change. You'll learn how to do this shortly. Embedded commands appear only on the screen, not on the printout.

Let's type the command to center the title of the report. Make sure you begin with the period on the first space in the line.

```
Fill justified text looks more like a page in a book or magazine.
                       But there may be gaps between the words.

When text is center justified, each line extends the same number
of characters to the left and to the right from the center of the
                                                            page.

   Right justified text lines up against the right margin, but the
                                      left margin is uneven.
```

Figure 7-5.   *Right justified text*

Type: **.CJ**
Press **RETURN**.
Now enter the title of the report: **Project Committee Report**
Press **RETURN**.
Then type **Lee Herman** and press **RETURN**. The screen should now look like Figure 7-6. When the report is printed, both of these lines will be centered.

Leave a blank line and then enter the command that will restore the Print Mode to left justified for the rest of the report.
Type: **.LJ**
Press **RETURN**.

Embedding Paragraph Margins

You can set the value for Paragraph Margin (PM) on the Print/ Program Commands menu or embed it. If your document will

```
<   Z Mem:46805 Len:    40 Pos:    40 Tab:    0 File:report
.cj
Project Committee Report
Lee Herman
```

Figure 7-6.   *Report title with embedded command*

have the first line of each paragraph indented the same amount, it's simpler to set this value on the menu. However, if the value for PM will vary in a document, embedding the command as needed lets you see the command on the screen immediately preceding the paragraph it affects. The first paragraph and all the normal paragraphs in our report will have indented first lines, so we'll embed a command for the first paragraph now.

On the line immediately below the LJ command, type **.PM5** and press **RETURN**.

The value for the paragraph margin (PM5) will indent the first line five spaces beyond the left margin, which is set on the Print/ Program Commands menu to 5; the paragraph margin is always relative to the left margin.

Another way to enter the value for the paragraph margin in the report is PM+5; this emphasizes that 5 is added to the current left margin value. Apple Writer II assumes that the value for PM is positive, whether or not you use the plus sign. The minus sign can also be used to specify a negative value for the paragraph margin relative to the value for the current left margin. For example, if the left margin value were LM10, a paragraph margin set to PM−5 would produce a paragraph in which the first line would be five spaces closer to the left edge of the paper than the rest of the lines in that paragraph.

Now enter the following paragraph:

> Our committee has been working hard to guarantee that the upcoming auction for the Las Madres School will be a great success. This report summarizes our activities to date and what remains to be done.

The screen should now look like Figure 7-7.

Now give the Adjust Screen Display command to change the length of the line of text on the screen. Notice that the left and right margins appear on the screen as they will look when printed, but the first line of the paragraph is not indented. The Adjust Screen Display command displays only the left and right margins specified on the Print/Program Commands menu, not the specified paragraph margin. Even if the paragraph margin were set to 5 on the Print/Program Commands menu, [A] would not indent the first line five spaces on the screen.

Insert a blank line after this paragraph and after each of the other paragraphs in the report.

```
>   Z Mem:46593 Len:   252 Pos:     0 Tab:     0 File:report
.cj
Project Committee Report
Lee Herman

.lj
.pm5
Our committee has been working hard to guarantee that the
upcoming auction for the Las Madres School will be a great
success.  This report summarizes our activities to date and what
remains to be done.
```

Figure 7-7.   *Title and first paragraph of report with embedded commands*

Often a report or a document that is divided into sections will need subheadings; embedded commands can specify the format for this text. You might want to center a subheading (by embedding the CJ command) or to print it flush against the left margin. You might also decide to put a subheading in boldface or to underline it for visual impact. By the end of this chapter, you'll be able to choose among these options. For now, the subheadings will be left justified.

Creating a subheading that begins at the left margin does not require changing the current Print mode. However, Apple Writer II considers any text entered after a RETURN to be a new paragraph. Therefore, unless we embed a command to override the current paragraph margin value (PM5), the program will assume that the subheading is a paragraph and indent it five spaces when it is printed.

In order to make the subheading an exception to the normal paragraph format and then to restore the normal value for the paragraph margin, type **.PM0** and press **RETURN**.

Then type the subheading: **Donations**

And on the next line, type **.PM5** and press **RETURN**.

Because the value, PM0, is relative to the left margin setting (LM5), Apple Writer II will not indent the line for the subheading. However, unless the previous value for the paragraph margin is embedded again after the subheading, none of the remaining paragraphs will have indented first lines.

```
 <    Z Mem:46195 Len:  650 Pos:  650 Tab:  157 File:report
.pm0
Donations
.pm5
A letter went out to potential donors in the business community
on November 3 and was followed up with phone calls and
solicitations in person from members of the committee.  We are
continuing to contact new sources.

The response has been positive so far.  We should have an
interesting assortment of items, gift certificates, and donated
services by the day of the auction.
```

Figure 7-8.   *"Donations" section of report with embedded commands*

Now enter the following text:

A letter went out to potential donors in the business community on November 3 and was followed up with phone calls and solicitations in person from members of the committee. We are continuing to phone new sources.

The response has been positive so far. We should have an interesting assortment of items, gift certificates, and donated services by the day of the auction.

The screen should now look like Figure 7-8.

Embed the command to make another subheading, type the following subheading, reverse the command (restore the previous value), and then type in the following paragraph. Figure 7-9 shows how the screen will look.

Grand Prize

The Las Madres students have been selling tickets for a grand prize drawing to be held during the auction. But we are still looking for something spectacular to give away. Anyone who can help us out with this should contact one of the committee members immediately.

```
<   Z Mem:45904 Len:  941 Pos:  941 Tab:  267 File:report
The response has been positive so far.  We should have an
interesting assortment of items, gift certificates, and donated
services by the day of the auction.

.pm0
Grand Prize
.pm5
The Las Madres students have been selling tickets for a grand
prize drawing to be held during the auction.  But we are still
looking for something spectacular to give away.  Anyone who can
help us out with this should contact one of the committee members
immediately.
```

Figure 7-9.   *"Grand Prize" section of report with embedded commands*

Reformatting Part of a Document

For various reasons, you may want to format a part of a document that is different from the rest. For example, a list of rules might consist of a series of short lines indented from the left margin. A long quotation should be indented from both the normal left and right margins.

You may want to create a portion of text in which the first line of a paragraph is longer than the other lines and extends more to the left. Text formatted like this is called a *hanging indent* or an *outdented* paragraph. You might recognize this as a format used in bibliographies: the first line is flush against the left margin and succeeding lines are indented several spaces from the left margin.

In the next section of the report, you will create a series of out-dented first lines for a portion of text. This text is also indented further from both the normal left and right margins of the other paragraphs.

First, type the new subheading with the appropriate embedded commands and then type the following paragraph:

Volunteers
During the week prior to the auction, volunteers will be needed to collect and store the donated items. Please set aside some time and let us know if you

Press **RETURN** twice to end the last line and to insert a blank line before the outdented text to follow.

In order to indent the entire portion of text, the left and right margins must be changed. Embed the commands to make the left margin value 15 and the right margin value 60.

Type **.LM15** and press **RETURN**.

Then type **.RM60** and press **RETURN**.

The paragraph margin must also be changed. If not, the current default (PM5) will indent the first lines five spaces past the present left margin setting (LM15). To make the first line longer, or outdented, it has to be indented less than the left margin.

To outdent a paragraph, you use the minus sign (the hyphen) to set the value for the paragraph margin. We'll embed the Paragraph Margin command so that the first lines of the next part of the report will be outdented three spaces from the embedded left margin.

Type **.PM—3** and press **RETURN**.

Then enter the following:

- have access to a station wagon or a small truck or are willing to drive someone else's
- have space in your garage where large items can be safely stored
- are willing to put up posters in your neighborhood

Since this is the only paragraph of its kind in the report, the margins must now be changed again before any more text is entered.

Type **.LM5** and press **RETURN**.

Then type **.RM70** and press **RETURN**.

The next line of text, however, is another subheading, which should not be indented. So we need to specify the paragraph margin.

Type **.PM0** and press **RETURN**.

Figure 7-10 shows how this section of the report should look on the screen with the embedded commands entered.

So long as you keep in mind how most of a document is formatted, changing margins to specify a different format for part of the document is not complicated. If you like, you can embed relative values for the left and right margins; that is, you can add or subtract from the current left or right margin using the plus and minus signs.

```
  <   Z Mem:45478 Len: 1367 Pos: 1130 Tab:     4 File:report
help us out with this should contact one of the committee members
immediately.

.pm0
Volunteers
.pm5
During the week prior to the auction, volunteers will be needed
to collect and store the donated items.  Please set aside some
time and let us know if you

.lm15
.rm60
.pm-3
-  have access to a station wagon or a small truck or are willing
to drive someone else's
-  have space in your garage where large items can be safely
stored
-  are willing to put up posters in your neighborhood

.lm5
.rm70
.pm0
```

Figure 7-10.   *"Volunteers" section of report with embedded commands*

For example, instead of LM15 and RM60 for the indented list you just formatted, the values could have been embedded as LM+10 and RM−10. To return to the normal left and right margins, LM−10 and RM+10 would have the same effect in this case as LM5 and RM70. But LM10 and LM+10 are two different commands: LM10 always means 10 spaces from the left edge of the paper, while LM+10 means 10 spaces beyond the current left margin.

USING THE UNDERLINE
AND BACKSPACE COMMANDS

When you want a group of characters to be underlined, you insert the underline token before and after the text. Similarly, you insert a backspace command in order to eliminate an unwanted space or to combine two characters, such as the "ñ" in many Spanish words.

These commands, like embedded commands, do not appear in the printed copy.

Inserting Underline Tokens

The underline token tells the printer that the text it marks off is to be underlined. On the Print/Program Commands menu the default for the underline token is the backslash (\).

Type the next subheading in the report and the following paragraph. Embed the commands for the paragraph margin and insert the backslashes as indicated:

> Publicity
> The \Las Madres Journal \has agreed to do a feature story on the auction that will appear on Friday, March 21. A photographer will also cover the event, so don't be surprised if you see yourself the next day in the \Journal \!

On the printout, the text between the underline tokens will be underlined.

Unless you are using the backslash for some other purpose in a document, it can remain the sign for the command to underline text. But should you want to use a different token throughout a document, change the default on the Print/Program Commands menu.

The UT command can be embedded in the text if only one part of the document will be affected. For example, the exclamation point can be used instead of the backslash, either by changing the default on the Print/Program Commands menu or by embedding ".UT!" on the line above the text that will be marked with the exclamation point for underlining.

Inserting a Backspace

Although the underline token does not appear in the printout, many printers insert a space for each UT command. If your printer responds this way, you'll probably want to remove some of the spaces.

Often, the underline token can be inserted where a space would otherwise occur. There should be a space before and after "Las Madres Journal", since the title occurs in the middle of the sentence. However, in the second set of underline tokens around "Journal", a space between the underlined word and the exclamation point is undesirable.

To eliminate such a space, you can insert a backspace that will have the effect of moving the exclamation point one space to the left when it is printed. When you insert a backspace character, it will appear on the screen so that you can check a document before it is printed and make certain that you have removed any spaces that shouldn't be there.

Because different makes and models of printers behave differently, you may have to experiment to find out how yours treats the UT command. Some do not insert an unwanted space; others do not have the ability to backspace. If you know your printer can't backspace, you can skip the following exercises in this section, which demonstrate how to remove spaces with the Backspace command.

You give the Backspace command in one of Apple Writer II's modes that you have not yet used: Control Character Insertion mode. This mode tells the printer to execute the command the character represents, instead of printing the command character in the text.

You enter and leave Control-Character Insertion mode by pressing [V]. In other words, [V] is a toggle, like [R] for Replace mode; and when Control-Character Insertion mode is on, a "V" appears on the data line.

The first step in removing the extra space after "Journal" is to put the cursor on the character that should be moved over, in this case the exclamation point. Then you enter Control-Character Insertion mode and give the Backspace command: you press the LEFT ARROW key once. An inverse "H" appears on the screen. Then you leave Control-Character Insertion mode and move the cursor to the right one space.

It all sounds much more complex than it actually is. Take it one step at a time:

1. Put the cursor on the exclamation point.
2. Press [V] and the "V" appears on the data line.
3. Press the **LEFT ARROW** key once (the Backspace command) and the inverse "H" appears.
4. Press [V] again and the "V" disappears from the data line.

5. Press the **RIGHT ARROW** key once to move the cursor past the exclamation point.

When you give the Backspace command, the inverse "H" indicates in the text on the screen that a Backspace command will go to the printer. The screen should now look like Figure 7-11.

The Backspace command also allows you to combine two characters in one space. This is useful for reproducing such characters as the accented "a" and "e" in French, the "ñ" in Spanish ("n" with a tilde), and other signs used in foreign languages. (Even if your printer does not insert a space for the underline token, you need the Backspace command in the following exercise.)

To see how this works, enter a new subheading and the following paragraph. Type the tilde after the second "n" in Montana, as indicated:

Entertainment
The popular musicians from the Casa Montaña restaurant will be strolling about the schoolgrounds. If any of you can juggle or would like to be a clown for a day, this is your chance.

Now put the cursor on the tilde. Press [V], press the **LEFT ARROW** key once, and press [V].

```
<   Z Mem:45238 Len: 1607 Pos: 1607 Tab:    0 File:report
-   are willing to put up posters in your neighborhood

.lm5
.rm70
.pm0
Publicity
.pm5
The\Las Madres Journal\has agreed to do a feature story on the
auction that will appear on Friday, March 21.  A photographer
will also cover the event, so don't be surprised if you see
yourself the next day in the\Journal\H!
```

Figure 7-11. *Underline tokens and Backspace commands embedded*

```
<   Z Mem:45027 Len: 1818 Pos: 1818 Tab:     0 File:report
The\Las Madres Journal\has agreed to do a feature story on the
auction that will appear on Friday, March 21.  A photographer
will also cover the event, so don't be surprised if you see
yourself the next day in the\Journal\H!

.pm0
Entertainment
.pm5
The popular musicians from the Casa MontanH~a restaurant will be
strolling about the schoolgrounds.  If any of you can juggle or
would like to be a clown for a day, this is your chance.
```

Figure 7-12.   *"Entertainment" section of report with embedded commands*

To move the cursor off the "H", use the **RIGHT ARROW** key. The screen should now look like Figure 7-12.

Since the report will be used again in a later chapter, save it now in a file named REPORT. Then save the settings on the Print/Program Commands menu in a print values file also named REPORT.

PRINTING TO THE DISPLAY

Before printing a document, you may want a better idea of how the printout will look than the screen provides at this point. The left and right margins reflect the values on the Print/Program Commands menu, but the first lines of paragraphs are not indented, the title is not centered, and the outdented paragraph is still formatted like all the others.

You can see on the screen how these formatting commands will affect the printout by "printing" to the editing display. To do this, you change the print destination.

When you give the command to print to the display, the text will scroll by on the screen. To stop the scrolling, press [S]. Then press [S] again to resume the scrolling. At the end of the "printing," a prompt will ask you to press RETURN. If you did not catch everything you wanted to see, give the command again.

```
    The response has been positive so far.  We should have an
interesting assortment of items, gift certificates, and donated
services by the day of the auction.

Grand Prize
    The Las Madres students have been selling tickets for a
grand prize drawing to be held during the auction.  But we are
still looking for something spectacular to give away.  Anyone who
can help us out with this should contact one of the committee
members immediately.

Volunteers
    During the week prior to the auction, volunteers will be
needed to collect and store the donated items.  Please set aside
some time and let us know if you

        -  have access to a station wagon or a small
           truck or are willing to drive someone else's
        -  have space in your garage where large items
           can be safely stored
        -  are willing to put up posters in your
           neighborhood

Publicity
```

Figure 7-13.   *Part of report "printed" on editing display*

Press [P] and type **PD0**. Press **RETURN**.

Then give the New Print command: [P]**NP**

Press **RETURN**. Figure 7-13 shows the outdented paragraph "printed" on the editing display.

Now that you've had a glimpse of how the document will look, you can print it out. Press [P] and change the print destination back to the correct port or slot for your printer.

Then turn on the printer and give the New Print command. The printout will look like Figure 7-14.

USING SPECIAL
FORMATTING COMMANDS

If your printer has the capability, text can be printed in boldface type, which creates a strong contrast against the white of the page or against the text surrounding it. Numbers can be printed as

```
                    Project Committee Report
                          Lee Herman

        Our committee has been working hard to guarantee that the
    upcoming auction for the Las Madres School will be a great
    success.  This report summarizes our activities to date and what
    remains to be done.

    Donations
        A letter went out to potential donors in the business
    community on November 3 and was followed up with phone calls and
    solicitations in person from members of the committee.  We are
    continuing to contact new sources.

        The response has been positive so far.  We should have an
    interesting assortment of items, gift certificates, and donated
    services by the day of the auction.

    Grand Prize
        The Las Madres students have been selling tickets for a
    grand prize drawing to be held during the auction.  But we are
    still looking for something spectacular to give away.  Anyone who
    can help us out with this should contact one of the committee
    members immediately.

    Volunteers
        During the week prior to the auction, volunteers will be
    needed to collect and store the donated items.  Please set aside
    some time and let us know if you

            - have access to a station wagon or a small
              truck or are willing to drive someone else's
            - have space in your garage where large items
              can be safely stored
            - are willing to put up posters in your
              neighborhood

    Publicity
        The Las Madres Journal has agreed to do a feature story on
    the auction that will appear on Friday, March 21.  A photographer
    will also cover the event, so don't be surprised if you see
    yourself the next day in the Journal!

    Entertainment
        The popular musicians from the Casa Montaña restaurant
    will be strolling about the schoolgrounds.  If any of you can
    juggle or would like to be a clown for a day, this is your
    chance.
```

Figure 7-14.   *Printout of report*

superscript characters (above the line) and as subscript characters (below the line). Figure 7-15 shows examples of text printed in boldface, superscript, and subscript characters.

Printers vary as to which special formats they can produce. The Apple Imagewriter printer can print boldface type, and the Apple Daisy Wheel printer can print superscripts and subscripts. Some

Boldface text makes a strong visual statement

Footnotes often use superscript numbers[2]

Chemical terms, like H_2O, often use subscript numbers

Figure 7-15.   *Printing boldface, superscripts, and subscripts*

---

printers can do all of these and more—including italics, for instance.

Many of the commands for special effects are entered with the ESC key and another character or characters. You enter Control-Character Insertion mode to put the character for the ESC key on the screen and then leave Control-Character Insertion mode and type the other character or characters for the command. The characters, including the character that represents ESC on the screen, do not appear in the printed text. Some commands may require one command at the beginning of the text to turn on the special format and a different command at the end to turn it off.

Your printer may treat the characters you enter for special formatting commands as it would the underline token and leave a space. Not all printers do this, but if yours does, insert a backspace to remove any spaces that you don't want in the printed text.

You should consult your printer's manual to determine the commands it can execute and the form each command must take. These will differ between makes and models of printers.

If you are printing with either an Apple Imagewriter or an Apple Daisy Wheel, you can use the SPECIAL file that is on the Apple Writer II Master disk. This file provides shortcuts for commands that work with these printers. You can load SPECIAL as a glossary file from the Master disk by selecting "Load Glossary File" from the Additional Functions menu and then entering the file name SPECIAL at the prompt. If the prefix has been set to another volume name, you'll have to include the name of the Master disk: /AW2MASTER/SPECIAL.

Then use the OPEN APPLE key and the character that represents the definition for the command you want to insert. For instance, to insert a command to print boldface type on the Apple Imagewriter, you would press OPEN APPLE-B; to turn off the command, you would press OPEN APPLE-b. Several commands can be used when **SPECIAL** is loaded in the Glossary buffer. They are listed in the section called "A Built-In Glossary of Printer Commands" in Chapter 2 of the *Apple Writer II User's Manual*.

REVIEW EXERCISES

1. Embed the commands to format a paragraph that would have a left margin of 10, a right margin of 68, and a first line indent of 3.

2. Embed the commands that would follow the paragraph in the preceding exercise to return to a left margin value of 5, a right margin of 75, and a paragraph margin of 5.

3. Use the Backspace command to print:

   mañana
   señorita

4. Insert the underline token and the backspace in this sentence:

   Has anyone seen my copy of <u>War and Peace</u>?

8
MAKING TABLES AND OUTLINES

Neat columns of text can enhance the visual appeal of a document and can present information concisely. But getting a table or an outline from the initial to the finished stage is ordinarily time-consuming. Adding information or rearranging it can be especially irksome on a typewriter. At times the only option is to start over. Word processing, however, takes much of the drudgery and guesswork out of the process.

Even if you have little or no experience putting together a table, Apple Writer II will help you to do it in a few simple stages. First determine how the information should be distributed on the page; then enter the table; and, finally, edit it until the result is exactly right.

In this chapter you'll first create a table. Then you'll learn how to use Apple Writer II's tabular formats to create a resume, a kind of outline.

SETTING TABS

To lay out a table, you set tabs and then enter text, using the TAB key to move across a line to the designated columns. When you start up Apple Writer II, default tab settings are automatically put into the Tab buffer, which, like the Glossary buffer and the Print Values buffer, is an area for temporary storage in the computer. You can keep some or all of the default tabs, or you can set your own, whichever is suitable for the particular table you are creating.

The default tab settings can be seen from the editing display. After starting up Apple Writer II and setting the prefix for /PRACTICE/AUCTION, press **ESC** once from the editing display. The data line is now replaced by a ruler divided into eight segments, with each space, or column, marked off on the 80-column screen.

The columns for tabs already set are highlighted, as if each one had a stationary cursor on it. These default tabs are set 10 columns apart, beginning with the first column, 0, and ending at column 69. Figure 8-1 shows the ruler on the editing display screen.

In making your own tables, decide the number of columns needed, the width of each, and the amount of space between columns. If the table will become part of a longer document, you may want to format the left and right margins to match the other pages. If so, it is also a good idea to adjust the screen margins in order to see how the shorter line will print out.

There are three ways to change tab settings:

- Remove all tabs at once (the defaults will be restored next time you start the program).
- Remove some selectively.
- Add tabs.

To remove all tab settings at once, you can give a command to

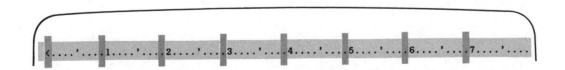

Figure 8-1.   *Default tabs on the ruler*

purge the Tab buffer. To remove one tab at a time, you put the cursor in the column for which the tab is set and then give the command to clear a tab. Similarly, you set a new tab by moving the cursor to the column where the tab will be and giving the command to set a tab. These commands can be used to change the default tab settings and to reset any tabs you have previously set.

For the table you are going to create in this chapter, some tab settings should be removed and one new one added. Use the TAB key to move from one tab setting to the next.

Press **TAB** once and the cursor jumps to the ninth column, 10 spaces past column 0.

Press [**T**] and the prompt appears, asking whether you want to set a new tab, clear a tab, or purge all the current tabs.

Type **C** to clear a tab. Notice that the highlight no longer appears on column 9 of the ruler, indicating that this tab has been cleared.

Now press **TAB** once to move to the next tab setting (at column 19) and remove it the same way: give the Tab Clear command.

Leave the tab set at column 29; it is one of the settings for the table. But clear the tabs at columns 39 and 49.

At this point you could continue clearing the other tabs, but it is easier to set the new one first. It will be on column 57.

Press **TAB** once and then move back two columns by pressing the **LEFT ARROW** key twice.

Now press [**T**] and type **S** to set this tab. As you can see, the highlight appears in column 57 directly above the blinking cursor.

Because the TAB key always moves the cursor to the next tab setting, pressing it now will put the cursor on column 59. Clear this tab and then clear the last one in column 69. The screen should look like Figure 8-2, with the tabs set only at columns 29 and 57.

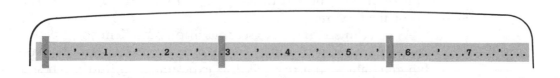

Figure 8-2.   *Ruler with two tabs set*

The ESC key is a toggle for turning both the data line and the ruler on and off. Pressing ESC once puts the ruler on the screen; pressing ESC again leaves the screen blank; pressing ESC one more time brings back the data line. Once all the tabs for a particular document have been set, the ruler is no longer necessary. The data line is more useful on the screen while you are entering text.

Press **ESC** twice to put the data line back on the screen. Whenever you want to check the tab settings or to change them, use the ESC key to view the ruler again.

There is another method for turning the data line on and off. On the Additional Functions menu the selection "Toggle Data Line Display" has the same effect as the ESC key. If the data line is on the screen, selecting this option on the menu turns on the ruler, and selecting it again turns both the data line and the ruler off; selecting it a third time brings back the data line. However, it is usually faster simply to press ESC on the editing display.

CONSTRUCTING A TABLE

Because the TAB key not only moves the cursor to the next tab setting, but also inserts characters for blank spaces wherever there is no text, there is now a top line of blank spaces on the screen. Delete them to the Word and Paragraph buffer. When the cursor is back at the beginning of the first line, type the heading for the first column of the table.

Type: **Donation**

Press **TAB** once. The cursor moves to the first tab setting (col. 29).

Type: **Donor**

Now press **TAB** again to move to the second tab setting (col. 57).

Type: **Value**

Leave two blank lines and then enter the items for the table as shown in Figure 8-3. Under "Value", enter the amounts so that the decimals line up. The easiest way is to insert one more space in front of all but the fourth amount. Do not press RETURN at the end of the last line.

As you can see, these tab settings allow sufficient space between the columns of text and create a symmetrical layout. For more elaborate tables, you may need to experiment to find the best tab settings. But if you enter a line or two and find that the settings

```
>    Z Mem:46462 Len:   383 Pos:    0 Tab:    0 File:table
Donation                    Donor                  Value

portable telephone          Essential Gadgets       50.00
dinner for two              The Jade Palace         35.00
10 aerobics classes         Healthy Bods            70.00
oil painting                a friend               200.00
imported cheeses            Gourmet Emporium        50.00
```

Figure 8-3.   *Entire text of table*

don't produce a workable layout, you can clear the screen and set new tabs with a minimum of effort.

Moving Across Text and Spaces

The column headings would make a more distinct impression if they were underlined. In fact, it would be effective to put an underline across the entire line on which the headings are entered. But adding characters into a table is slightly different from initially entering text in columns. Once columns have been set up and the space between them filled with space characters, you don't want to distort the columns.

To format the top line so that it will be underlined, move the cursor to the "D" in "Donation" by giving the command to go to the beginning of the document. Insert the underline token in front of the "D".

Now move the cursor to the space after the "n" in "Donation". You may notice that the headings "Donor" and "Value" have moved over one space to the right; however, on the printout they will be lined up as you originally entered them.

If you pressed TAB now to move across the line in order to insert the other underline token, new spaces would be entered and "Value" would be pushed down onto the next line. You could use the RIGHT ARROW key to move to the end of "Value", but there is a faster method.

Hold down the **SOLID APPLE** key while you press the **TAB** key

```
>    Z Mem:46460 Len:  385 Pos:   64 Tab:    64 File:table
\Donation                    Donor                   Value\

portable telephone           Essential Gadgets        50.00
dinner for two               The Jade Palace          35.00
10 aerobics classes          Healthy Bods             70.00
oil painting                 a friend                200.00
imported cheeses             Gourmet Emporium         50.00
```

Figure 8-4.   *Underline tokens in table heading*

twice. Pressing SOLID APPLE-TAB moves the cursor over the spaces from one tab setting to the next without inserting more spaces.

Now use the **RIGHT ARROW** key to put the cursor on the space after "Value", insert the underline token, and move the cursor back to the end of the document. The screen should look like Figure 8-4, with the two underline tokens in the top line of the table.

Setting Margins for Tables

When you are making a table, it is useful to know how many more characters can be entered on a line. Since the default margins on the Print/Program Commands menu have not been changed, 78 characters could have been entered before word wraparound would break the line.

Once you have entered a table, the number after Tab: indicates whether the margins can be changed for a shorter line. This table can fit on a line shorter than 78 columns, and reducing the margins will make it more readable. Give the command to change the left margin to 5.

The number after Tab: serves another function. The ruler shows only the 80 columns that can be displayed on the screen at one time. However, tabs can be set up to column 240. Although the columns from 81 to 240 cannot be displayed on the screen, you can print out long lines if you have a printer that accommodates extra-wide paper.

To set tabs past column 80 you would first change the margins on the Print/Program Commands menu. For the widest possible margins, you would leave LM0 as the value for the left margin and enter RM240. Then you would insert spaces with SPACEBAR until Tab: indicates the column where you would like to set a tab. Giving the Tab Set command would then set that tab. You can enter a total of 64 tabs with this method. Tabs set past column 80 do not, however, show up on the ruler.

If you adjust the margins on the editing display after setting RM240, you can scroll horizontally across the screen with the LEFT ARROW and RIGHT ARROW keys. Scrolling allows you to see all the text on the long line by putting as much on the screen as it can display at one time.

SAVING TABS WITH TABLES

Tables are saved in a text file, like any other document. Save this one now in a file named TABLE, since it will be used again in the next chapter. Even if you don't think you'll need a table in the future, you should save it on a data disk before printing it.

But saving the table did not save the tabs that were set in order to create it. Like the other buffers in Apple Writer II, the Tab buffer is an area of memory in the computer that temporarily stores tab settings. When you turn off the computer or purge the buffer to reset tabs, whatever settings were in the buffer are lost. The next time you start up Apple Writer II, the default settings are loaded into the Tab buffer again.

However, tab settings can be saved in a file to be used again, much the way print values and glossaries are saved. If you might later add information to a table, saving the tab settings and loading them with the text file avoids having to set them again. You may also find that the tab settings for one table work for other tables as well. In that case you would simply load the tab file and create another table.

To save a tab file, you go to the Additional Functions menu and select "Save Tab File". Then you name the file. To load the file, you select "Load Tab File" from the menu.

When the Additional Functions menu is on the screen, select "Save Tab File" and name the tab file TABLE. The screen will look like Figure 8-5.

Then press **RETURN** and the file is saved.

```
       ADDITIONAL FUNCTIONS MENU

    A.  Load Tab File
    B.  Save Tab File
    C.  Load Print/Program Value File
    D.  Save Print/Program Value File
    E.  Load [G]lossary File
    F.  Save [G]lossary File
    G.  Toggle Carriage Return Display
    H.  Toggle Data Line Display
    I.  Connect Keyboard to Printer/Modem
    J.  Quit Apple Writer

        Press RETURN to Exit

        Enter your selection (A - J) :b

    Enter File Name :table
```

Figure 8-5.   *Saving a tab file*

On the catalog for the AUCTION subdirectory, the tab file will be listed as TABLE.TAB to distinguish it from the text file TABLE. But in loading or saving a tab file, the extension .TAB need not be typed.

PRINTING A TABLE

The margins have already been set, so there is little else to do before printing a table as brief as this one. However, it will be more readable if it is double-spaced.

Begin by going to the Print/Program Commands menu and changing Line Interval to LI1. Then set the printing commands for your printer. The Print/Program Commands menu should look like Figure 8-6, except for your specific printing values.

Now print the table. The printout should be like Figure 8-7.

Notice that the double-spacing not only left a blank line in between each line of the table, but also put three blank lines after the headings because of the extra RETURN.

```
Print/Program Commands:

Left      Margin     (LM) = 5
Paragraph Margin     (PM) = 0
Right     Margin     (RM) = 78
Top       Margin     (TM) = 1
Bottom    Margin     (BM) = 1
Page Number          (PN) = 1
Printed Lines        (PL) = 58
Page Interval        (PI) = 66
Line Interval        (LI) = 1
Single Page          (SP) = 0
Print Destination    (PD) = 1
Carriage Return      (CR) = 0
Underline Token      (UT) = \
Print Mode (LJ,FJ,CJ,RJ) = LJ
Top Line             (TL) :

Bottom Line          (BL) :

Press RETURN to Exit

[P]rint/Program :
```

Figure 8-6.   *Line Interval set for double-spacing*

Donation	Donor	Value
portable telephone	Essential Gadgets	50.00
dinner for two	The Jade Palace	35.00
10 aerobics classes	Healthy Bods	70.00
oil painting	a friend	200.00
imported cheeses	Gourmet Emporium	50.00

Figure 8-7.   *Printout of table*

CONSTRUCTING AN OUTLINE

Tab settings allow you to enter text for outlines consistently and easily. For example, the standard outline form can be set with tabs, as in Figure 8-8. The cursor can then be moved to each subheading with the TAB key.

Outlines often contain more text than do tables. How many characters to fit on a line, how much blank space to leave, and how large to make margins are therefore important considerations that will affect the appearance of the printed copy.

A resume is one example of an outline in which information is organized to produce a meaningful grouping of text that is also visually pleasing. There are many possibilities for formatting a resume or any similar document — centered headings, underlining, titles in capital letters, blocks of text in paragraphs, fill justified margins, to mention just some of the variations. Let your imagination and Apple Writer II lead you to experiment with various layouts.

The resume you'll create next will demonstrate a simple format: a centered block of text at the top and two tab settings for the main body of text. You'll also see how to edit the text easily.

Entering Text in an Outline

Deciding how text should be distributed in a resume is to some extent a matter of trial and error. Therefore, tab settings can be determined after some preliminary estimates have been made and

```
>   Z Mem:46699 Len:  146 Pos:   22 Tab:   21 File:history

                     The History of the World

    I.  Prehistoric era
        A.  Art and Artifacts
            1.  Stone tools
            2.  Cave paintings
```

Figure 8-8.   *An outline created with tabs*

after part of the resume has been put on the screen. If necessary, the tab settings can be changed later.

However, the tabs set for the table are still in the Tab buffer. They won't be correct for the resume, so we'll purge them all.

Press [**T**] and then type **P**. Now give the New Screen command to clear the table from the editing display.

Embed the command to center justify the following three lines and then type them:

Lee Herman
123 Shadyslope Drive
Las Madres, California

The main body of the resume will have blocks of text grouped into three categories: Education, Experience, and Professional Associations. These categories will line up against the left margin as one column of text.

Press **RETURN** twice after "California" and embed the left justify command.

Then type: **Education**

The screen should now look like Figure 8-9. A tab can now be set by figuring out how many characters must be entered in the first column and how many blank spaces should separate it from the next group of text. The last category, Professional Associations, would take up too much room on one line. So when we get that far, we'll enter it on two lines, each starting at the left margin.

Even so, "Professional" is a longer word than "Education".

```
<     Z Mem:46771 Len:     74 Pos:     73 Tab:      9 File:resume
.cj
Lee Herman
123 Shadyslope Drive
Las Madres, California

.lj
Education ▪
```

Figure 8-9.   *Heading and first column of resume*

The cursor is now on the space after "Education", and the number after Tab: is 9, whereas the word "Professional" has 12 letters.

Press **SPACEBAR** until 12 appears after Tab: on the data line. The first column must be able to hold this number of characters.

But if the tab is set at column 13, there won't be any space in between the category and the information in that line. So press **SPACEBAR** until Tab: indicates 16. (You can't move the cursor where no text or spaces have been entered.) Then give the command to set a tab at this position.

Press **ESC** to view the ruler. As you can see, the new tab at column 16 is set.

Now with the cursor at column 16, enter the following:

B.A., State University

Some of the other entries in this column will be longer, and we must leave space between this column and the next one. Turn the data line back on to see the position of the cursor.

Let's try setting the next tab at column 53, which is 15 spaces past the current position of the cursor at column 38. Watch the data line while you press **SPACEBAR** and set a tab at column 53.

Now type: **1972**

Press **RETURN**.

Enter the following information in the second and third columns on the next line:

M.B.A., Mt. Tamalpais University   1983

The screen should now look like Figure 8-10.

Leave a blank line and continue using TAB to enter text for the rest of the resume in the appropriate columns, as is shown in Figure 8-11.

When you create an outline or any other document that will require text to be entered close to the end of the line, you'll get better results if you turn off word wraparound. Without word wraparound, you can enter as many characters as the margins allow. But with word wraparound on, any word that goes over the number of characters is moved down in its entirety to the next line.

The "Z" on the data line that indicates word wraparound is in effect a toggle. Pressing [Z] turns word wraparound off, and pressing [Z] again turns it back on.

```
<    Z Mem:46665 Len:    180 Pos:    179 Tab:    57 File:resume
.cj
Lee Herman
123 Shadyslope Drive
Las Madres, California

.lj
Education          B.A., State University              1972
                   M.B.A., Mt. Tamalpais University    1983
```

Figure 8-10.   *Two lines of text in resume*

Editing Text in an Outline

Because you do not want to disturb the placement of text and blank spaces in a table or an outline, deleting text can be somewhat tricky. For every character deleted, the text on a line will move one space to the left, and the columns will no longer line up

```
>    Z Mem:46334 Len:    511 Pos:      0 Tab:     0 File:resume
.cj
Lee Herman
123 Shadyslope Drive
Las Madres, California

.lj
Education          B.A., State University               1972
                   M.B.A., Mt. Tamalpais University      1983

Experience         Project Manager, XYZ Co.             1984-
                   Ass't Project Manager, XYZ Co.       1983-84
                   Corporate Communications, A&B Co.    1976-82
                   Ass't Editor, Las Madres Journal     1973-76

Professional       Young Executives Association
Associations       Movers and Shakers
```

Figure 8-11.   *Text of entire resume*

```
                          Lee Herman
                       123 Shadyslope Drive
                       Las Madres, California

        Education       B.A., State University              1972
                        M.B.A., Mt. Tamalpais University    1983

        Experience      Project Manager, XYZ Co.            1984-
                        Ass't Project Manager, XYZ Co.      1983-84
                        Corporate Communications, A&B Co.   1976-82
                        Ass't Editor, Las Madres Journal    1973-76

        Memberships     Young Executives Association
                        Movers and Shakers
```

Figure 8-12.   *Printout of modified resume*

properly. You can use the DELETE key or the other Delete commands, but you must insert more spaces.

However, Replace mode avoids altering the number of characters and spaces on a line. So when you want to change some numbers in a table, correct errors, or even retype a whole column of text, use Replace mode.

For example, changing the text in the resume from "Professional Associations" to "Memberships" is a simple operation in Replace mode.

Put the cursor on the "P" in "Professional" and press [**R**].

Then type **Memberships** and press **SPACEBAR** once.

```
        Item                    Amount          Description

        widget                    32            fills needs
        widget holder              4            holds 8 widgets
        widget manual              1            standard reference
                                                on widgets
```

Figure 8-13.   *Review exercise table*

Now put the cursor on the "A" in "Associations". Since moving the cursor takes you out of Replace mode, enter Replace mode again.

Then press **SPACEBAR** until "Associations" has been replaced with blank spaces.

Save the resume now as the file RESUME. A printout of the resume would look like Figure 8-12.

REVIEW EXERCISES

1. Create the table in Figure 8-13.

2. Reproduce the outline in Figure 8-8.

9

COMBINING DOCUMENTS AND FORMATTING THE FINISHED PAGE

Once a document has been stored as a file on a disk, it may prove to be of no further use except as a permanent copy for future reference. Other documents may ultimately be used — in part or in whole — in ways you didn't imagine when you first created them.

Apple Writer II offers an array of features that allow you to recycle text for different purposes: two documents can be combined into one, a portion of one document can be saved separately or incorporated into a new document, two documents can be printed together, and a portion of one document can be printed together, and a portion of one document can be printed by itself.

In this chapter you learn how to combine documents by using variations on the Save, Load, and Print commands. You'll see how to split the screen of the editing display. This is a useful feature when you're working with two documents or considering whether to save part of a document. You'll also learn to make page breaks and add page numbers and footnotes, giving your documents the final touches that enhance them.

SAVING DOCUMENTS

There are four options for saving a document in Apple Writer II. You are already familiar with the first: enter the text on the editing display, give the Save command, and name the file. The other options provide considerable flexibility about what is stored on a disk and where:

- An entire document on the screen can be added to the end of a file document.
- Part of a document can be saved at the end of a file.
- Part of a document can be saved in its own file.

Each of these Save options reduces the number of commands you would otherwise need to produce the desired results. For example, if you want to add a piece of text at the end of a file, you can enter the text, edit it, and then save it to that file without loading the original file. Saving part of the document on the screen in its own file eliminates having to delete on the screen text that should not be saved. And saving part of a newly created document to an existing file avoids both loading the file and deleting extraneous text.

Moreover, while the document is on the screen, it can be saved in multiple files. You can save all of it in one file, part of it in a separate file, and part or all of it in an existing file.

Saving a Document at the End of a File

When you want to add on to a file, it is convenient to create the new text and then save it to that file. Many people find an empty editing display less distracting than a screen filled with text. It is easier to concentrate on the addition until it is ready to be saved.

The report you saved in Chapter 7 is almost finished, but it lacks a conclusion. Adding one final subheading and a brief paragraph will demonstrate how to save text at the end of a file.

Set the prefix for the volume and subdirectory on the ProDOS Commands menu. Load the REPORT print values file on the

Additional Functions menu. Then open up the editing display.

As you have probably noticed, when a file is loaded the cursor is positioned after the final character at the end of the text. If the REPORT file were loaded now, the cursor would be in the middle of a line after the period in the last sentence. The new text would be added at this point.

To add space between the preceding paragraph of the report and the addition, press **RETURN** twice at the top of the editing display.

The last portion of text in the report was formatted as a normal paragraph with an indented first line (PM5). To prevent the new subheading from being indented, it should be preceded by an embedded command, like the other subheadings.

Type **.PM0** and press **RETURN**.

Then type the subheading **Conclusion** and embed the formatting command for the normal (indented) paragraph that will follow. The screen should look like Figure 9-1.

Now type the following paragraph:

So far the preparations are proceeding on schedule. With one month remaining, we will be able to tie up any loose ends. Plan to be there on March 22 for a good time in support of a worthwhile activity.

To add text onto the end of a file, you give the Save command as usual and type in the name of the file. But before pressing RETURN, you type the plus sign.

Give the Save command and then type: **REPORT+**.

The screen will look like Figure 9-2.

Press **RETURN** and the prompt will ask whether you want to

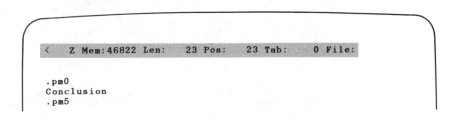

```
< Z Mem:46822 Len:    23 Pos:    23 Tab:    0 File:

.pm0
Conclusion
.pm5
```

Figure 9-1.   *"Conclusion" subheading with embedded commands*

```
 <    Z Mem:46619 Len:   226 Pos:   226 Tab:    203 File:

.pm0
Conclusion
.pm5
So far the preparations are proceeding on schedule.  With one
month remaining, we will be able to tie up any loose ends.  Plan
to be there on March 22 for a good time in support of a
worthwhile activity.




[S]ave :report+
```

Figure 9-2.   *Saving a document to the end of a file*

delete the old REPORT file. You do, because the new file will contain both the old file and the addition.

Type **Y** and press **RETURN**.

```
 <    Z Mem:44802 Len:  2043 Pos:  2043 Tab:    203 File:report
.pm5
The popular musicians from the Casa MontanH~a restaurant will be
strolling about the schoolgrounds.  If any of you can juggle or
would like to be a clown for a day, this is your chance.

.pm0
Conclusion
.pm5
So far the preparations are proceeding on schedule.  With one
month remaining, we will be able to tie up any loose ends.  Plan
to be there on March 22 for a good time in support of a
worthwhile activity.
```

Figure 9-3.   *"Conclusion" section appended to REPORT*

The "Conclusion" section has now been added at the end of the REPORT file. The next time you load REPORT, it will appear on the screen, as shown in Figure 9-3.

When you add text to your files, you can save the new text and make any formatting changes later. Or, if you know that blank lines or embedded commands will be necessary, you can include these in the new text, as you just did.

Saving Part of a Document
At the End of a File

Suppose that after putting some text on the screen you decide to save only part of it to an existing file. In that case, you would enter the file name and the plus sign, but the selected portion would have to be marked off. The cursor marks the beginning of the text to be saved. The end of the selection is indicated as part of the Save command entry.

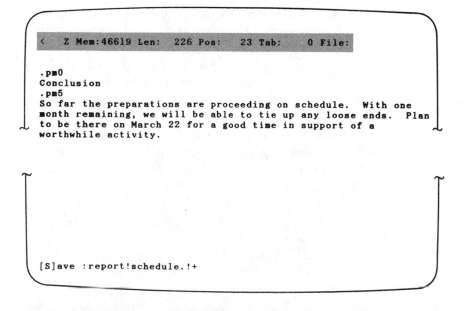

Figure 9-4.   *Saving part of a document to end of a file*

For example, instead of the entire document that is on the screen now, you could have saved just the first sentence. To do so, the cursor would be moved to the "S" in "So" at the beginning of the sentence. Then, after the file name had been typed in the Save command prompt, the end of the text would be indicated between exclamation marks. In this instance it would be "!schedule.!" and then the plus sign. Figure 9-4 shows the screen as it would look if the first sentence were about to be added to the end of REPORT.

Saving all or part of a document to an existing file is most convenient when the addition belongs at the end. When it belongs elsewhere, you can save the new text to the end of the file and then move it by deleting it to the Word and Paragraph buffer and retrieving it at the correct location. However, you can also save the addition in a separate file and then load it exactly where it should occur in the old file, as you will see later in this chapter.

Saving Part of a Document In a Separate File

Rather than saving part of a document into an existing file, you can make a new file for it. This option enables you to create a second document quickly. One of the other sections of the report, "Volunteers", can form the basis for a new document. By saving it separately, it can be printed and used as a sign-up sheet.

Clear the screen and load the REPORT file. As you can see, the new section, with its embedded commands, now ends the report.

Put the cursor on the "D" in "During". The fastest method is to give the Find command. The first subheading and the embedded commands need not be saved.

Now give the Save command and type a different name for the new file. Type **SIGNUP** over the old name that appears in the prompt.

Indicate the end of the selected text by enclosing the last word in exclamation points. Type: **!neighborhood!**

The screen now looks like Figure 9-5.

Next, press **RETURN** and this paragraph is saved to its own file, SIGNUP. Meanwhile the REPORT file is unchanged on the screen and is still intact on the data disk.

The exclamation point used to mark off the end of the text to be saved in this exercise, as well as in the previous example, is a delimiter. The text between the delimiters is called a *marker*. When you enter a marker, make sure that it is sufficiently distinctive. If "neighborhood" had appeared elsewhere in the selection, Apple Writer II would have saved only up to the marker's first occurrence. If punctuation or spaces are to be included, they must be entered as part of the marker (as in "!schedule.!").

The exclamation point is the standard delimiter in Apple Writer II, and it is commonly used with both the Save and Load commands to mark off text. However, if an exclamation point occurs within the marker itself, it cannot be used as the delimiter for that word or phrase. Other signs can become delimiters when the exclamation point cannot be used. The asterisk (*), the less than sign (<), the ampersand (&), and the pound sign (#) can substitute for the exclamation point. Although these signs take on special meanings when used as delimiters with the Find command,

```
<   Z Mem:44802 Len: 2043 Pos:   964 Tab:    0 File:report
Grand Prize
.pm5
The Las Madres students have been selling tickets for a grand
prize drawing to be held during the auction.  But we are still
looking for something spectacular to give away.  Anyone who can
help us out with this should contact one of the committee members
immediately.

.pm0
Volunteers
.pm5
During the week prior to the auction, volunteers will be needed
to collect and store the donated items.  Please set aside some
time and let us know if you

.lml5
.rm60
.pm-3
-  have access to a station wagon or a small truck or are willing
to drive someone else's

[S]ave :signup!neighborhood!
```

Figure 9-5.   *Saving part of a document in a separate file*

as will be explained in Chapter 11, they can be used just like the exclamation point with the Save and Load commands.

The slash is another delimiter that Apple Writer II recognizes. You have been using the slash (/) to delimit volume, subdirectory, and file names and to delimit text for finding and replacing. But because the slash is the delimiter that marks off the parts of a file name, it cannot be used to mark off text with the Save and Load commands.

LOADING FILES

There are several options for loading that allow you to combine all or part of multiple documents. Simply loading a file while another one is already loaded allows you to join them as one continuous document on the screen. The second file will be loaded at the end of the first. If it is desirable to store the documents in this combined form, you can save it in a new file with a different name. Or if the object was merely to view them together, you can clear the screen afterward.

Documents can also be combined so that text from one file is loaded anywhere in the text that is already on the screen. Unlike text saved to an existing file, text can be loaded into a document at precisely the spot you specify. A selected portion of a file can also be loaded into a document using delimiters and markers.

Loading One File Into Another

Loading the table you saved in Chapter 8 into the report will demonstrate how to incorporate a second file into the document in memory at a particular location. After you add a connecting sentence, the table will be inserted at the end of the "Donations" section.

Leave a blank line after the last line of the "Donations" section and type the following:

Here is a sampling of the donations we have been promised:

Now put the cursor after the embedded command ".PM0" and press **RETURN**. This command will now apply to the table as well as to the next subheading.

The cursor should be at the beginning of the line between ".PM0" and "Grand Prize". When you give the Save command, the table will be loaded where the cursor is positioned on the screen.

Give the load command and type: **TABLE** (Figure 9-6 shows how the screen should look.)

Press **RETURN** and the table is inserted into the text of the report at the cursor's position, as in Figure 9-7.

When loading one file into another, you may have to adjust formatting commands or add blank lines, just as when saving text to the end of a file. If you have not anticipated these adjustments before loading, you can always make them afterward. As you can see in Figure 9-7, there should be another blank line between the table and the next subheading, so press **RETURN**. Then add two blank lines between ".PM0" and the heading of the table.

Save this document as a new file. Type: **REPORT2**

Now both REPORT and TABLE still exist as separate files on the data disk and REPORT2 combines them in one file. If you have no reason to keep the originals once they have been com-

```
>     Z Mem:44742 Len: 2103 Pos:   716 Tab:    0 File:report
A letter went out to potential donors in the business community
on November 3 and was followed up with phone calls and
solicitations in person from members of the committee.  We are
continuing to contact new sources.

The response has been positive so far.  We should have an
interesting assortment of items, gift certificates, and donated
services by the day of the auction.

Here is a sampling of the donations we have been promised:
.pm0

Grand Prize
.pm5
The Las Madres students have been selling tickets for a grand
prize drawing to be held during the auction.  But we are still
looking for something spectacular to give away.  Anyone who can
help us out with this should contact one of the committee members
immediately.


[L]oad :table
```

Figure 9-6.   *Loading TABLE into REPORT*

bined, instead of saving a new file, just save the combined file under the name of the original file on the screen and you can delete the other original file from the disk later.

Although loading one file into another is often convenient, you should proceed cautiously if one or both files are long. There must be enough room in the computer's available memory to hold both files at once. If you try to load two files when there is insufficient memory, the beeper will sound and a zero will appear after Mem: on the data line. To avoid this, check the data line to see how much memory is still available and check the catalog to see how much memory the second file requires before loading it.

If the combined document will be too long, try cutting down the length of the document on the screen by deleting some of it or load only part of the second file, as explained in the next section. In cases where the second file will be added to the end of the first, you can achieve the same effect by printing them as one file without loading them together. You'll learn how to do this at the end of this chapter.

```
<    Z Mem:44357 Len: 2488 Pos:    710 Tab:    58 File:report
Donations
.pm5
A letter went out to potential donors in the business community
on November 3 and was followed up with phone calls and
solicitations in person from members of the committee.  We are
continuing to contact new sources.

The response has been positive so far.  We should have an
interesting assortment of items, gift certificates, and donated
services by the day of the auction.

Here is a sampling of the donations we have been promised:
.pm0
\Donation                     Donor                     Value\

portable telephone            Essential Gadgets          50.00
dinner for two                The Jade Palace            35.00
10 aerobics classes           Healthy Bods              70.00
oil painting*                 a friend                  200.00
imported cheeses              Gourmet Emporium           50.00
Grand Prize
.pm5
The Las Madres students have been selling tickets for a grand
```

Figure 9-7.   *TABLE loaded into REPORT*

Loading Part of a File

Sometimes you'll find it useful to load part of a file into a document on the screen. The Load command, like the Save command, can specify a selected portion of text. The procedure for loading part of a file is similar to the one used to save part of a document. Delimiters and markers indicate the text to be loaded.

Part of the conclusion in the report is appropriate to put in a memo that describes the current status of the project. Since the report is on the screen, go to the end of the document and note the first and last words of the selection, together with any punctuation. In this case, the markers will be "So" and "ends."

Now clear the screen and on the Additional Functions menu load the glossary file MEMO.GLOSS into the glossary buffer. Then retrieve the glossary entry that sets up the heading for a standard memo:

Press **OPEN APPLE**-h

Fill in the items in the heading as in Figure 9-8. Leave a blank line after the heading. Now type

This is to let you know how the auction project is coming along.

Press **RETURN** twice.

Give the Load command and type the name of the file. Between exclamation points type the markers for the first and last words of the text to be loaded: **REPORT!So!ends.!**

```
<   Z Mem:46753 Len:    92 Pos:    92 Tab:     0 File:
Date:   February 19, 1986

To:  Dr. Tracy Fontenrose

From:  Lee Herman

Subject:  Auction
```

Figure 9-8.   *Memo heading*

```
 <     Z Mem:46686 Len:   159 Pos:   159 Tab:      0 File:
Date:  February 19, 1986

To:  Dr. Tracy Fontenrose

From:  Lee Herman

Subject:  Auction


This is to let you know how the auction project is coming along.




[L]oad :report!So!ends.!
```

Figure 9-9.   *Loading part of a file*

The screen looks like Figure 9-9. Check that "So" is properly capitalized; otherwise, the text would be loaded from the word "so" in the "Publicity" section. If any other words in the report started

```
 <     Z Mem:46566 Len:   279 Pos:   279 Tab:    120 File:report

To:  Dr. Tracy Fontenrose

From:  Lee Herman

Subject:  Auction


This is to let you know how the auction project is coming along.

So far the preparations are proceeding on schedule.  With one
month remaining, we will be able to tie up any loose ends.
```

Figure 9-10.   *Part of REPORT loaded into memo*

with these letters, such as "Someone", the beginning marker could include a space after "So" to distinguish it, or the phrase "So far" could be used as the marker. Also check that the period is included after "ends".

Press **RETURN** and the two sentences from the report become part of the new memo, as in Figure 9-10.

Since this document has not yet been saved, no file name has been shown on the data line. But now the data line shows "REPORT" after "File:", merely indicating that part of the REPORT file has been loaded.

Save this document now as MEMO2.

If the text to be loaded starts at the beginning or extends to the end of a file, you can use a shortcut in typing the markers:

- To load text from the beginning of a file to a specific marker, only the delimiters for the beginning marker need be typed and then the marker that ends the selection.

- To load text from a specific marker to the end of a file, only the beginning marker is required.

Thus, to load all of the report from the beginning up to the first sentence of the last paragraph, "REPORT!!Conclusion!" would be the entry, with no text between the first delimiters. To load the entire last paragraph in the report into MEMO2, only the first marker would be entered ("REPORT!So!) without an ending marker.

There are two more ways to specify how marked text is loaded. You can select text so that the markers themselves are not loaded by adding "n" to the load command entry. In addition, you can load all the text in a file that occurs between the same markers by adding "a" as well as "n" to the entry.

For example, in Figure 9-11 any of the items could be selected without the number. The numbers preceding and following each item would be the markers, and "n" would specify loading only the text between the markers from the file.

To load only the second item, "several pairs of jeans", the entry would be "!(2)!(3)!n". And if you wanted to load every item in Figure 9-11, but not any of the numbers, the entry would be "!)!(!an". Each item is delimited by these unique markers.

Loading part of a file, like saving part of a document, is also a way to separate one section of text and make it a separate file.

```
(1) sleeping bag
(2) several pairs of jeans
(3) three towels
(4) hiking boots
```

Figure 9-11.   *Items to load without markers*

Simply load the text onto an empty editing display and save it again under a new file name.

Peeking at a File

Before taking advantage of the various options for loading part of a file, you must be able to specify the beginning and ending markers. But most people can't determine which markers should be used unless they can see the source file. A feature in Apple Writer II called *peeking* allows you to find the words or phrases for markers while another document is in memory.

Peeking at a file is also a quick method for refreshing your memory about its contents without actually loading it. Perhaps you have saved a file containing a list of activities to be done according to a schedule. Suppose that in the midst of creating a document, you want to include some dates or other information from the list. By peeking at the file, you can see what you need to know and continue working on the document.

To peek at a file, you give the Load command, type the file name, and then type a backslash (\ ). With MEMO2 on the screen, we'll peek at the NOTES file.

Give the Load command and type: **NOTES **

When you press **RETURN**, the memo moves up to the top of the screen and the NOTES file is displayed at the bottom, under the Load command entry (as illustrated in Figure 9-12).

Ordinarily, when you peek at a file, it will scroll by, much like the scrolling when you print to the display. But NOTES is so short that it all fits on the bottom of the screen. To stop the scrolling you press [S], and you press [S] again to continue viewing the rest of

```
This is to let you know how the auction project is coming along.

So far the preparations are proceeding on schedule.  With one
month remaining, we will be able to tie up any loose ends.




[L]oad :notes\
10/15/85  Sent memo to TF
Finance committee meets 10/23/85
Assign someone to handle publicity
Also, someone in charge of volunteers
I'll prepare a letter for potential donors
What indoor facilities if it rains the day of the auction?      (Press RETURN)
```

Figure 9-12.   *Peeking at a second file*

the file. After peeking at the contents of a file, you press RETURN to resume working on the document in memory.

Press **RETURN** and NOTES disappears, leaving the memo as it appeared before.

Copying With the Load Command

The Load command offers one more option: you can "load" part of a document that is in memory to another location in that document. The text on the screen must have been previously saved, however. In effect, this option duplicates some text in the same document.

For example, if you create a table that is longer than a page, you would probably want the column headings reproduced on the second page as well. You could copy the headings to the Word and Paragraph buffer, or you could copy them with the Load command.

To load part of a document elsewhere in the same document,

you would enter the beginning and ending markers preceded by the pound sign (#). The copy would be inserted at the position of the cursor. In general, you can accomplish the same results with the Copy command, explained in Chapter 3. This Load option is particularly useful in WPL programs, when the Copy command would not be feasible.

SPLITTING THE SCREEN

The editing display can be divided into equal halves, each with its own data line. When the screen is split, you can look at two parts of a document that would not otherwise be on the screen simultaneously. Text can be moved or copied from one display on the screen to the other. You can also load a second document into one half of the screen or peek at it as it scrolls past.

It is often helpful to see two parts of a long document on the

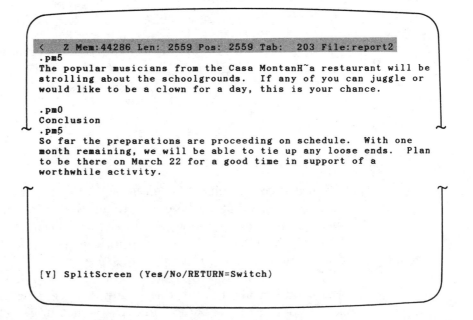

Figure 9-13. *The Split Screen command prompt*

screen while you are editing it. For example, if you are deciding whether to move a paragraph, you can view the text in its old and new locations. You can also check for unnecessary repetitions and inconsistencies in the document.

Clear the screen and load the REPORT2 file and then give the Split Screen command:

Press [**Y**]

The prompt appears, as in Figure 9-13.

In response to the prompt, type **Y** to split the screen. Press **RETURN** and the editing display should now look like Figure 9-14.

Notice that the cursor in the lower display is blinking, but the one in the upper display is not. The blinking cursor can be moved, just as you move it with a full screen, and the text in that display can be edited.

Press [**B**] to move the cursor in the lower display to the beginning of the report, as in Figure 9-15. As you can see, the data line for the lower display is no longer showing the same information as the one at the top.

The cursor can be moved quickly through the text by using the SOLID APPLE key and the UP and DOWN ARROW keys. Press **SOLID**

```
<     Z Mem:44286 Len:  2559 Pos:  2559 Tab:    203 File:report2
Conclusion
.pm5
So far the preparations are proceeding on schedule.   With one
month remaining, we will be able to tie up any loose ends.   Plan
to be there on March 22 for a good time in support of a
worthwhile activity.



<     Z Mem:44286 Len:  2559 Pos:  2559 Tab:    203 File:report2
Conclusion
.pm5
So far the preparations are proceeding on schedule.   With one
month remaining, we will be able to tie up any loose ends.   Plan
to be there on March 22 for a good time in support of a
worthwhile activity.
```

Figure 9-14.   *Split screen with REPORT2 in both sections*

APPLE-DOWN ARROW. Notice that the cursor jumps down to the last line that was on the screen, while the lower text scrolls up.

The display containing the blinking cursor is called the *active display.* You can add and delete text in the active display just as you do when there is a full screen. To make the other display active, you press [Y] and **RETURN**.

Press [Y] and **RETURN** to activate the other display. The cursor starts blinking in the upper half of the screen.

Text can be moved or copied from one display to the other. To move a paragraph from the active display, you would first delete it to the Word and Paragraph buffer. Then you would activate the other display, put the cursor where you want the paragraph inserted, and retrieve the paragraph from the Word and Paragraph buffer. If you just want to see how text would look in both locations, instead of deleting it, you can copy it to the Word and Paragraph buffer. Remember, any changes made to the document will not be preserved unless you save them.

```
<    Z Mem:44286 Len: 2559 Pos: 2559 Tab:   203 File:report2
Conclusion
.pm5
So far the preparations are proceeding on schedule.  With one
month remaining, we will be able to tie up any loose ends.  Plan
to be there on March 22 for a good time in support of a
worthwhile activity.



>    Z Mem:44286 Len: 2559 Pos:     0 Tab:     0 File:report2
.cj
Project Committee Report
Lee Herman

.lj
.pm5
Our committee has been working hard to guarantee that the
upcoming auction for the Las Madres School will be a great
success.  This report summarizes our activities to date and what
remains to be done.
```

Figure 9-15.   *Displaying two parts of a file on split screen*

When you have finished viewing the document on the split screen, you give the Split Screen command again and, in response to the prompt, you type N.

Restore the full screen now: press [Y] and type N. Then press **RETURN**.

A split display also allows you to compare two different documents by following the steps to load a file while a document is in memory. The file will be loaded at the end of the document, and then you can split the screen and move the text in either display. Figure 9-16 shows the REPORT2 file in the upper display and the MEMO2 file in the lower.

Loading another file into one of the displays on a split screen has the same effect as loading a file while one is already in memory: the files are joined together. So do not save the results unless you want a combined file. To avoid joining the files, you can load the second one with the backslash and compare it as it scrolls past in the active display.

```
<     Z Mem:44005 Len: 2840 Pos: 2344 Tab:     4 File:report2
The popular musicians from the Casa MontanH~a restaurant will be
strolling about the schoolgrounds.  If any of you can juggle or
would like to be a clown for a day, this is your chance.

.pm0
Conclusion
.pm5
So far the preparations are proceeding on schedule.  With one
month remaining, we will be able to tie up any loose ends.  Plan
to be there on March 22 for a good time in support of a
worthwhile activity.
<     Z Mem:44005 Len: 2840 Pos: 2632 Tab:     0 File:report2
Date:  February 19, 1986

To:  Dr. Tracy Fontenrose

From:  Lee Herman

Subject:  Auction


This is to let you know how the auction project is coming along.
```

Figure 9-16.   *Displaying two files on split screen*

ADDING PAGE BREAKS, PAGE NUMBERS, AND FOOTNOTES

Some of your documents will be several pages long. With Apple Writer II, you can decide where to end a printed page and where to print a page number. You can also format footnotes to appear at the bottom of a page.

Making Page Breaks

Apple Writer II sets up the number of printed lines per page according to the value for "Printed Lines" (PL) on the Print/Program Commands menu. If the default value is left unchanged, 58 single-spaced lines of text will be printed on each page, including any text in the top or bottom line (TL and BL), any footnotes, blank lines for the top and bottom margins (TM and BM), and any blank lines inserted between paragraphs. This value can be changed on the Print/Program Commands menu to print fewer lines per page.

However, there are times when the PL value is correct in general for a document but not for a particular page. You can then embed a formatting command that tells the printer to end a page earlier, or in other words, to break the page at a certain point and go on to the next page. This command helps prevent awkward divisions of text.

For example, the outdented text in the "Volunteers" section of the report would look better printed all together on the same page. To make sure that part of this text won't be printed at the bottom of a page and continued on the next page, let's embed a Form Feed command on the line above the outdented text.

Move the cursor to the hyphen on the first line of outdented text and press **RETURN**.

Type a period and the Form Feed command: **.FF**

Then press **RETURN** again.

As with any other embedded command, the Form Feed command must begin with a period at the beginning of a line and end with **RETURN** when it appears in a document. Figure 9-17 shows how the screen should look.

Embedding the Form Feed command forces the printer to break the page at a specified location. But perhaps the text would not have been separated between pages. Form Feed can be embedded as a *conditional form feed,* which will take effect only if there isn't enough room at the bottom of a page for all the text.

To embed a conditional Form Feed command, you count the number of lines needed to keep the text intact and specify that number as part of the command. However, the number of lines of text on the screen should be the same as the number of lines that will actually be printed. That is, if necessary, you should give the Adjust Screen Display command so that the display margins match the print values. Because the print value file for the original **REPORT** file was already loaded when you loaded the **REPORT2** file, the screen margins are correct.

Since the text requires five lines, change the Form Feed command by inserting the conditional specification. The command should be ".FF5".

You can see where a page will break by putting the page and line count on the screen. The Page and Line Count command is

```
<    Z Mem:44282 Len: 2563 Pos: 1657 Tab:     3 File:report2
.pm0
Volunteers
.pm5
During the week prior to the auction, volunteers will be needed
to collect and store the donated items.  Please set aside some
time and let us know if you

.lm15
.rm60
.pm-3
.ff
-   have access to a station wagon or a small truck or are willing
to drive someone else's
-   have space in your garage where large items can be safely
stored
-   are willing to put up posters in your neighborhood

.lm5
.rm70
.pm0
Publicity
.pm5
```

Figure 9-17.　*Embedded Form Feed command*

[_]. To give this command, you hold down the CONTROL key and the SHIFT key while you press the key that has the underline on top and the hyphen on the bottom. The page and line count remains on the screen and reflects the cursor's position until you type in more text.

Press [_]

As Figure 9-18 shows, the last line of the outdented text will be printed on the first page, provided that more text is not added to the report ahead of it. Therefore, the conditional form feed you just entered will probably not cause a page break.

As the report is presently formatted, the second page will begin with the second line in the paragraph under "Entertainment".

However, even a few words added anywhere on the first page might alter the line count so that "Entertainment" would be the last line of the first page. To avoid cutting off the subheading from its paragraph, embed another conditional form feed that will guarantee at least one line of the paragraph after the subheading:

```
>    Z Mem:44281 Len: 2564 Pos: 1870 Tab:    53 File:report2
to collect and store the donated items.  Please set aside some
time and let us know if you

.lm15
.rm60
.pm-3
.ff5
-  have access to a station wagon or a small truck or are willing
to drive someone else's
-  have space in your garage where large items can be safely
stored
-  are willing to put up posters in your neighborhood

.lm5
.rm70
.pm0
Publicity
.pm5
The\Las Madres Journal\has agreed to do a feature story on the
auction that will appear on Friday, March 21.  A photographer

[_] Page 1 Line 46
```

Figure 9-18.   *Checking the page and line count*

Type **.FF2** in front of "Entertainment" and press **RETURN**. See Figure 9-19.

The Form Feed command should be embedded at the end of a document below the last line of text to force the printer to stop at the top of a new page. Also a Form Feed command at the end of a document is necessary whenever page numbers or footnotes are to be printed on the last page, as you'll see in the next two exercises.

Formatting Page Numbers

Page numbers are obviously useful in a long document. With Apple Writer II you can put the page number either at the top or the bottom of the page. It can be printed on the left, in the center, or on the right side, top or bottom. If you prefer not to have a page number on the title page, you can specify this also.

```
<    Z Mem:44272 Len: 2573 Pos: 2226 Tab:    68 File:report2
.pm5
The\Las Madres Journal\has agreed to do a feature story on the
auction that will appear on Friday, March 21.  A photographer
will also cover the event, so don't be surprised if you see
yourself the next day in the\Journal\H!

.pm0
.ff2
Entertainment
.pm5
The popular musicians from the Casa MontanH~a restaurant will be
strolling about the schoolgrounds.  If any of you can juggle or
would like to be a clown for a day, this is your chance.

.pm0
Conclusion
.pm5
So far the preparations are proceeding on schedule.  With one
month remaining, we will be able to tie up any loose ends.  Plan
to be there on March 22 for a good time in support of a

[_] Page 2 Line 1
```

Figure 9-19.   *Conditional form feed to join heading and text*

The page number will be printed on the line reserved for text at the top (TL) or at the bottom (BL). Therefore, to format a page number, you enter the specification on the Print/Program Commands menu.

The standard delimiter for the page number is the slash (/). Since there are three choices for the position of the page number, the delimiters indicate your decision. The pound sign (#) inside a set of slashes tells the printer where to put the page number. The six possible formatting commands entered on the Print/Program Commands menu for the page number are

1. TL/#/// (page number printed at top in left margin)
2. TL//#// (page number printed at top in center)
3. TL///#/ (page number printed at top in right margin)
4. BL/#/// (page number printed at bottom in left margin)
5. BL//#// (page number printed at bottom in center)
6. BL///#/ (page number printed at bottom in right margin)

To print the page number on all the pages except the first page, you use the backslash (\) as the delimiter. Thus, "TL \ \ \# \" would format the page number on the top of the page at the right margin, beginning with the second page; "BL \# \ \ \" would format a page number at the bottom of the page at the left margin, beginning with the second page.

With the Print/Program Commands menu remaining on the screen, type: **BL**

Then type: \ \# \ \ (as shown in Figure 9-20)

Press **RETURN**. The report is now formatted with a centered page number that will be printed on the bottom of the second page.

But there is one more step before the document can be printed. When a document will have page numbers in the bottom line, you must embed the Form Feed command at the end of the text; otherwise, the printing will stop before it reaches the bottom of the page.

Go to the end of the report, press **RETURN**, and type: **.FF**

Although an embedded command should always end with RETURN, the Form Feed command at the end of a document is an exception to this rule. Do not press RETURN after embedding the command at the end of the report.

The page number can be formatted so that other characters are also printed in the top or bottom line. For example, to print the word "page" with the number on the right side at the top of a page, you would type "TL///page#/"; similarly, to print the number between hyphens centered at the bottom of a page, you would specify "BL//-#-//".

The top line of a page can also contain text for a *header,* and the bottom line can contain text for a *footer.* Headers or footers in a long document might include the name of the author and an abbreviation of the title, as well as other pertinent information. Text can be distributed across the page by entering it between the delimiters.

For example, suppose that you want to format a header for each page of the report, except for the first (or title) page. The text for the header would contain the author's last name on the right side of the page and an abbreviation of the title in the center. The

```
Print/Program Commands:

Left      Margin      (LM) = 5
Paragraph Margin      (PM) = 0
Right     Margin      (RM) = 70
Top       Margin      (TM) = 1
Bottom    Margin      (BM) = 1
Page Number           (PN) = 1
Printed Lines         (PL) = 58
Page Interval         (PI) = 66
Line Interval         (LI) = 0
Single Page           (SP) = 0
Print Destination     (PD) = 1
Carriage Return       (CR) = 0
Underline Token       (UT) = \
Print Mode (LJ,FJ,CJ,RJ) = LJ
Top Line              (TL) :

Bottom Line           (BL) :

Press RETURN to Exit

[P]rint/Program :bl\\#\\
```

Figure 9-20.   *Page number formatted on Print/Program commands menu*

command entered on the Print/Program Commands menu for this header would be "TL \ \Report \Herman \".

The page number can be combined with a header or a footer. Figure 9-21 shows the bottom line text changed on the Print/Program Commands menu if a footer for the report that includes the word "page" and a number in the center and a name on the right side were to be printed.

The report is all ready for printing. Save it with [S]= and print it out now. The page number will be at the bottom of the second page, as in Figure 9-22. Then save the revised print values, including the page number format, as a new print values file named REPORT2.

Notice that the conditional form feed above "Entertainment" keeps the subheading together with its paragraph on the second page. Had this command not been embedded, the subheading would have become the last line of the first page. When the page

```
Print/Program Commands:

Left       Margin    (LM) = 5
Paragraph Margin    (PM) = 0
Right      Margin    (RM) = 70
Top       Margin    (TM) = 1
Bottom     Margin    (BM) = 1
Page Number          (PN) = 1
Printed Lines        (PL) = 58
Page Interval        (PI) = 66
Line Interval        (LI) = 0
Single Page          (SP) = 0
Print Destination    (PD) = 1
Carriage Return      (CR) = 0
Underline Token      (UT) = \
Print Mode (LJ,FJ,CJ,RJ) = LJ
Top Line             (TL) :

Bottom Line          (BL) :
  \\page#\Herman\
Press RETURN to Exit

[P]rint/Program :
```

Figure 9-21.   *Footer specified on Print/Program commands menu*

was reformatted to allow room for a page number on the bottom line, the number of lines of text that could be printed was less per page, even where the page number was not printed.

Formatting Footnotes

If you wish to put footnotes at the bottom of a page, Apple Writer II can do this. A footnote, unlike a footer, does not put the same text on each page; instead, a *footnote* explains a portion of text on a particular page in a document. The body text to which the footnote refers is marked by a number or other sign. Footnotes are, of

```
Entertainment
     The popular musicians from the Casa Montaña restaurant
will be strolling about the schoolgrounds.  If any of you can
juggle or would like to be a clown for a day, this is your
chance.

Conclusion
     So far the preparations are proceeding on schedule.  With
one month remaining, we will be able to tie up any loose ends.
Plan to be there on March 22 for a good time in support of a
worthwhile activity.
```

2

Figure 9-22.   *Printed report with page number*

course, appropriate in research papers. They appear in business documents as well to provide additional or clarifying comments. Footnotes are also used to clarify the information in a table.

To see how footnotes are formatted, let's add a note to the table. Clear the screen and load TABLE. Since there will be only one footnote, an asterisk can signify that a note will be found at the bottom of the page.

Put the cursor on the space after "painting". Enter Replace mode and type an asterisk (*).

Since the table has been created with inserted tab spaces, Replace mode keeps the table aligned when the footnote reference is added. When you move the cursor to enter the text for the footnote, you will leave Replace mode.

Ordinarily, if a footnote reference appears in a paragraph of text, you should enter the text for the footnote right after the reference. This helps ensure that the footnote appears on the same page as the reference. The text for the footnote is enclosed within the footnote symbols, which are (<>). However, in this instance, even with Replace mode, the text would not fit in the table without rearranging the columns.

When it is not feasible to enter the footnote text immediately after its reference, you can type it on a separate line nearby. So move the cursor to the end of the document and press **RETURN**.

Then type: (**<* a seascape with clouds>**)

```
 <   Z Mem:46357 Len:   488 Pos:   488 Tab:     3 File:table

\Donation                    Donor                  Value\

portable telephone           Essential Gadgets       50.00
dinner for two               The Jade Palace         35.00
10 aerobics classes          Healthy Bods            70.00
oil painting*                a friend               200.00
imported cheeses             Gourmet Emporium        50.00
(<* a seascape with clouds>)
.ff
```

Figure 9-23.   *TABLE formatted with footnote*

The footnote will be printed exactly the way the text appears between the footnote symbols. There will be a space between the asterisk and the rest of the footnote.

Now press **RETURN** and embed a Form Feed command. Otherwise, since this is the only page of the document, the printer would not go on to the bottom of the page and would not print the footnote. Figure 9-23 shows how the screen should look at this point. Figure 9-24 shows how the table would look if it were printed.

Save the footnoted table with [S]=.

When a footnote is entered, it is put in a buffer with a maximum size of 1024 characters per page. WPL programs share this buffer, which is described in Chapter 10. For the most part, however, there should be plenty of room for several footnotes on a page.

If a footnote is longer than the number of characters set for a line of text in the body of a document, it should be broken into segments and entered on separate lines. The left and right margin values do not affect footnotes; nor does word wraparound break a

Donation	Donor	Value
portable telephone	Essential Gadgets	50.00
dinner for two	The Jade Palace	35.00
10 aerobics classes	Healthy Bods	70.00
oil painting*	a friend	200.00
imported cheeses	Gourmet Emporium	50.00

* a seascape with clouds

Figure 9-24.   *Printout of TABLE with footnote*

line of footnote text. Therefore, you must match the lines of a footnote to the left and right margins. For example, if the document is formatted with a 65-character line, enter 65 characters or less between each set of footnote symbols.

To format multiple footnotes on one page, enclose each in footnote symbols, breaking lines where necessary. To leave a blank line between footnotes, put a set of footnote symbols between them, enclosing only one or more spaces. If your printer can print superscripts, you can use superscript numbers to identify the body text and the corresponding footnote.

PRINTING DOCUMENTS

Two or more documents that have been combined and then saved in a file will be printed as one continuous series of pages. Apple Writer II will keep track of the page numbers and print them in the position on the page you have chosen.

Instead of combining two files into one, you can print them as one document with the Print command. This option is an especially useful alternative when the total length of the documents may be greater than the computer's available memory. Moreover, there may be other good reasons for maintaining separate files yet printing them out together.

In order to print two or more documents as one, you load the first file in the sequence and print it, as usual, with the New Print command, [P]NP. Then you load a second file and give the command for Continue Print, [P]CP. To add subsequent files, repeat the [P]CP command after loading each one into memory.

Even if each file in the sequence has previously been printed with page numbers, Apple Writer II will renumber the pages and print consecutive page numbers on the new combined document. However, to print the final page of the last file with a page number or any footnotes, the Form Feed command must be embedded at the end of the text.

The table, complete with its footnote, can be printed together with MEMO2 as one document. The memo should be printed first, however, so clear the screen and load MEMO2.

Add this sentence to the memo in a new paragraph:

The following list will give you an idea of the kinds of donations we'll have on hand.

Then press **RETURN** twice to leave space before the table.

```
Date:   February 19, 1986

To:  Dr. Tracy Fontenrose

From:  Lee Herman

Subject:  Auction


This is to let you know how the auction project is coming along.

So far the preparations are proceeding on schedule.  With one
month remaining, we will be able to tie up any loose ends.

The following list will give you an idea of the kinds of
donations we'll have on hand.


Donation_____Donor_____Value

portable telephone        Essential Gadgets          50.00
dinner for two            The Jade Palace            35.00
10 aerobics classes       Healthy Bods               70.00
oil painting*             a friend                  200.00
imported cheeses          Gourmet Emporium           50.00




* a seascape with clouds
```

Figure 9-25.   *MEMO2 and TABLE printed as one document*

It is always wise to save a document before printing it. Since new text has been added to the MEMO2 file, save it with [S]=.

You should also always check the Print/Program Commands menu before giving any print commands. Checking this menu is even more important when you are about to print more than one file, because each document will be formatted according to the current print values. If a document later in the sequence requires different formatting, make the changes to the menu before continuing to print that particular document.

Put the Print/Program Commands menu on the screen. Notice that Paragraph Margin is now PM5. When you printed REPORT2, the last embedded command was .PM5 and that value is now reflected on the menu. Reset Paragraph Margin to PM0. Otherwise, the heading of the memo and the columns of the table will be indented. The left and right margin values will be appropriate for the memo and the table, so they need not be changed.

Now return to the editing display and print the memo with the New Print command.

When the memo has been printed, clear the screen and load the table. The Form Feed command is already embedded. If it were not, you would add it at this point.

Press [P] and type: **CP**

As Figure 9-25 illustrates, the two files are printed together.

There is one more printing option. The Enable Print command can be used to print part of a file. Like the Form Feed command, it is embedded in a document to identify the selected text for the printer.

The Enable Print command can be either .EP0 or .EP1, embedded at the beginning of a line and ended with a RETURN.

An embedded EP0 tells the printer to skip over all the following text until it reaches an embedded EP1. Then all the text will be printed unless another EP0 is embedded. Figure 9-26 shows the report with the Enable Print command embedded so that only the "Publicity" section will be printed.

In the next two chapters you will learn more methods for combining documents and for giving Print commands in WPL programs.

```
< Z Mem:44262 Len: 2583 Pos: 2137 Tab:     4 File:report2
.epl
.lm5
.rm70
.pm0
Publicity
.pm5
The\Las Madres Journal\has agreed to do a feature story on the
auction that will appear on Friday, March 21.  A photographer
will also cover the event, so don't be surprised if you see
yourself the next day in the\Journal\H!
.ep0

.pm0
.ff2
Entertainment
.pm5
The popular musicians from the Casa MontanH~a restaurant will be
strolling about the schoolgrounds.  If any of you can juggle or
would like to be a clown for a day, this is your chance.

.pm0
Conclusion
```

Figure 9-26.　　*REPORT2 with Enable Print commands embedded*

REVIEW EXERCISES

1. Save the paragraph in the "Publicity" section of **REPORT2** as a separate file.

2. Print the "Grand Prize" section of the report as a separate document.

3. Enter the list in Figure 9-11 and save it as a file. Then load the third item without loading the markers.

AUTOMATED WORD PROCESSING: PRODUCING DOCUMENTS WITH WPL

P art III introduces Apple Writer II's own word processing language, WPL. With WPL, you can print customized copies of a form letter automatically. The WPL programs provided for you on the Master disk are ready for you to use. WPL is easy to learn, and you can write your own programs to run with Apple Writer II.

10

USING WPL PROGRAMS STORED ON THE MASTER DISK

WPL, which stands for *word processing language*, is one of Apple Writer II's most remarkable features. You can run one of the four WPL programs provided for you as files on the Master disk, and you can write your own WPL programs. WPL programs streamline such routine word processing activities as printing a series of documents.

When you run a WPL program, you start it and instruct it to perform certain Apple Writer II functions. Then the program carries them out automatically. In some instances, the instructions are already written into the program and you can give just one command—to run the program. As you gain practical experience with Apple Writer II, you'll soon identify the tasks you regularly perform that require several command sequences a WPL program could do automatically.

A particularly useful application of a WPL program is to produce customized form letters. Imagine giving a single command and printing one hundred letters, one after the other, each to a different address on your mailing list. One of the WPL programs on the Master disk, AUTOLETTER, can do this; it is ready for you to set up and print as many copies of your form letters as you wish.

For many people new to computers, the idea of learning a programming language may seem intimidating. There's no need, however, to become fluent in WPL in order to use AUTOLETTER to print your form letters or to run the three other programs on the Master disk. In fact, no programming expertise at all is required. Here are the four WPL programs:

- AUTOPRINT automatically prints as many as 30 files as separate documents.
- CONTPRINT automatically combines as many as 30 files into one printed document.
- COUNTER counts the total number of words in a file.
- AUTOLETTER prints form letters.

The Master disk also includes a demonstration program, DEMOS. DEMOS is not a program you can use for your own work; it demonstrates two very practical applications of WPL. One is to produce a form letter with a program similar to AUTOLETTER. The other application is to produce a contract with a program that loads and combines specified portions of prepared text (sometimes called "boiler plate").

This chapter gets you started using WPL. First, you'll run the DEMOS program. Next, you'll try out AUTOPRINT and COUNTER, using files from the PRACTICE disk. Then you'll create and print a form letter with AUTOLETTER. Should you wish to learn more about WPL, Chapter 11 illustrates step-by-step some useful programs you can create with WPL.

RUNNING WPL PROGRAMS

To run any WPL program, you follow the same procedure:

1. Type the [P] command from the editing display.
2. Type DO.

You have been typing [P] to give print commands, such as [P]? and [P]NP, but [P] followed by DO means a program command. That's why the prompt that appears on the screen after you type [P] reads "[P]rint/Program".

You can run WPL programs only from the editing display. Do

not try to type DO after the prompt on the Print/Program Commands menu.

3. Leave a space. (The space is not strictly necessary; however, it is allowed and it makes checking the spelling of the program file name easier.)

4. Enter the file name of the WPL program. (Depending on the default prefix, you may have to enter the complete volume and file name.)

When you give the command to run a WPL program, Apple Writer II loads the file containing that program into the buffer reserved for WPL programs and for footnote text. This buffer can hold 2048 characters of a WPL program. However, if a footnoted document is to be printed while a WPL program is loaded, half the space in this buffer is reserved for footnotes; even if the document has only one footnote, the space available for the WPL program is then only 1024 characters. As you learned in Chapter 9, the maximum number of characters for footnotes, whether or not a WPL program is also sharing the buffer, is 1024 per page.

None of the WPL programs on the Master disk exceeds 1024 characters. You should keep in mind, however, that AUTOPRINT, CONTPRINT, and AUTOLETTER cannot print documents that have more than 1024 characters of footnotes per page. (Even so, 1024 characters allow about a half page of single-spaced footnotes.)

5. Press RETURN to go back to the editing display and Apple Writer II when a WPL program ends.

To stop a WPL program while it is running, you press the ESC key. When the program stops, you can clear the screen on the editing display.

Let's look at a demonstration of WPL on DEMOS. It shows vividly the speed and ease with which WPL can produce custom documents.

RUNNING THE DEMONSTRATION
PROGRAMS ON DEMOS

Start up Apple Writer II and leave the Master disk in drive 1. To run any of the WPL programs that are on the Master disk, the Master disk must be in drive 1. The Master disk must also be inserted if you want to view any of the programs on the Master disk as text files on the editing display. If you have only one disk drive, you'll be instructed when to insert the data disk, if necessary.

Go to the editing display. The prefix has not been set, so the default prefix, AW2MASTER, is in effect. Thus, only the program's file name need be entered to run DEMOS.

Press [**P**]

Then type: **DO** (lowercase is acceptable for WPL commands and file names)

Press **SPACEBAR**.

Type: **DEMOS**

Press **RETURN**.

The data line disappears, and the following prompt is at the top of the screen:

Would you like to see this
demonstration in a 40
column display (Y/N)?

If you can display only 40 columns, type "Y"; for wider displays, type "N".

Press **RETURN**. Now you see the Demonstrations menu, as shown in Figure 10-1.

Demonstrating a Form Letter Program

Select the form letter demonstration and press **RETURN**. This program takes names and addresses from a separate file and automati-

```
        DEMONSTRATIONS MENU

   1. FORM LETTER
   2. CONTRACT

      Enter Your Selection (1 or 2) :
```

Figure 10-1.   *The DEMOS menu*

cally fills them in as the recipients of a form letter. It also inserts the name of the sender and the date from information you provide. The characters you enter will be reproduced exactly in the form letter in uppercase or lowercase or any combination.

In response to the first prompt, type your name as the sender of the form letter and press **RETURN**.

For the second prompt, enter a date and press **RETURN**.

You now see on the screen the form letter shown in Figure 10-2, with a place for the date to be inserted and a place for your name as the signature. The places where each recipient's name and address will be inserted are indicated by "(Name)", "(FirstName)", and "(Address)".

Press **RETURN** and watch the program fill in each item for the first letter. Figure 10-3 shows the letter addressed to "John Blanko", the first name in the name and address file.

After viewing the letter, press **RETURN** and the program inserts the name and address of the next recipient on the list, "Harry Q.

```
>   Z Mem:46255 Len:   590 Pos:     0 Tab:     0 File:FORMLET
 Here's the original form letter
 Press RETURN to modify:
                                   1444 Ridgeway
                                   Hayward, Ind. 40294
                                   (Date)

(Address)


Dear (Name):

Thank you for your recent request concerning our new product line.  We believe
that soon people all over the U.S. will recognize its benefits, as you already
have.

We will soon be shipping a trial unit to the above address.  Please let us
know, (FirstName), if it satisfies your requirements.

                                   Sincerely,

                                   (Signature)
```

Figure 10-2.   *Original DEMOS form letter*

```
>   Z Mem:46206 Len:  639 Pos:     0 Tab:     0 File:FORMLET
"E" stops; Press RETURN for next letter
                                    1444 Ridgeway
                                    Hayward, Ind. 40294
                                    September 25, 1985

John Blanko
1984 Orwell Place
Future, PA 14151


Dear John Blanko:

Thank you for your recent request concerning our new product line.  We believe
that soon people all over the U.S. will recognize its benefits, as you already
have.

We will soon be shipping a trial unit to the above address.  Please let us
know, John, if it satisfies your requirements.

                                    Sincerely,
```

Figure 10-3.   *Form letter filled in with a name from file*

Public". Your name and the date you entered appear again in the appropriate places.

As you can see, running a program such as this one can make quick work of a mailing list. Each name and address from your list would be automatically filled in for each letter. Since this is only a demonstration program, you cannot edit it or supply it with your own list of names and addresses. However, later in this chapter you learn how to modify the AUTOLETTER program to use for form letters.

Now, if you have seen enough of this part of DEMOS, you can press E (SHIFT-E) and then press RETURN to interrupt the program at this point. (If DEMOS were in the process of putting together a letter, you could press ESC to interrupt it.) If you would like to see the program create one more letter, just press RETURN. Either way, before you leave the demonstration, the program displays the list from which it loaded the names and the addresses, as you can see in Figure 10-4.

```
<    Z  Mem:46686 Len:   159 Pos:   159 Tab:      0 File:ADDRESSES
(1)John Blanko
1984 Orwell Place
Future, PA 14151
(2)Harry Q. Public
1953 Warren Court
Sublime, WI 09876
(3)Susan Kremcheez
0000 Null Result
Meander, OH 54637


  The letters were prepared
from the addresses on this list.

  Press RETURN to continue.
```

Figure 10-4.   *DEMOS name and address file*

After viewing the address list, press **RETURN**. The Demonstrations menu reappears.

Demonstrating a Contract Program

Select the demonstration of a boilerplate contract program. Then press **RETURN**. This part of DEMOS loads text from several files to put together a complete document. It produces a rental contract and fills in the name of the tenant and other specific details from information you provide.

The first prompt asks you to enter a name for the imaginary tenant. Do so, and press **RETURN**.

The next prompt asks you to designate an apartment number, from 1 to 340. Enter a number and press **RETURN**.

The last prompt asks for the amount of a month's rent. Type any whole number, but do not use a dollar sign or a decimal figure. Figure 10-5 shows the screen when responses to all three prompts have been entered.

```
Tenant's name? George Washington
Apartment number? (1 through 340) 76
Monthly rental rate in dollars?  (Don't type $ sign.) 500
```

Figure 10-5.   *Information entered for DEMOS contract*

Press **RETURN**. The menu of options appears, as in Figure 10-6. Each option is the subject of a paragraph from a separate file. By choosing an option, you are deciding to include that subject or paragraph in a particular contract.

To choose any combination of options, you type the number from 1 to 4 and press RETURN after each number. The program

```
Contract ---------------------

OPTIONS:

    1  Cleaning deposit
    2  Rent due the 15th
    3  No pets
    4  Renter pays utilities




Type numbers of clauses
to include (1-4):
RETURN stops:
```

Figure 10-6.   *Menu for DEMOS contract*

then loads the text for each option and combines it to create the rental contract. Let's choose the first and third options.

Type 1 and press **RETURN**.

When the prompt reappears, type 3 and press **RETURN**.

Press **RETURN** again to indicate that no more options are to be included in the contract. The screen instructs you to press **RETURN** once more to view the completed document. As you can see, the program scrolls through the text of the contract. Then it displays the first screen, as shown in Figure 10-7.

To return to the editing display in Apple Writer II, press **RETURN** twice.

This demonstration program cannot be used to create an actual contract. You can't edit the text of the sample contract to put in, for example, a different address (or to correct the typing error, "deposity"). But such a program could be written in WPL that would have a menu from which to load prepared text.

```
>   Z Mem:45784 Len: 1061 Pos:     0 Tab:     0 File:STARTCON
                Press RETURN to continue.

ADDRESS:   1094 Drury Lane, Apt. #76, Cupertino, Ca.   95014

RENT: $500.00 per month.

Tenant agrees to the following terms and conditions:


DEPOSIT:  A security deposit of fifty percent (50%) of one month's rent will
be required.  The deposity is fully refundable after tenancy for one year, or
upon inspection of the unit at surrender.

PETS:  No pets are allowed inside the rental unit.  This includes hamsters,
dogs, cats, felines of any sort, rodents, birds, or other animals.  Small fish
in aquaria are exempt.

The above parties further agree that there are no additional obligations over
and above the ones explicitly set forth in this contract.  In witness whereof
the undersigned have affixed their signatures.
```

Figure 10-7.   *Completed DEMOS contract*

Unlike the demonstration programs on DEMO, you can use the four ready-made WPL programs on the Master disk for your own documents. Let's see now how to apply two of them, AUTO-PRINT and AUTOLETTER, to your word processing in Apple Writer II.

PRINTING MORE THAN ONE FILE AUTOMATICALLY

Both AUTOPRINT and CONTPRINT load files from your data disk for automatic printing. To run either program, the Master disk must be in drive 1; and before printing starts, the data disk containing the files to be printed must be in one of the disk drives.

Printing Separate Documents With AUTOPRINT

AUTOPRINT is a WPL program for printing up to 30 files in succession as separate documents. By running AUTOPRINT, you can enter all the file names at the outset; you don't have to give a Load and Print command for each file. Running AUTOPRINT is the equivalent of giving the [P]NP command for as many files as you have to print.

To streamline your work routine, you can wait to print until you have saved several files on a data disk. Then you can let AUTOPRINT take charge of printing them all.

When you start AUTOPRINT, it prompts you for the names of the files. If the prefix has been set to the volume (and subdirectory, if there is one) name of the disk containing the files, you need type only the file names. Setting the prefix reduces typing considerably when you have more than a couple of files to print.

There is another reason for setting the prefix to your data disk before starting AUTOPRINT. When this program runs, it creates a second WPL program, PRINTIT, which contains the commands to print the files you specified. AUTOPRINT saves PRINTIT on the disk to which the prefix is set. If you don't set the prefix to your data disk, PRINTIT will be saved on the Master disk. PRINTIT is a small file, only one block in length; still, it is better not to add files unnecessarily to the Master disk. (AUTOPRINT creates PRINTIT only once per disk, so it never takes up more than one block.)

To see how AUTOPRINT works, we will print two of the files you completed in Chapter 9, TABLE and REPORT2.

Set the prefix now for /PRACTICE/AUCTION. Then load the REPORT2 print value file from the Additional Functions menu.

As you know, before printing any document, you should check the Print/Program Commands menu to make certain the values are set correctly for your printer and for the specific formatting requirements of the document to be printed. With AUTOPRINT, the values must be correct for all the files, since once the program begins printing, all the files will be printed in succession automatically. Obviously, the REPORT2 print value file is set up to print the REPORT2 file. But it may not be equally correct for the TABLE file.

Put the Print/Program Commands menu on the screen now (as in Figure 10-8), and check whether any of the values for the report

```
Print/Program Commands:

Left        Margin      (LM) = 5
Paragraph Margin        (PM) = 0
Right       Margin      (RM) = 70
Top         Margin      (TM) = 1
Bottom      Margin      (BM) = 1
Page Number             (PN) = 1
Printed Lines           (PL) = 58
Page Interval           (PI) = 66
Line Interval           (LI) = 0
Single Page             (SP) = 0
Print Destination       (PD) = 1
Carriage Return         (CR) = 0
Underline Token         (UT) = \
Print Mode (LJ,FJ,CJ,RJ) = LJ
Top Line                (TL) :

Bottom Line             (BL) :
  \\#\\
Press RETURN to Exit

[P]rint/Program :
```

Figure 10-8.   *REPORT2.PRT loaded*

will have an undesirable effect on the table. As you see, the left and right margin settings (LM5, RM70) are suitable for both the table and the report. The bottom line setting, for a centered page number to begin on the second page of a document (\ \# \ \), will not affect the table, which is only one page in length. Therefore, with the values currently set, the REPORT2 print value file is also correct for the table.

However, the current settings of the Print/Program Commands menu are not the only values to consider when you are about to print more than one file with AUTOPRINT. Any embedded formatting commands in the first document printed update the Print/Program Commands menu and remain in effect for the next document, and so on.

If, for example, the report were printed first, the paragraph margin value would be changed to PM5 on the menu for the next document, since that is the last PM command embedded in the report. Because of possible changes to the Print/Program Commands menu during printing, you may get peculiar results with AUTOPRINT unless you foresee the effects of embedded commands in each document.

To avoid formatting the table with a paragraph margin that would rearrange its columns, you could embed a PM0 command at the end of the report. Then, if you printed the report first, the Print/Program Commands menu would still reflect PM0. Printing the table first, however, won't change any values on the menu.

Press **RETURN** to go back to the editing display, since you can't give a WPL command from the Print/Program Commands menu screen. Give the command to print AUTOPRINT.

Type: [**P**]

Then type: **DO /AW2MASTER/AUTOPRINT** (The volume name is required because the prefix is set to the data disk.) Check that you have entered the volume and file names with no errors.

Notice that, unlike printing a file in Apple Writer II, you do not load the file into memory. Had another document been in memory, you would not have had to clear memory before giving the command to run AUTOPRINT. The AUTOPRINT program would clear memory for you. You should, therefore, first save any valuable work left in memory when you run AUTOPRINT.

Press **RETURN**.

The title of the program replaces the data line. A prompt instructs you to enter a file name.

Type: **TABLE** (Uppercase or lowercase is acceptable.) The screen should now look like Figure 10-9.

Press **RETURN** and the same prompt appears.

Type: **REPORT2** and press **RETURN**.

The prompt will continue to reappear for up to 30 file names. When you have entered the names of all the files to be printed, you press RETURN without entering a file name to start the printing. If you have only one disk drive, you remove the Master disk and insert the data disk before pressing RETURN for the last time.

With the data disk in one of the disk drives, turn on the printer.

Press **RETURN** now.

While the program runs and the files are printed, you'll see the first file, TABLE, on the screen for a moment and then the end of the REPORT2 file briefly. A beep signals that the program has finished running. The screen announces "End of Automatic Print" and instructs you to press RETURN when you wish to go back to the editing display in Apple Writer II.

If you look at the printout, you'll see that each file has been printed separately. The report is not joined to the table, but begins on a new page. Because page numbering starts over for each file this program prints, the page number is printed on only the second page of the report, even though that is the third page of the printout.

In order to get similar results when you run AUTOPRINT, embed a Form Feed command at the end of each document, without a final carriage return. Both TABLE and REPORT2 already have this command embedded. If you do not embed the Form Feed command at the ends of documents, AUTOPRINT may join them on the same page. Also, the printer will not stop on a new page after printing the last page of the last document. When your pur-

```
**** AUTOMATIC PRINT ****
Enter name of file to be printed: table
```

Figure 10-9. *AUTOPRINT title and first prompt*

pose is to join separate files into one printed document, you can use the CONTPRINT program.

Joining Files with CONTPRINT

Another WPL program provided for you on the Master disk, CONTPRINT, prints up to 30 files in succession combined into one document. Running CONTPRINT achieves the same results as if you had given the [P]CP command in Apple Writer II for each succeeding file. When there are a number of files to be printed in one document, CONTPRINT eliminates the need to clear memory and give the Load and Print command for each file. Like the [P]CP command, CONTPRINT prints the document with continuous page numbers, if the page number has been formatted.

CONTPRINT runs the same way AUTOPRINT does. On the editing display, you would give the command [P] DO and the file name /AW2MASTER/CONTPRINT (assuming the prefix is set for the data disk). In response to the prompts, you would enter the names of the files in the order you wish them to be printed. If you have only one disk drive, you would insert and remove the Master disk just as you did to run AUTOPRINT.

Like AUTOPRINT, CONTPRINT is simpler to run when the prefix is set for the volume containing the document files. Also like AUTOPRINT, CONTPRINT clears any document currently in memory in Apple Writer II when it runs.

You will follow the same preliminary steps before running CONTPRINT:

1. Set the prefix to your data disk.
2. Set the Print/Program Commands menu so that the values are compatible for all the documents to be printed.
3. Adjust or add any embedded formatting commands in individual files.
4. Save any document in memory that you want to keep.

Follow these additional steps for CONTPRINT:

5. Remove any embedded Form Feed commands at the end of a document, if the next file is to be printed on the same page.

6. Also remove any carriage returns after the last line of text in a document in order to avoid a blank space between two joined files.

COUNTING WORDS IN A FILE WITH COUNTER

The third WPL program on the Master disk, COUNTER, adds the total number of words in a file. This information can be useful when you are preparing a document that must meet certain word length requirements.

COUNTER is quite simple to run. Since it, too, clears memory, you should first save any work you may need again. From the editing display you give the command to run the program, [P] DO followed by the file name COUNTER (or /AW2MASTER/COUNTER, if the Master disk is not the default prefix). Then in response to the prompt, you enter the name of the file that you want to use with COUNTER (including the volume and possibly the subdirectory name, if the Master disk is the default prefix).

To see COUNTER in operation, let's find out how many words are in the REPORT2 file. Since the prefix has been set to the data disk, the volume name of the Master disk must be entered with the program name in the WPL command. If you have only one disk drive, remove the data disk and insert the Master disk now.

Type: **[P] DO** and press **SPACEBAR**.

Then type: **/AWZMASTER/COUNTER** and press **RETURN**.

When the prompt appears, type **REPORT2** (as shown in Fig-

```
     Word Counter

Enter Disk File Name:report2
```

Figure 10-10.   *COUNTER title and first prompt*

```
      Word Counter

Enter Disk File Name: report2
Total number of words in file "report2" = 403.  (Press RETURN)
```

Figure 10-11.   *COUNTER displays number of words in REPORT2*

ure 10-10). With the data disk in one of the disk drives, press
RETURN.

The light goes on and off over the disk drive. After a short wait,
the screen displays the number of words in REPORT2, as shown
in Figure 10-11. If you ask the program to count the words in a
large file, the wait will be longer. It may seem that nothing is hap-
pening, but when the program is finished counting, it will display
the results.

Press **RETURN**. COUNTER is ready to go on processing
another file for you at this point. If you wanted to know the
number of words in another file on the same data disk, you would
enter its name now.

To leave COUNTER and go back to Apple Writer II on the
editing display, you press RETURN three times, after it has completed its operation on one file. Since you already pressed RETURN
once, press **RETURN** twice now to go back to the editing display.

As you no doubt just noticed, when you indicate that you are
leaving the program, the beeper sounds. A message on the screen
confirms that the program is ended.

CREATING FORM LETTERS
WITH AUTOLETTER

The last WPL program on the Master disk, AUTOLETTER, goes
beyond eliminating tedious steps in Apple Writer II. Like the form
letter program you saw on DEMOS, the AUTOLETTER program
loads names and addresses into the text of a form letter; unlike the

demonstration program, AUTOLETTER can actually print form letters, making as many copies as you like. Once you have provided the program with the text of your letter and your list of names and addresses, it does the rest.

The fastest way to see what AUTOLETTER can accomplish for you is to run it as a demonstration. Then in the rest of this chapter, you'll learn how to prepare the files so that you can make AUTOLETTER print your form letters.

Demonstrating AUTOLETTER

The Master disk contains sample text and address files to demonstrate how AUTOLETTER prints a form letter automatically when it runs. The program does not specify the volume name for these files. Consequently, AUTOLETTER looks for them on the disk to which the prefix is set. The Master disk must be the default prefix when AUTOLETTER runs as a demonstration program. Otherwise, it looks fruitlessly for the files and you'll get an error message: "ProDOS Error: File Not Found." Should this happen, you may have to restart Apple Writer II to recover.

Change the prefix now so that the Master disk is the default volume. If you have only one disk drive, put the Master disk in drive 1.

Select "Set Prefix" on the ProDOS Commands menu. Then type: **/AW2MASTER**

Press **RETURN** twice to set the prefix and return to the editing display.

Next check the Print/Program Commands menu. Notice that printing the REPORT2 file with AUTOPRINT has changed the value for the paragraph margin to PM5. Change the margin value back to PM0.

Turn on the printer and you are ready to run AUTOLETTER from the editing display.

Type: **[P]DO**

Then type **AUTOLETTER** and press **RETURN**.

The first form letter is filled in on the screen. When the first letter has been printed, the screen looks like Figure 10-12.

The top line of the screen informs you that the recipient's name and address have been loaded and inserted in the form letter. To print the next letter, you press **RETURN**. The Form Feed command

```
John Smith
123 Elm Street
Anytown, U.S.A. 12345

Dear John:

Congratulations on your purchase of an Apple computer.  You and
your family will spend many enjoyable and instructive hours with
your new personal computer.  In today's fast-paced
high-technology world, John, you can't afford to be without one.
And you can rest assured that when you use an Apple computer,
you're using the best there is.

Best wishes,


The Folks at Apple Computer
```

Figure 10-12.   *First AUTOLETTER form letter*

embedded at the end of the letter is not carried out until you press RETURN.

Press **RETURN** now and notice that the printer starts the next letter on a new page.

It isn't necessary to print all five sample letters; however, you cannot leave AUTOLETTER while it is waiting for a RETURN, only when it is running. To interrupt before it has finished printing all five letters, you press RETURN to start it again and then press ESC.

Press **RETURN**.

Press **ESC** as soon as the next letter appears on the screen. The program and the printer stop. Now clear the screen and turn off the printer.

If you had not stopped the program, AUTOLETTER would have continued printing until it completed the last letter on the list. When AUTOLETTER had printed the last letter, the screen would display this message:

Done at address 6 (Press RETURN)

The message informs you that the next letter the program would print—if the list were longer—would be the sixth letter.

Pressing RETURN would then end the program and would put you back in Apple Writer II on the editing display.

CREATING A FORM LETTER

The form letter just printed was created with three files on the Master disk:

- A file named FORMLETTER (shown in Figure 10-13) that contains the text of the letter with "(Name)" and "(Address)" in the place of the recipient's name and address.
- A file named ADDRS (shown in Figure 10-14) that contains the list of recipients.
- A file named AUTOLETTER (shown in Figure 10-15) that contains the set of instructions the program carries out to insert the names and addresses into the text and print the form letter.

```
>    Z Mem:46392 Len:   453 Pos:    0 Tab:    0 File:formletter

(Address)

Dear (Name):

Congratulations on your purchase of an Apple computer.  You and
your family will spend many enjoyable and instructive hours with
your new personal computer.  In today's fast-paced
high-technology world, (Name), you can't afford to be without
one.  And you can rest assured that when you use an Apple
computer, you're using the best there is.

Best wishes,


The Folks at Apple Computer

.inAddress number (X) (press return)
.FF
```

Figure 10-13. *The FORMLETTER file*

```
>    Z Mem:46582 Len:  263 Pos:      0 Tab:      0 File:addrs
<1>John Smith
123 Elm Street
Anytown, U.S.A. 12345
<2>Terry Jones
321 Palm Lane
Centerville, FL 54321
<3>Egbert Q. Manly
1984 Orwell Place
Future, PA 14151
<4>Harry Q. Public
1953 Warren Court
Sublime, WI 09876
<5>Mary Sanders
0000 Null Result
Meander, OH 54637
<
```

Figure 10-14.   *The ADDRS file*

```
>    Z Mem:46528 Len:  317 Pos:      0 Tab:      0 File:autoletter
START    PSX 1
LOOP     NY
         LFORMLETTER
         B
         F/(Address)//
         Y?
         LADDRS!<(X)>!<!N
         PGO FOUND
         PGO QUIT
FOUND    PLSADDRS!<(X)>! !N=$A
         B
         F/(Name)/$A/A
         PNP
         PSX +1
         PGO LOOP
QUIT     PINL   Done at address (X) (press RETURN)
         NY
```

Figure 10-15.   *The AUTOLETTER program file*

Printing your own form letter with a modified version of AUTOLETTER is not difficult. The rest of this chapter demonstrates the three steps in preparing files to load your text and your mailing list:

1. Prepare a text file, similar to FORMLETTER.

2. Prepare a list file, similar to ADDRS.

3. Make a few simple changes in the AUTOLETTER program and save it on your data disk so that it loads your prepared files from the same disk, instead of FORMLETTER and ADDRS.

Preparing a text file is the first step. The FORMLETTER file is the model for a text file that AUTOLETTER can use. As Figure 10-13 shows, AUTOLETTER can fill in the recipient's address (including the name), and it can fill in the recipient's first name separately in the salutation and in the body of the letter. Unlike the form letter in the DEMOS program, AUTOLETTER does not prompt you for the date, so you must include it in your text file.

Your own text file can be longer than FORMLETTER. The only limits on the form letter's length are that it must fit in Apple Writer II's memory and it must fit on the same disk with the program file and the list file. Printing many long form letters will, of course, take time.

Let's prepare a text file. The following text can be the basis for a form letter that might be sent out to thank those who donated to the auction.

Type in the following date: **March 7, 1986**

Press **RETURN** twice to leave space before the address.

Now type (**Address**) and press **RETURN** twice.

Next, type **Dear (Name)**, and press **RETURN** twice. The screen should look like Figure 10-16. Now type the rest of the form letter text, as shown in Figure 10-17.

Make certain that the Form Feed command is embedded on the last line. Do not put in a final carriage return.

Before saving the file, set the prefix again to /PRACTICE/ AUCTION. If you have only one disk drive, remove the Master disk now and insert the data disk. Then save this text on the data

```
<    Z Mem:46805 Len:    40 Pos:    40 Tab:    0 File:
March 7, 1986

(Address)

Dear (Name),
```

Figure 10-16.   *Heading of Auction form letter*

disk as the file WPLLETTER.

Preparing a list file that AUTOLETTER can use to fill in the name and address is the next step. So clear the screen before continuing.

AUTOLETTER prints as many letters as there are names and

```
>    Z Mem:46559 Len:   286 Pos:    0 Tab:    0 File:wplletter
March 7, 1986

(Address)

Dear (Name),

Thank you for your donation to the auction.  We appreciate your
generosity.

Your name will be listed in the auction catalogue so everyone
attending will know that you, (Name), are a true friend of Las
Madres School.

Sincerely,


Lee Herman
.ff
```

Figure 10-17.   *Complete text of Auction form letter*

addresses in the list file. After it loads the last name and address from the file and prints that letter, the program ends. The size of a list file can be as large as your requirements dictate, provided there is room on the data disk for it together with the letter file and the program file.

When AUTOLETTER runs, it identifies each name and address from the list by loading the text between delimiters. It uses the Load command you learned in Chapter 9 to load part of a document without loading the delimiters. Chapter 11 explains how AUTOLETTER finds and distinguishes each address.

Your list file should meet the following requirements:

- The list must be numbered sequentially, beginning with 1.
- The numbers must be enclosed in angle brackets (< >).
- No spaces can separate the right angle bracket (>) from the name on the first line.
- Each line must end with RETURN, and a left angle bracket (<) must be on the line immediately below the last address.

Type the first name and address:

<1>Buzz Cord
Essential Gadgets
911 Bell Street
Las Madres, CA

The screen should look like Figure 10-18.

Check to make sure you did not type a space after the right angle bracket. Then complete the list as shown in Figure 10-19.

Save this list on the data disk with the file name WPLLIST. After saving the file, clear the screen again.

Preparing the AUTOLETTER program is the last step in creating a form letter. You alter the AUTOLETTER program so that it loads your text file and list file, instead of the sample files, FORM-LETTER and ADDRS. Then the new version of AUTOLETTER is saved on the same data disk.

To edit the AUTOLETTER program, you load it on the editing display with the Load command in Apple Writer II. If you have only one disk drive, insert the Master disk now. Since the

```
<     Z Mem:46784 Len:    61 Pos:    61 Tab:    14 File:
<1>Buzz Cord
Essential Gadgets
911 Bell Street
Las Madres, CA
```

Figure 10-18.   *First name and address for Auction address list*

prefix is set for the data disk, you must give the volume name and the file name to load AUTOLETTER as a file.

Notice that AUTOLETTER loads like any other document file you load on the editing display with the Load command in Apple Writer II. When you load a WPL program file to edit it—or perhaps just to look at it—it does not run as a program. What you see displayed on the screen are the characters that constitute the contents of the program, that is, its commands and instructions.

```
>     Z Mem:46664 Len:   181 Pos:    0 Tab:    0 File:wpllist
<1>Buzz Cord
Essential Gadgets
911 Bell Street
Las Madres, CA
<2>Mimi Furst
Healthy Bods
Madres Mall
Las Madres, CA
<3>Manny A. Goode
Gourmet Emporium
10 Pound Way
Las Madres, CA
<
```

Figure 10-19.   *Complete address list for Auction form letter*

Because AUTOLETTER is not running as a WPL program, it does not look for FORMLETTER and ADDRS. Thus a prefix other than the Master disk causes no error message.

Move the cursor to the beginning of the AUTOLETTER program. Now the entire program is on the screen.

You need not understand what these WPL commands mean or how to write a program in order to prepare AUTOLETTER for printing your form letters. All that is necessary is to delete the file names FORMLETTER and ADDRS where they occur in the program and type in the names of your text file and list file. (If you would like to understand WPL commands and learn to write a simple program, read Chapter 11.)

Here is how to change AUTOLETTER so that it will print the form letter for the auction donors:

1. Move the cursor to the space after "LFORMLETTER" in the third line of the program. Delete "FORMLET-TER", but leave the "L".

Now type: **WPLLETTER** (the name of the text file)

2. Move the cursor to the space after "LADDRS" in the seventh line of the program. Cursor should be on the first exclamation point. Delete "ADDRS", but leave the "L".

Type: **WPLLIST** (the name of the list file)

3. Move the cursor to the tenth line of the program and delete "ADDRS" from this line.

Type: **WPLLIST**

That's all you have to do to change the program. The screen should now look like Figure 10-20.

Give the Save command and save this version of the program on the data disk with the file name WPLAUTOLET. (If you have only one disk drive, first insert the data disk.)

Since the modified file is being saved on the data disk to which the prefix is set, you need not type the volume and subdirectory name between slashes. The new name, WPLAUTOLET, won't entirely cover the old name, /AW2MASTER/AUTOLETTER, that appears when you give the Save command. Type only the letters

```
>    Z Mem:46525 Len:   320 Pos:      0 Tab:      0 File:wplautolet
START    PSX 1
LOOP     NY
         LWPLLETTER
         B
         F/(Address)//
         Y?
         LWPLLIST!<(X)>!<!N
         PGO FOUND
         PGO QUIT
FOUND    PLSWPLLIST!<(X)>! !N=$A
         B
         F/(Name)/$A/A
         PNP
         PSX +1
         PGO LOOP
QUIT     PINL   Done at address (X) (press RETURN)
         NY
```

Figure 10-20.   *Edited AUTOLETTER program*

needed and press **RETURN** when the cursor is immediately to the right of the last letter in the new name.

The time has come to enjoy the rewards of this small effort. Turn on the printer and give the WPL command to run the new version of the program.

Type: **[P]DO**

Then type **WPLAUTOLET** (make sure you type the new file name, not AUTOLETTER) and press **RETURN**.

As you can see, the program WPLAUTOLET loads the WPLLETTER file and fills in the first name and address from the WPLLIST file. Then it prints three letters. Figure 10-21 shows the first letter printed.

If more names and addresses were added to the WPLLIST file, WPLAUTOLET would print them, too. At the end, the program announces what the number of the next letter would be. To go back to Apple Writer II and the editing display, you press RETURN.

The AUTOLETTER file on the Master disk has not been

```
March 7, 1986

Buzz Cord
Essential Gadgets
911 Bell Street
Las Madres, CA

Dear Buzz,

Thank you for your donation to the auction.  We appreciate your
generosity.

Your name will be listed in the auction catalogue so everyone
attending will know that you, Buzz, are a true friend of Las
Madres School.

Sincerely,


Lee Herman
```

Figure 10-21.   *Printout of WPLAUTOLET*

altered. You can run it in its original state to see it print the sample form letter again from the FORMLETTER and ADDRS files. When you have prepared the text file for your form letter and the file with your address list, you can load the original program file, AUTOLETTER, on the editing display; then you can modify it by replacing the names of the FORMLETTER file and the ADDRS file with the names of your text file and your list file in exactly the same way you just did.

One cautionary reminder: your modified version of the AUTOLETTER program will look for your text file and your list file on the disk to which the prefix is set. Since you must save your version of AUTOLETTER on the data disk that contains your text file and list file, always set the prefix for that data disk before running your form letter program.

The WPL programs demonstrated in this chapter are just the beginning of what WPL can accomplish. In the next chapter, you'll learn more about WPL.

REVIEW EXERCISES

1. Run COUNTER to find the total number of words in the MEMO2 file and in the TABLE file.

2. Run CONTPRINT to combine the MEMO2 file and the TABLE file in one printed document.

11

PROGRAMMING IN WPL

Now that you've seen how running a WPL program lets you sit back while it takes over repetitive activities, you can begin writing your own WPL programs. By the end of this chapter, you'll be able to write a simple, short WPL program.

Programming in WPL is not as difficult as you may imagine. Many Apple Writer II commands serve the same function in WPL programs. WPL uses these Apple Writer II commands and a few new commands.

Some people find programming an exciting challenge in itself; designing a complex program often combines creativity, skill, and persistence. Although you may feel justifiably proud of writing your own WPL program, that is a bonus. The main point of this chapter is more practical: to show you step-by-step how you can apply simple WPL programs to automate time-consuming word processing tasks.

In this chapter you'll learn the exact rules for writing WPL programs. The WPLAUTOLET program you saved in Chapter 10 will illustrate how commands function in WPL. You'll also see how to modify this program further by inserting new information into the text of the form letter. Then you'll create two versions of a

WPL program you can use for printing multiple copies of a document automatically.

WRITING WPL STATEMENTS

A WPL program consists of a series of *statements,* each ending with RETURN. Statements are single, complete instructions that may include labels, commands, and arguments.

The command is the core of a WPL statement. There are three main types of commands used in WPL:

- Apple Writer II CONTROL-character commands, which are typed as one character without the CONTROL key. For example, the Load command is [L] in Apple Writer II, but L in a WPL statement.

- Apple Writer II Print/Program commands, which, like the other CONTROL-character commands, are typed without the CONTROL key in WPL. These commands always have three-character names. For example, the New Print command in Apple Writer II is [P]NP in Apple Writer II, but PNP in a WPL statement.

- WPL commands, which are used only in WPL programs. Like the Print/Program commands, WPL commands begin with P followed by two characters. For example, one of the WPL commands you'll learn, the No Display command, is PND.

All of the Apple Writer II commands that are used in WPL, including the Print/Program commands, perform the same functions in a WPL statement. The difference is that they are not carried out immediately. In Apple Writer II, as you know, a command given with the CONTROL key is executed at once. In WPL, commands only take effect when the program runs.

As you might expect, a statement must at least contain a command; however, a statement can have two more parts: a label and an argument. Commands, labels, and arguments must conform to *syntax* rules in WPL. These rules determine where text is positioned on the line, whether spaces are allowed, and whether case matters.

A *label* is a name given to a statement. It always occurs first, beginning on the first space. Labels form a left-hand column identifying major segments of the program and clarifying its execution. Figure 11-1 shows four labels in the WPLAUTOLET program from Chapter 10.

A label can be any combination of characters, excluding spaces. It can be any length. In practice, you'll probably write short labels to conserve space. The label can be written in uppercase or lowercase or mixed letters; however, any reference to it elsewhere in the program must match the case of each character exactly.

At least one space must separate the label from the command. A simple way to ensure that this syntax rule won't be violated is to set a tab a few spaces beyond the longest label. Then each command will line up and the program will, incidentally, be easier to read.

The third part of a statement, the *argument*, provides additional information for some commands. For example, in the Find command, the delimiters and the text between them make up the

```
<    Z Mem:46525 Len:   320 Pos:   212 Tab:    21 File:wplautolet
START    PSX 1
LOOP     NY
         LWPLLETTER
         B
         F/(Address)//
         Y?
         LWPLLIST!<(X)>!<!N
         PGO FOUND
         PGO QUIT
FOUND    PLSWPLLIST!<(X)>! !N=$A
         B
         F/(Name)/$A/A
         PNP
         PSX +1
         PGO LOOP
QUIT     PINL    Done at address (X) (press RETURN)
         NY
```

Labels

Figure 11-1.   *Labels in WPLAUTOLET program*

argument. Similarly, delimiters and text in Load and Save commands are arguments. When such arguments identify text in files, the case of the text between delimiters must match exactly the text to be located. All other arguments in WPL statements can be either uppercase or lowercase.

Some Apple Writer II CONTROL-character commands require an argument in WPL statements because when you give the command in Apple Writer II, you must respond to a prompt. For example, the New Screen command [N] is not complete until you type Y or N in response to the prompt. In WPL the New Screen command, N, is always accompanied by its argument, Y. (You would not write a statement containing this command unless you wanted to clear memory.) No space is allowed between an Apple Writer II CONTROL-character command and its argument in a WPL statement.

Spaces are allowed between both Print/Program commands and WPL commands and their arguments, but not between the P and the two-character command name. For example, the Print/ Program command to run a WPL program, [P]DO (file name) is PDO (file name) in a WPL statement; the name of the file containing the program to run is the argument. As you may recall, when you give this command in Apple Writer II, you can type a space between DO and the program's file name; the space is also allowed in a WPL statement for this type of command and for WPL commands.

Each statement must end with RETURN. Always press RETURN immediately after typing an argument. Some commands do not require an argument. For example, the command to go to the beginning of a file, [B] in Apple Writer II, is a complete statement in WPL: B (no CONTROL key). Where a statement does not contain an argument, always press RETURN immediately after the command name.

The syntax of a WPL statement conveys necessary information to make the program work smoothly. Frequently, novice programmers commit syntax errors. You should always check a program carefully for this problem, because syntax errors are simple to correct.

Any statements that do not conform exactly to the syntax rules are ignored when the program runs. Consequently, you can annotate your programs by inserting *comments*. Comments are statements that don't affect the program's execution, but they can be read when you load the program file on the editing display or print it out. Comments that remind you what functions the program performs are particularly helpful when you haven't run a program for a while.

To put in a comment, you type P in the command section, and then type a space. Since a space after P is not valid command syntax, the program ignores the comment when it runs. (Obviously, you would not put a space after P in a command you do want the program to execute.)

Let's put some WPL statements on the screen. Later we'll write a program to print five copies of the RESUME file you saved in Chapter 8. We can begin it now, so start up Apple Writer II and set the prefix to /PRACTICE/AUCTION. Then go to the editing display.

The first statement is a comment, describing the program's function. The label is the name of the program.

Beginning on the first space, type: **WPLCOPY**
Then set a tab at column 12 and tab to that position.
Type **P** and press **SPACEBAR**.
Now type: **This program prints 5 copies of RESUME**
Press **RETURN**.

The second statement has no label and no argument. It is the No Display command (PND). This WPL command, which turns off screen display, is often one of the first commands in a WPL program. With the screen display turned off, programs run faster and the entire screen can be devoted to screen messages.

Tab to the command column. Then type **PND** and press **RETURN**.

Now add a statement that clears memory if any document is in the text buffer when the program starts. Type only the command and its argument.

Type **NY** and press **RETURN**.

Your screen should match Figure 11-2. Save these statements as the file WPLCOPY and then clear the editing display.

USING COMMANDS IN STATEMENTS

Each WPL program is a unique series of commands in statements designed to accomplish a desired task. Looking at how the function commands perform in a program and how a particular pro-

```
<   Z  Mem:46762 Len:    83 Pos:    83 Tab:    14 File:wplcopy
WPLCOPY       P This program prints 5 copies of RESUME
              PND
              NY
```

Figure 11-2.   *First three statements of WPLCOPY*

gram organizes command sequences can illustrate basic principles of WPL programming. In this section we'll examine some of the statements in two WPL programs you used in Chapter 10, the WPLAUTOLET program and the AUTOPRINT program. The examples illustrate the three types of commands and their functions.

Using Apple Writer II CONTROL-Character Commands

Because Apple Writer II CONTROL-character commands perform the same functions in a WPL program, you can write statements that duplicate a series of actions you take at the keyboard. When the program runs, the RETURN at the end of a statement indicates that the command is to be carried out, just as when you press RETURN at the end of a command given at the keyboard. Most of the commands you give at the keyboard in Apple Writer II with the CONTROL key to take immediate effect can also be commands issued when a WPL program runs.

A program can, for example, load and save Apple Writer II files, search for text in a document, and move the cursor to the beginning and end of a document. Two commands that cannot be used in WPL statements are the Replace mode command ([R]) and the Control Character Insertion mode command ([V]). With the exception of [R] and [V], any CONTROL-character command you've used in Apple Writer II can become a command in a WPL statement, when typed without the CONTROL key. Table 11-1 shows some examples of Apple Writer II CONTROL-character commands as they are written in WPL.

Command	In Apple Writer II	In WPL
Load	[L]	L
Save	[S]	S
Beginning of	[B]	BDocument
Direction Arrow	[D]	D
New Screen	[N]Y	NY
Create Subdirectory	[O]I	OI

Table 11-1. *Examples of Apple Writer II CONTROL-Character Commands Used in WPL Statements*

The WPLAUTOLET program contains some of the Apple Writer II commands commonly used in WPL statements. Let's look at the first six lines. Figure 11-3 shows WPLAUTOLET loaded on the editing display with the lines numbered.

Each line of the program is a statement. The first statement ("PSX 1") probably does not make sense to you yet. You'll understand all the statements in WPLAUTOLET by the end of this chapter.

```
<   Z Mem:46525 Len:  320 Pos:  212 Tab:   21 File:wplautolet
START  1 PSX 1
LOOP   2 NY
       3 LWPLLETTER
       4 B
       5 F/(Address)//
       6 Y?
       7 LWPLLIST!<(X)>!<!N
       8 PGO FOUND
       9 PGO QUIT
FOUND 10 PLSWPLLIST!<(X)>! !N=$A
      11 B
      12 F/(Name)/$A/A
      13 PNP
      14 PSX +1
      15 PGO LOOP
QUIT  16 PINL   Done at address (X) (press RETURN)
      17 NY
```

Figure 11-3. *WPLAUTOLET program with lines numbered*

The second statement, which is repeated in the last line of the program, is the New Screen command with its argument. This statement clears any document that may be in Apple Writer II's memory when the program starts. Remember, the commands are not executed until you run the program; you can't respond to the New Screen prompt while the program runs. The prompt acts as a safety feature in Apple Writer II in case you change your mind about clearing memory. However, in writing a WPL program, you decide in advance that clearing memory is desirable. Otherwise, you do not put a New Screen command in a statement. Note that no space separates the command (N) from the argument (Y).

Other CONTROL-character commands that require typing in another character in response to a prompt are handled similarly to the New Screen command in WPL. For example, the statement "OI" in a WPL program would give the command to go to the ProDOS Commands menu and select "Create a Subdirectory".

The third statement simply gives the Load command in WPL; its argument is the name of the file to be loaded, WPLLETTER. The fourth statement is the familiar Apple Writer II command to go to the beginning of a document. It is a complete command, needing no argument. The same command appears in line 11 also.

The statements in the second, third, and fourth lines of the WPLAUTOLET program make up a sequence of commands:

NY	The screen is cleared of any document that may be in memory when the WPLAUTO-LET program starts.
LWPLLETTER	The program gives the command to load the WPLLETTER file into memory.
B	The program gives the command to put the cursor at the beginning of the WPLLET-TER document.

Look now at the fifth and sixth lines of WPLAUTOLET:

F/(Address)//
Y?

In the fifth line you should recognize the Find command,

without the CONTROL key. The delimiters and the text make up its argument, which is an instruction to find and replace text in the WPLLETTER file. The statement in line six, "Y?", is actually part of the Find command here. It takes a separate line because in giving the Find command to replace text in Apple Writer II, you must press RETURN before responding to the prompt. The Find command is very versatile and useful in WPL programs. You'll learn how this command and its arguments function in a later section.

Using Print/Program Commands

All of the commands you give in Apple Writer II with [P] can also be given as WPL commands. The [P] that you press before each of these commands means both Print command and Program command. Like the other CONTROL-character Apple Writer II commands, the Print/Program commands are written in WPL without the CONTROL key.

But Print/Program commands must be written in statements according to the syntax rules for WPL commands, not for Apple Writer II CONTROL-character commands: Print/Program commands are always three characters long and may be separated by spaces from their arguments. Table 11-2 shows examples of Print/Program commands in Apple Writer II and in WPL.

Line 13 of the WPLAUTOLET program contains the familiar New Print command written in WLP: PNP. This statement causes the program to begin printing the form letter.

Command	In Apple Writer II	In WPL
New Print	[P]NP	PNP
Continue Print	[P]CP	PCP
Set Left Margin	[P]LM	PLM
Set Right Margin	[P]RM	PRM
Run WPL Program	[P]DO	PDO
Input	.IN	PIN

Table 11-2. *Examples of Print/Program Commands Used in WPL Statements*

As you know, Print/Program commands in Apple Writer II that set the printing and formatting values can be given either on the editing display after pressing [P] or after pressing [P]? to go to the Print/Program Commands menu. A Print/Program command in a WPL statement need not include the question mark; it is sufficient to type P (without the CONTROL key), the two characters that represent the rest of the command and the argument, which usually sets the value.

For example, to set the left margin in a document to be printed five spaces from the left edge of the paper, in Apple Writer II you would first press [P]? (assuming you wished to change several values at once on the Print/Program Commands menu) and then enter the two characters and the value: LM5. In a WPL statement the same command would be PLM and its argument would be 5.

Most of the commands you can embed in a document are commands from the Print/Program Commands menu, which can be used in WPL statements. Two commands, however, are used only as embedded commands: the Form Feed command (.FF) and the Enable Print command (.EP); these two commands cannot appear in WPL statements. As with all the other embedded commands, the Form Feed command and the Enable Print command can, of course, be used in document files that a WPL program prints. The WPLLETTER document ends with a Form Feed command, as do the documents you printed with AUTOPRINT in Chapter 10.

One command that you have not yet learned, the Input command, can be embedded in Apple Writer II document files and can be used in WPL statements. The Input command prints a message on the screen during printing. When the printer reaches the Input command, either embedded in a document or as a statement in a WPL program, printing stops until you press RETURN.

You embed the Input command in a document by typing .IN. In a WPL statement, the Input command is PIN. (Although you don't press [P] in Apple Writer II to embed the Input command, in WPL it is always preceded by P, never by a period.)

The WPLAUTOLET program uses the Input command in line 16 as follows:

PINL Done at address (X) (press RETURN)

You may recall that at the end of printing with WPLAUTOLET, the screen shows you the next number of the address that would be loaded and instructs you to press RETURN in order to go back to

Apple Writer II. The Input command subsequently causes this message to be printed on the screen when the program reaches this point in the sequence of commands. The message is the command's argument.

The Input command will be an important part of the program you'll create later in this chapter. Notice the character after "PIN" in this statement; it is not the Load command, but a special WPL command that can be used with the Input command. It will be explained shortly.

Using WPL Commands

The WPL commands that have no counterparts in Apple Writer II all begin with P followed by a two-character designation. Table 11-3 lists five commands that are used exclusively in WPL statements. They will be covered in this section.

The Go command affects the sequence in which commands are executed in a program. Ordinarily, program commands are executed one after the other. The Go command identifies a command not immediately following it as the next to be executed, if certain conditions apply.

The Go command is never complete without an argument. The required argument always refers to the label of the command which is to be executed next. For example, the statement "PGO PRINT" would consist of the command "PGO", followed by an allowed space, and the argument "PRINT", which would be the label of a command to be executed out of sequence in the program.

Command	In WPL	Meaning
Go	PGO + label	Alter command sequence
Quit	PQT	End program
No Display	PND	Turn off screen
Yes Display	PYD	Turn on screen display
Print a Line	PPR	Print program message on screen

Table 11-3. *Examples of Commands Used Exclusively in WPL*

Three statements that are in the WPLAUTOLET program are Go commands:

PGO FOUND   the argument in line 8 identifies the statement labeled "FOUND" in line 10 as the next to be executed

PGO QUIT   the argument in line 9 identifies the statement labeled "QUIT" in line 16 as the next to be executed

PGO LOOP   the argument in line 15 identifies the statement in line 2 labeled "LOOP" to be executed next

The labels—"FOUND", "LOOP", and "QUIT"—mark major segments of the WPLAUTOLET program. The Go commands provide for a sequence of execution that prints as many form letters as there are names and addresses in WPLLETTER. When no more names and addresses can be found, the program stops instead of printing again.

The Quit command, which is PQT, is used to end a program. The Quit command stops a program, returning you to the editing display in Apple Writer II. If a file is loaded while the program runs, it remains on the screen after the Quit command.

You won't find PQT in the WPLAUTOLET program, because this program ends in two stages. The Input command first puts the message on the screen; and when you press RETURN, the New Screen command clears the file in memory. If there is no final message in a program, you can use the Quit command to end it.

The Go command in combination with the Quit command can illustrate an important feature in WPL called *conditional execution*. Conditional execution means that a command is not executed unless the previous command is carried out successfully. Conditional execution is a logical process. Essentially, it decrees: "If this occurs, do that. If not, skip it. Do that other thing instead."

Imagine that you are going shopping for a pair of athletic shoes, size 8 1/2, grey with white stripes. Your mission could be described according to the logic of conditional execution:

1. Enter shoe store.
2. Look for one pair of athletic shoes, size 8 1/2.

3. If found, go to cashier.

4. If not found, leave store.

5. Pay cashier.

In the example, you skip paying for shoes that are not found. But if they are found, you don't leave the store before paying for them. Go and Quit commands and conditional execution are an important, powerful part of WPL.

Conditional execution determines whether the Go commands in WPLAUTOLET are skipped or are executed in the course of printing the form letters. If a name and address are found in the WPLLIST file, the "PGO FOUND" statement is executed. If not, the statement is skipped, and the next statement, "PGO QUIT", is executed instead. If the program finds a number larger than the number of the last name and address in WPLLIST, the "PGO LOOP" statement is skipped, and the program prints no more form letters. The next statement, the Input command announcing the end of printing, is executed instead.

The No Display command (PND), as you know, turns off the screen display so that the entire screen can be devoted to screen messages. The WPLAUTOLET program does not make use of this command because the original program, AUTOLETTER, from which it was adapted, displays the text of the form letter and its changes while the program runs.

The Yes Display command (PYD) is only used to turn the screen display on again after a PND command. Unless you turn the display off with PND, it is already on. When the screen display is on, only one line of the screen is available for program messages.

The Print a Line command (PPR) prints various kinds of messages on the screen. It's commonly used to print a program title. The Print a Line command can also insert blank lines between messages to make them more readable. Printed messages can be 128 characters in length.

The argument of the Print a Line command is the text for the message. Like other WPL commands, spaces can be inserted between the command and the argument. If you want a title to appear centered on the screen, insert spaces that accomplish this effect before the text of the argument. A statement that contains only the command PPR prints a blank line on the screen. This can be useful to make preceding and following messages more readable.

The text of a Print a Line command flashes on and off the screen if it is followed by another PPR command. Often the PPR command is followed by a PIN command, which stops the program and keeps the preceding message on the screen until you press RETURN.

The [G] and [L] commands are two CONTROL-character WPL commands that can be combined with both the PPR and PIN commands. These are not the Apple Writer II commands for viewing the Glossary buffer and loading a file; they are commands exclusive to WPL. The [G] command in WPL causes the beeper to sound. The [L] command in WPL clears the screen of program messages. In line 16 of WPLAUTOLET, the "L" after "PIN" is this command.

When you put [G] or [L] in a WPL statement, you must use [V] to enter and leave Control Character Insertion mode. To insert [G] in a WPL statement, you would press [V], then [G], and press [V] again. To insert [L] you would do the same: press [V], [L], and [V] again. Either of these commands entered with the CONTROL key is shown on the screen in inverse. If you print the program file, however, the characters look normal.

Figure 11-4 shows the first five statements in the AUTOPRINT program you ran in Chapter 10. Let's examine these commands:

NY	clears Apple Writer II's memory of any document
PND	turns off the screen display
PPRL	prints a [L]; i.e., clears the screen of any program messages
PPR **** AUTOMATIC PRINT ****	prints line of text for program's title
PIN Enter name of file to be printed: =$A	prints a message requiring a response; stops until RETURN pressed

Notice in Figure 11-4 that the first statement in AUTOPRINT is labeled to indicate the beginning of the program. The fifth line

```
>    Z Mem:46342 Len:  503 Pos:    0 Tab:    0 File:/aw2master/autoprint
START    NY
         PND
         PPRL
         PPR **** AUTOMATIC PRINT ****
NAME     PIN Enter name of file to be printed: =$A
```

Figure 11-4.   *First five lines of AUTOPRINT*

is also labeled, indicating the response the Input message requests.

By using PPR and PIN commands to print information and ask for responses, you can create menus. Depending on the response, conditional execution determines which commands the program executes. The program that creates the ProDOS Commands menu, for example, is a series of PPR commands that print the options on the screen and an Input command that asks for your selection.

Other WPL commands will be discussed as they come up in the exercises. Two WPL commands are not covered in this chapter; they are the Subroutine Call command (PSR) and the Return from Subroutine command (PRT); nor are all the commands introduced in this chapter explained at length. For further information about more advanced programming, consult the WPL manual.

USING DELIMITERS IN WPL STATEMENTS

Although you have been using delimiters in Find, Save, and Load commands in Apple Writer II, marking off text for these commands takes on special importance in WPL programs. This section demonstrates new ways to use some of the options available with these commands in WPL statements that you can use for your form letters.

Load the WPLAUTOLET program on the editing display now. We'll first examine the arguments that contain delimiters. Then we'll modify the program to add information from another list file, using options with the Find and Load commands.

Deleting and Replacing Text

WPLAUTOLET uses Find and Load commands to delete and replace text in the WPLLETTER file, prior to printing the form letters. Let's look again at the Find command in the fifth line of WPLAUTOLET:

F/(Address)//

This statement searches from the beginning of the WPLLETTER document for the text "(Address)". If it finds the text, it replaces it with nothing. (There's no text between the second set of delimiters.)

The statement in line 6, "Y?", is also part of the Find command.

As you know, after you enter the text between delimiters for the Find command and press RETURN, the prompt asks you to type Y if you wish to replace the found text. Then you can press any key, usually SPACEBAR, to discontinue searching. Here the RETURN required to end a statement (in line 5) activates the prompt. The Y in line 6 responds to the Find prompt and the question mark substitutes for the space character (which would not show up in the program).

You can try this out, if you like, on the text of the program. Press [E] and then [F]. This sets the direction arrow and positions the cursor to search backward from the end of the program.

Type: /NY// and press **RETURN**.

When the Find prompt appears, press Y and the last statement of WPLAUTOLET is replaced with nothing; in other words, it is deleted.

Type a question mark to discontinue the Find command. Then restore the statement in the program.

The command to find a specific portion of text and replace it with no text prepares the document in memory for the address to be loaded. The text "(Address)" does not belong in the printed form letters, so it is removed.

When the command replacing "(Address)" with nothing is executed, the cursor is positioned where it should be for the next statement in line seven:

LWPLLIST!<(X)>!<!N

This statement, which looks so complicated, actually consists of mostly familiar instructions:

- L   the Load command
- WPLLIST   the file to be loaded
- !   the sign used for the delimiters
- <>   the angle brackets used to enclose each number in the WPLLIST file
- N   the option to load text between delimiters without loading the markers

Thus the statement means: Load the text in the WPLLIST file that occurs between the beginning marker <(X)> and the end marker <.

There is no "(X)" between angle brackets in the WPLLIST file; this sign stands for any number that may be between angle brackets. How "(X)" functions is explained in the section on numeric variables later in this chapter. The right angle bracket between the second set of delimiters marks the end of each address in WPLLIST.

The other use of the Find command in WPLAUTOLET in line 12 is slightly different:

    F/(Name)/$A/A

At line 12 the command is given to find the text "(Name)" in the WPLLETTER document that is loaded in memory and to replace all occurrences ("A"). When you find and replace all occurrences in Apple Writer II, you don't have to respond to a prompt. Therefore, this Find command statement is complete in one line. The RETURN at the end of this statement carries out the command for the two places in the form letter where "(Name)" occurs.

The text between the second set of delimiters in line 12, "$A", allows a different name to be loaded in each printed letter. (How "$A" operates is explained in the section on string variables.)

Using a Second List File With WPLAUTOLET

Let's modify the WPLAUTOLET program to make the Find and Load command options do more work for us. It would seem more personal if each donor's gift were mentioned in the letter. First, we'll make a place in the WPLLETTER document for each donation to be inserted.

Clear the screen and load WPLLETTER. Change the words "your donation" to "donating". (Finding and replacing is the fastest method.)

Then type: **(Gift)** (Leave a space before and after "(Gift)".) Save this edited file with [S]=.

Now clear the screen and type the text shown in Figure 11-5. This is the list of gifts to be inserted.

Save this document as WPLGIFT, clear the screen, and load WPLAUTOLET. Now we can prepare the program to replace "(GIFT)" with the appropriate item from each donor in the WPLLIST file.

Move the cursor to the beginning of line 13 and press **RETURN**. Now move the cursor up to the blank line. Set a tab at column 8 and use the TAB key to line up the commands.

In the command column, type **B** and press **RETURN**. Now the Find command will start the search from the beginning of the document.

In the next line, type a label: **GIFT**

Then tab to the command column and type **F/(Gift)//**.

Press **RETURN**. This statement replaces "(Gift)" in WPLLETTER with nothing, but it is not yet complete.

In the command column on the next line, type **Y?** and press **RETURN**.

The screen should now look like Figure 11-6.

When the program runs, the cursor in the WPLLETTER document is now positioned to insert the text from WPLGIFT, so on

```
<    Z Mem:46775 Len:    70 Pos:    70 Tab:    70 File:wplgift
<1>a portable telephone<2>the aerobics classes<3>the imported cheeses<
```

Figure 11-5.   *WPLGIFT list*

```
<    Z Mem:46485 Len:    360 Pos:    252 Tab:    10 File:wplautolet
            B
            F/(Address)//
            Y?
            LWPLLIST!<(X)>!<!N
            PGO FOUND
            PGO QUIT
FOUND    PLSWPLLIST!<(X)>! !N=$A
            B
            F/(Name)/$A/A
            B
GIFT     F/(Gift)//
            Y?
            PNP
            PSX +1
            PGO LOOP
QUIT     PINL    Done at address (X) (press RETURN)
            NY
```

Figuro 11 6.   *Three new statements in WPLAUTOLET*

the next line in the command column, type

LWPLGIFT!<(X)>!<!N

Press **RETURN**.

Suppose the text can't be located in WPLGIFT? This could happen if you make any syntax errors or type the text incorrectly. We'll give the program an alternative, using the conditional execution feature in WPL.

In the command column on the next line, type **PGO** and the argument **PRINT** and press **RETURN**.

Then on the next line in the command column, type **PGO** and the argument **QUIT**. Do not press RETURN.

There's one more modification to make. No label exists for the argument of the first Go command. You must type a label for the command PNP. Move the cursor to the first space on the next line. Enter Replace mode and type the label **PRINT**.

Now if the text is loaded, the next command is PNP. If not, the next command is the Input command.

When you have finished modifying WPLAUTOLET, the screen

should look like Figure 11-7. (Note that the entire program does not fit on the screen.)

Save this edited file with [S]=. If you run this program the first letter printed will look like Figure 11-8.

Using Alternative Delimiters

You might wish to modify WPLAUTOLET (or a form letter program you create) so that the person's full name is inserted ("Dear Albert Einstein" instead of "Dear Al"). Since each line in the WPLLIST file containing the full name of a recipient ends with RETURN, one way to accomplish this is to make a carriage return character the end marker in a Load command. Then the entire first line of each entry in the list file could be loaded without the markers.

Currently in WPLAUTOLET the text is loaded up to the first space in the first line. The command used to do this is in line 10, in the statement labeled FOUND:

PLSWPLLIST!<(X)>! !N=$A

The command to load the first name from WPLLIST into WPLLETTER is not the Load command, but a similar WPL command, the Load String command (PLS). You'll learn about this command later in the next section, along with (X) and $A. Notice that the delimiter used is the exclamation point and the ending marker is a space. Because the first space in each entry in WPLLIST is between the first and last name of the recipient, only the person's first name is loaded into WPLLETTER.

In order to use a sign for carriage return as the end marker, you must use a delimiter that allows for this. (If you simply pressed RETURN after a left angle bracket, the line would be broken before you could complete the command's argument.) As you know, the slash and the exclamation point are the delimiters commonly used in Apple Writer II. However, other characters can be delimiters, and certain delimiters allow a character to represent a carriage return. Table 11-4 shows the characters that can represent carriage returns with other delimiters.

As Table 11-4 illustrates, when the left angle bracket (<) is the delimiter, the right angle bracket (>) means a carriage return character. Therefore, if we were to use the left angle brackets to load the

```
<   Z Mem:46423 Len:  422 Pos:  342 Tab:    0 File:wplautolet
FOUND    PLSWPLLIST!<(X)>! !N=$A
         B
         F/(Name)/$A/A
         B
GIFT     F/(Gift)//
         Y?
         LWPLGIFT!<(X)>!<!N
         PGO PRINT
         PGO QUIT
PRINT    PNP
         PSX +1
         PGO LOOP
QUIT     PINL   Done at address (X) (press RETURN)
         NY
```

Figure 11-7. *The screen after final modifications to WPLAUTOLET*

```
March 7, 1986

Buzz Cord
Essential Gadgets
911 Bell Street
Las Madres, CA


Dear Buzz,

Thank you for donating a portable telephone to the auction.  We
appreciate your generosity.

Your name will be listed in the auction catalogue so everyone attending
will know that you, Buzz, are a true friend of Las Madres School.

Sincerely,


Lee Herman
```

Figure 11-8. *First letter printed out with modified WPLAUTOLET*

Delimiter	Carriage Return Character
/	none
!	none
<	>
#	%
&	(
*	,

Table 11-4.   *Carriage Return Characters With Delimiters*

entire first line of an address list, the end marker for the carriage return could be <><.

To use the left angle bracket as the delimiter and the right angle bracket as the end marker, however, would rule out using the angle brackets anywhere else in the text that is to be identified for loading. The sign used as the delimiter cannot also appear in the marker or in the text marked off. In WPLLIST, the left and right angle brackets enclose each number, and the brackets are part of the beginning marker to load the name.

Taking account of these constraints, the solution would be to create an address file that distinguishes each number without using angle brackets. Then the left angle bracket could be the delimiter and the right angle bracket could be used as the end marker to load the entire name of each recipient of the form letter. Such a command and its argument might look like "LADDRESS<**(X)**<><N".

In this hypothetical example, the name of the file is ADDRESS. The left angle bracket is the sign for the delimiters. Each number in the ADDRESS file is preceded and followed by two asterisks, as in "**1**Buzz Cord".

The options you learned in Chapter 9 for the Save command can also be put to use in WPL statements. You can have a program save all or part of a file to the end of an existing file. Other powerful WPL commands that use delimiters are explained in the next section.

USING LOOPS AND VARIABLES

A *loop* is a sequence of commands that is repeated in a program. A loop makes it possible for WPLAUTOLET to print more than one form letter and for AUTOPRINT to print more than one document. *Variables* are placeholders that can be filled with different values during a program's execution. *String variables* are filled by text, and *numeric variables* are filled by numbers.

The string variable $A and the numeric variable (X) are both used in the WPLAUTOLET program. In this section you'll see how loops and variables in WPL programs can be used to automate repetitive tasks.

Designing a Loop

You can think of a loop as a series of actions performed from beginning to end repeatedly. For example, to reproduce several pages of a document on a copy machine, you go through the following actions in the same order again and again:

1. Place the first page of the original on the glass plate.
2. Push the button.
3. Remove the copy.
4. Replace the first page of the original with the second page.
5. Push the button.

When you identify comparable sequences for commands that Apple Writer II can perform, you can write a loop that causes the commands to be repeated. Since Apple Writer II can print several pages of a document from a file, a program could be written in WPL to perform these commands:

1. Load page one of the file.
2. Print the page in memory.
3. Load the next page of the file.
4. Go to the statement labeled Print.
5. Stop printing when all pages are printed.

The loop would consist of commands 2-4. The first command, to load the first page, would be done only once. The rest of the commands would be repeated until there were no more pages to load. Then conditional execution would cause the print command to be skipped and the program would end.

When you put a loop in a program, you must be careful to allow for an exit from the loop. Otherwise, it is possible for a loop to be written that would theoretically never end. We're going to need a loop in the WPLCOPY program to print RESUME five times. Consider what would happen if the loop looked like this:

Print PNP
GO PRINT

Such a loop would print more than five copies; it would continue repeating indefinitely — or until you pressed the ESC key to stop the program.

In designing a loop, you should make sure that it meets four essential requirements:

1. A sequence of commands that are to be repeated.

2. A label for the first command in the sequence.

3. A Go command to start the loop again.

4. An exit from the loop.

Setting Numeric Variables

One technique for exiting a loop is to set a numeric variable that establishes the number of times the loop repeats. A numeric variable can stand for zero or for any positive whole number from 1 to 65,535. By setting a numeric variable in a program, you can write commands that add or subtract from the number the variable represents. If in the course of a program's execution a variable is increased to 65,535+1 or decreased to zero, conditional execution is called into effect. The next command is skipped. (When the number filling a numerical variable reaches 65,535+1, the program resets it to zero.)

A program can have as many as three numeric variables: (X),(Y), and (Z). The command to set the value of (X) is PSX; the value set is the argument. The command to set (Y) is PSY; to set (Z), it is PSZ.

Let's finish the WPLCOPY program we began earlier. To print five copies of the RESUME file, we need statements to set the numeric variable, to load the RESUME file, to make a loop that prints the file five times, and to quit the program. By setting one numeric variable, (X), at the beginning, we can limit the number of times the loop is executed. When the numeric variable decreases to zero, the loop ends.

Clear the screen and load the file WPLCOPY on the editing display.

The last statement so far is the New Screen command (NY).

Press **RETURN** to end that statement line.

In the command column on the next line, type **PSX 5** and press **RETURN**.

Now on the next line in the command column, type the Load command and its argument **RESUME**, and press **RETURN**. Since we want to load and print the entire file, no delimiters are used.

It is advisable to build in conditional execution after a Load command, so add the next two statements:

    PGO PRINT
    PGO QUIT

The screen should now look like Figure 11-9.

We can now write the loop. It consists of a labeled Print command, a command to decrease the value of (X) each time a copy is printed, and a Go command to start the sequence again. Add the statements for the loop as shown in Figure 11-10.

The "PSX-1" changes the value of (X) each time the loop is executed. After one copy is printed, the value of (X) is reset to 4. When (X) is decreased to zero, conditional execution causes the "GO PRINT" statement to be skipped, ending the loop.

The Go command in line 7 refers to a label, "QUIT". Therefore, we must add a statement with such a label, rather than a simple PQT command alone. The final statements shown in Figure 11-11 end the program gracefully. Enter them now. Remember to

```
<   Z Mem:46681 Len:   164 Pos:   164 Tab:    20 File:wplcopy  <
WPLCOPY         P This program prints 5 copies of RESUME
                PND
                NY
                PSX 5
                LRESUME
                PGO PRINT
                PGO QUIT
```

Figure 11-9. *First seven statements of WPLCOPY*

```
<    Z Mem:46624 Len:   221 Pos:   221 Tab:    21 File:wplcopy
WPLCOPY        P This program prints 5 copies of RESUME
               PND
               NY
               PSX 5
               LRESUME
               PGO PRINT
               PGO QUIT
PRINT          PNP
               PSX -1
               PGO PRINT
```

Figure 11-10.   *Loop added to WPLCOPY*

enter the [G] command in Control-Character Insertion mode. Then save this edited file with [S]= and clear the screen.

Let's run the program now to test it. Set the Print/Program Commands menu for your printer and a left margin of 5. Turn on the printer. Since the prefix is set for /Practice/Auction, you need only enter the file name "**DO WPLCOPY**" after giving the PDO command.

As you just heard, the Quit statements first sound the beeper; then the message that the program is done appears on the screen.

```
<    Z Mem:46542 Len:   303 Pos:   121 Tab:    19 File:wplcopy
WPLCOPY        P This program prints 5 copies of RESUME
               PND
               NY
               PSX 5
               LRESUME
               PGO PRINT
               PGO QUIT
PRINT          PNP
               PSX -1
               PGO PRINT
QUIT           PPR 5 copies printed
               PIN G  (press RETURN)
               NY
```

Figure 11-11.   *Complete WPLCOPY program*

When you press RETURN, the screen is cleared on the Apple Writer II editing display.

To modify this program to print copies of your own file, you can change the fifth statement so that it contains your file name. You can set (X) initially to the number of copies you want to print.

Numeric variables are useful for executing various addition and subtraction commands in WPL programs. The value of the numeric variable can be increased as well as decreased during the program's execution. In WPLAUTOLET, the program sets the (X) variable initially to 1. Then, in loading the addresses, it loads the first address, because the number 1 in its marker matches the current value of (X). After printing the first address, the value of (X) is increased by one ("PSX+1" in line 17). In the next loop, the program looks for the new value of (X), the number 2 in the second address. When (X) is increased to a number greater than the number of the last address, the program exits the loop.

Setting a String Variable

Like numeric variables, string variables in a WPL program take the values you designate to them. A string is a sequence of up to 64 characters. It can include letters, numbers, spaces, and any other character that the keyboard can produce.

In effect, a string variable is a placeholder in a program that you fill with text, that is, with the string you specify. You can set up to four string variables in one program: $A, $B, $C, and $D.

Three WPL commands designate the contents of string variables.

- The Assign String command (PAS) lets you specify the content of a string variable as a statement within a program, using an equal sign: "PAS Lee Herman=$A".
- The Load String command (PLS) lets you load text marked off by delimiters from a file into a program: "PLSREPORT2!beginning marker!end marker!N =$B".
- The Input command (PIN) lets you designate a response from the keyboard as the content of a string variable: "PIN Select A-J =$C".

In addition, you can command a program to compare the contents of a string variable to another string. The WPL command is

Compare Strings (PCS). When you give the Compare Strings command, conditional execution results. If the two strings compared are equal, the next statement is executed. Any difference at all — in length or case or in any other particular — causes the next statement to be skipped.

String variables can also be used to set the value of a numeric variable. For example, you can write a statement "PSX $D".

String variables are a flexible, powerful feature of WPL. To demonstrate their usefulness, we'll put two string variables in a program and assign their values by means of responses to Input commands. We'll use the Compare Strings command to evaluate the keyboard responses and determine whether the program should proceed or quit. The value of (X) will be set from one of the string variables.

If the WPLCOPY program ran successfully, the screen should now be clear. The program you'll write is a more elaborate version of WPLCOPY. We can call it WPLCOPY2. It allows for any file name to be entered from the keyboard and for any number of copies to be specified, also from the keyboard.

Type the first three statements as follows. Remember to use [V] for the [L] command.

```
NY
PND
PPR [L] ****WPLCOPY2****
```

The first two commands clear memory and turn off the display. The Print a Line command clears the screen before printing the program's title.

Now enter the next three lines exactly as follows:

```
Name      PIN Enter Name of File      =$A
          PCS /$A//
          PGO QUIT
```

The screen should now look like Figure 11-12.

The Input command asks that a file name be entered. (It assumes that the prefix is set for the data disk containing both the file and the WPLCOPY2 program.) The program converts whatever text is entered for the file name to the string variable, "$A".

The next command compares the contents of "$A" to nothing ("/$A//"). If no file name is entered, "$A" contains nothing. Therefore, conditional execution causes the "GO QUIT" state-

```
  <    Z Mem:46685 Len:   160 Pos:   159 Tab:    20 File:wplcopy2
                NY
                PND
                PPR  L    ****WPLCOPY2****
   NAME         PIN   Enter Name of File        =$A
                PCS /$A//
                PGO QUIT
```

Figure 11-12.   *Six lines of WPLCOPY*

ment to take effect. If a file name is entered, "$A" does not equal nothing, and the next statement is skipped.

Add the next four lines:

```
Number    PIN     Enter Number of Copies    =$B
          PCS /$B//
          PGO QUIT
          PSX $B
```

These commands take the response from the keyboard for the number of copies, convert it to "$B", and compare "$B" to nothing. Again, if no number is entered, the program ends. If a number has been entered, that number is set as the value of "(X)".

Now type the next section of the program as follows:

```
          L$A
          PGO PRINT
          PGO QUIT
PRINT     PNP
          PSX −1
          PGO PRINT
```

As you probably recognize, these commands are the same as those in the earlier version, except that the Load command looks for the file name that "$A" represents, instead of RESUME.

The final lines of the program are the same as WPLCOPY. Add them now:

```
QUIT      PIN [G] Printing done (Press Return)
          NY
```

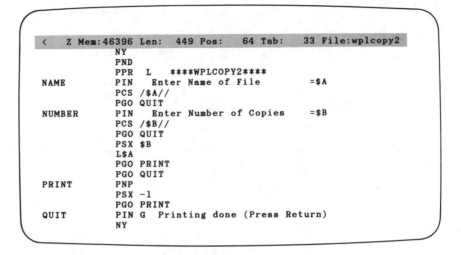

```
<   Z Mem:46396 Len:   449 Pos:    64 Tab:    33 File:wplcopy2
                 NY
                 PND
                 PPR   L   ****WPLCOPY2****
NAME             PIN    Enter Name of File         =$A
                 PCS /$A//
                 PGO QUIT
NUMBER           PIN    Enter Number of Copies      =$B
                 PCS /$B//
                 PGO QUIT
                 PSX $B
                 L$A
                 PGO PRINT
                 PGO QUIT
PRINT            PNP
                 PSX -1
                 PGO PRINT
QUIT             PIN G  Printing done (Press Return)
                 NY
```

Figure 11-13.   *Complete WPLCOPY2 program*

The screen should now look like Figure 11-13. After checking for typing and syntax errors, save this program as WPLCOPY2. Then clear the screen.

Turn on the printer and run the program. You can enter the name of any file in the AUCTION subdirectory and print it any number of times.

REVIEW EXERCISES

1. Modify the WPLAUTOLET program to insert the first and last name in "(Name)".

2. How would you modify the WPLCOPY2 program to enter a name for a second file and print (X) copies of both files?

IV

APPENDIXES

The appendixes are intended to be reference guides. Appendix A covers setting up a serial printer and a modem to work with Apple Writer II and using the keyboard together with the printer as a typewriter. Appendix B offers a comparison of Apple Writer DOS 3.3 and Apple Writer II ProDOS. Appendix C explains how to customize the Master disk for default print and tab settings. Appendix D summarizes Apple Writer II commands.

A

SERIAL PRINTERS, MODEMS, AND TERMINAL/PRINTER MODE

You can use one of the ProDOS commands in Apple Writer II to give the program the specifications for a particular serial peripheral device you are using: "Set Printer/Modem Interface". All modems are serial and some printers are. Once Apple Writer II is properly set to work with your modem, you operate it in Terminal/Printer mode. Both serial and parallel printers can also use Terminal/Printer mode. Terminal/Printer mode, as the name suggests, has a dual purpose. The "Terminal" part of this mode allows you to send and receive digital data over the telephone lines with a modem. The "Printer" part lets you use the keyboard to send typed characters directly to the printer. In effect, this turns the keyboard and printer into a typewriter.

With a modem and Apple Writer II, you can send document files to another computer. You can also receive documents from another computer and save them on your data disks. For example, if you have a computer at work and one at home, you can easily transfer information between them. Writers can send manuscripts electronically over long distances in a fraction of the time it would take to mail a printout of the text.

Other uses for modems are becoming increasingly popular. Information services to which you subscribe provide sources of data via modem. For example, you can obtain the latest stock market quotes. Specialized services include data bases for doctors and lawyers that provide information from reference materials. Students at certain colleges can search the campus library's resources from their dormitories.

If you don't have a modem, you can still use Terminal/Printer mode to make the keyboard and printer operate like a typewriter. This is convenient for typing addresses on envelopes. You can also type labels and type information on printed forms.

This Appendix explains the preliminary steps necessary to take advantage of Apple Writer II's Terminal/Printer mode. It also explains how to prepare Apple Writer II to communicate with a serial printer for any Print commands as well as in Terminal/Printer mode. If you have a parallel printer and no modem, you can skip the next two sections and just read the last section.

SETTING THE PRINTER/MODEM INTERFACE

To tell Apple Writer II how your modem or serial printer handles data, you select "Set Printer/Modem Interface" on the ProDOS Commands menu. The prompt appears as in Figure A-1.

You respond to the prompt by typing 1 or 2, depending on which serial device you are using and which slot has been assigned to it. For the Apple IIe, a serial interface card for a printer should be installed in slot 1 and a serial interface card for a modem installed in slot 2. (If you have serial interface cards installed in slots other than these, you cannot use the ProDOS commands menu to describe your device to Apple Writer II; instead, you or your dealer must make any adjustments on the serial interface card itself.)

The ports on the Apple IIc corresponding to the slot assignments on the Apple IIe are port 1 for a printer and port 2 for a modem. The Apple IIc does not require that you install interface

```
    ProDOS COMMANDS

A.  Catalog
B.  Rename File
C.  Lock    File
D.  Unlock File
E.  Delete File
F.  List Volumes On-Line
G.  Create Subdirectory
H.  Set Prefix Volume
I.  Format Volume
J.  Set Printer/Modem Interface

    Press RETURN to Exit

    Enter Your Selection (A - J) :j

Set Which Slot/Port (1 or 2) :
```

Figure A-1.   *ProDOS Commands menu with J selected*

cards; it comes equipped for you to plug in serial devices to the appropriate port.

In response to the prompt, choose slot 1 if you are using a serial printer with an interface card in slot 1 (Apple IIe) or if you are connecting a serial printer to port 1 (Apple IIc). Choose slot 2 if you are using a modem with an interface card in slot 2 (Apple IIe) or if you are connecting a modem to port 2 (Apple IIc).

When you type 1 in response to the prompt, the default settings for a serial printer appear on the screen, as in Figure A-2. Typing 2 in response to the prompt puts on the screen the default settings for a modem, as shown in Figure A-3.

In both cases, you can either accept the default settings or inform Apple Writer II about the correct values for the following:

- baud
- data bits
- parity
- stop bits.

The *baud rate* is the speed at which data is transmitted to or from your device. The three other specifications determine the length of

```
        ProDOS COMMANDS

A.  Catalog
B.  Rename File
C.  Lock    File
D.  Unlock File
E.  Delete File
F.  List Volumes On-Line
G.  Create Subdirectory
H.  Set Prefix Volume
I.  Format Volume
J.  Set Printer/Modem Interface

    Press RETURN to Exit

    Enter Your Selection (A - J) :j

Set Which Slot/Port (1 or 2) :1

Format: Baud,Data Bits,Parity,Stop Bits

Enter values :0,8,N,2
```

Figure A-2.   *Default serial settings for a printer*

```
        ProDOS COMMANDS

A.  Catalog
B.  Rename File
C.  Lock    File
D.  Unlock File
E.  Delete File
F.  List Volumes On-Line
G.  Create Subdirectory
H.  Set Prefix Volume
I.  Format Volume
J.  Set Printer/Modem Interface

    Press RETURN to Exit

    Enter Your Selection (A - J) :j

Set Which Slot/Port (1 or 2) :2

Format: Baud,Data Bits,Parity,Stop Bits

Enter values :0,8,N,1
```

Figure A-3.   *Default serial settings for a modem*

a unit transmitted, or the *data format*. The manual for your printer should state the correct baud rate and the specifications for data format.

The default value for baud rate is zero. If you accept this default and make no changes, Apple Writer II uses the switch settings on the interface card. But if the values are not correct for the device you are using, you can change them through the program to override the switch settings on the interface card.

Selecting Values for a Serial Printer

Apple Writer II's defaults may be correct for your printer. If you are using an Apple IIe with a printer interface card that has been set up for your printer, the defaults should be acceptable; Apple Writer II then uses the switch settings on the printer interface card. If you are using an Apple IIc with an Apple Imagewriter or with a Scribe printer, the defaults should also be acceptable.

However, if the switches on the printer interface card are set for a particular printer and you wish to use a different serial printer that requires a different baud rate or data format, you can make the changes in Apple Writer II rather than resetting the switches on the interface card. Should you need to find out exactly how the switches are set, the manual for your serial interface card should provide this information.

If you want to override any of the settings on the serial interface card, do not accept zero for baud rate. Make sure you also select the correct baud rate. A common rate for printers is 9600 baud.

To set new values, first type the baud rate followed by a comma. Then type the number of data bits (6, 7, or 8), followed by a comma. Next, type N, E, or O for parity, followed by a comma; the letters stand for "none," "even," or "odd." Finally, type a number for stop bits (1 or 2) and press RETURN.

Once you have changed the settings on the ProDOS commands menu, they remain in effect until you turn off the computer. Rather than changing the values every time you start up Apple Writer II, you can save your serial settings in a print value file and load the file when you are ready to print. You can also make your serial settings the defaults Apple Writer II loads automatically at start up. (See Appendix C.)

Selecting Values for a Modem

Apple Writer II needs to know about baud rate and data format when you use a modem. As it does for a serial printer, Apple Writer II can work either with the switch settings on the modem's serial interface card or the program can override the switches. By accepting the defaults for slot 2, you tell Apple Writer II to use the switch settings on the modem's interface card. For the Apple IIc, the default serial settings for a modem are correct for the Apple 300 Baud Modem.

Your modem operates either as a sender or receiver of data, or both. Consequently, the baud rate and data format of the device with which you communicate must be compatible with yours for successful data transmission. By setting the printer/modem interface for slot (or port) 2 in Apple Writer II, you can tell the program how to coordinate data transmission between your device and its intended sender or receiver.

Modems usually transmit data at 300 baud or 1200 baud. Most 1200 baud modems can also transmit at 300 baud; however, a 300 baud modem cannot send or receive at 1200 baud. Therefore, if you have a 1200 baud modem, you must transmit at 300 baud to another 300 baud modem.

Matching the data format so that both modems use the same number of data bits, parity, and stop bits is essential to the quality of transmission. When these values do not match, you may receive extra unrecognizable characters on the screen, or characters may even be lost. Similarly, the data you send may be less readable on the other end.

When you or your dealer installed the serial interface card in the Apple IIe, the switches were probably set to work with your modem. The manual for the serial interface card should explain these settings. If you are not certain how to interpret the switch settings, ask your dealer.

If you are communicating with a modem that uses the baud rate and data format set on your serial interface card, you can accept Apple Writer II's default serial settings for slot (or port) 2. Many of the information services can also accommodate your baud rate and data format without your making adjustments.

To communicate with another modem user, you should determine which values are mutually compatible and change Apple Writer II's settings on the ProDOS Commands menu. If you regularly communicate with a modem that requires changing the serial settings, you can save the settings in a print value file. Such a file can also include the correct print destination (PD2), which is explained in the next section. Unless you use your modem much more often than your printer, you probably would not want to make the serial and print values the default settings Apple Writer II loads automatically at startup. Should you wish to do so, see Appendix C.

USING A MODEM IN TERMINAL/PRINTER MODE

Before entering Terminal/Printer mode to use a modem with Apple Writer II, there are three preliminary steps:

1. Set the printer/modem interface (as explained in the preceding section), making any necessary changes to the defaults.

2. Give the Print Destination command (PD) on the Print/ Program Commands menu, setting the value that represents the slot (or port) for the modem (usually PD2).

3. Make sure that your modem is properly connected to the computer and to your phone line, according to the instructions that came with the modem.

Then turn on the modem and go to the Additional Functions menu. Select "Connect Keyboard to Printer/Modem". The screen will look like Figure A-4.

```
ESC-R)ecord E)cho F)ilter Q)uit
```

Figure A-4.   *Options in Terminal/Printer mode*

The top of the screen indicates four options: Record, Echo, Filter, and Quit. To choose any one of the options, you press ESC and then the first letter. Thus, to leave Terminal/Printer mode, you press ESC-Q.

If you select Record, the data you receive is stored in Apple Writer II's memory, providing sufficient memory is available. When you leave Terminal/Printer mode, you can edit the data, save it to your data disk, and print it.

The options Echo and Filter can be used to make text appearing on the screen more readable. Select Echo to change the way characters you type are displayed on the screen. If each character is displayed twice or no characters at all are displayed, press ESC-E for normal display. If you select Filter, CONTROL characters won't be displayed on the screen.

If when you enter Terminal/Printer mode the cursor does not blink, Apple Writer II and the modem are not working together properly. And if you give a command to the modem and get no response, you'll need to determine the cause. Leave Terminal/Printer mode by pressing ESC-Q. If the editing display does not appear, press CONTROL-RESET. Then turn off the computer.

Check first that the cable and phone wires are connected. If this is not the problem, consult your modem manual for potential sources of malfunctioning. One modification that frequently needs to be made is in the cable linking the serial interface card in the Apple IIe to the modem. If the modem manual and the serial interface manual do not provide clear instructions for altering the cable, let your dealer take care of it.

Sending a Document File via Modem

After setting the printer/modem interface and the print destination, you can prepare a document file to be sent to another modem. Follow these steps:

1. Load the file into Apple Writer II's memory in Text Entry mode.
2. Turn on your modem and enter Terminal/Printer mode.

3. Give the commands listed in your modem manual to dial the receiving modem's telephone number.

4. When you have been connected to the other modem, leave terminal mode (ESC-Q).

5. On the editing display, give the command to print a file: [P]NP.

6. When the file has been sent, reenter Terminal/Printer mode and command your modem to hang up your phone.

While the file is being sent, the editing display does not show a blinking cursor. The blinking cursor reappears when the file has been completely transmitted. The amount of time it takes to send a file varies. A 1200 baud modem transmits four times as fast as a 300 baud modem.

Receiving Data via Modem

To receive information from a data service or to receive files from another computer, follow these steps (after setting the printer/modem interface and the print destination):

1. Turn on your modem and then enter Terminal/Printer mode.

2. Give the commands that connect you to the information service, according to the instructions for that service; or give the commands that connect you to the other computer.

3. Select Echo if the characters you type are doubled or do not appear on your screen; select Filter if you want to eliminate CONTROL characters on the screen.

4. Select Record if you want to save the data.

5. When the data or file has been received, give the commands to sign off the information service, if necessary, and command your modem to hang up your phone.

6. Leave Terminal/Printer mode (ESC-Q) and, if you recorded the data, the text will be on the editing display where you can now edit it and save it.

USING KEYBOARD AND PRINTER AS A TYPEWRITER

To turn the keyboard and printer into a typewriter, you must first set the value for Print Destination (PD) on the Print/Program Commands menu to correspond to the slot (or port) for your printer (usually PD1). Also on the Print/Program Commands menu, set the value for Single Page (SP) for either single sheets or fanfold paper. Envelopes and printed forms are treated like single sheets of paper. Gummed labels on fanfold paper require the setting for continuous sheets. If you have a serial printer, the printer/modem interface must also be set on the ProDOS Commands menu.

Now turn on the printer. If the printer is not on when you try to enter Terminal/Printer mode, the program stops. In order to recover from this, you have to reset the program by pressing the CONTROL, OPEN APPLE, and RESET keys simultaneously. Once the program is reset, you will have to go through all of the preliminaries again.

With the printer on, enter Terminal/Printer mode by going to the Additional Functions menu and selecting "Connect keyboard to Printer/Modem". The options at the top of the screen apply only to a modem, not to a printer. Note, though, that to leave Terminal/Printer mode, you press ESC-Q.

You can now type. If the printer does not immediately print each character, it will print a complete line when you press RETURN. Different printers behave differently. You must press RETURN to end a line; word wraparound is not in effect in Terminal/Printer mode.

Whether or not the printer immediately prints typed characters, you cannot edit them in Terminal/Printer mode. The printer can only print exactly what you type, just like a typewriter.

You may need to experiment in order to coordinate line feeds between the computer and your printer. Try first with Carriage Return (CR) set on the Print/Program Commands menu as it is when you use the Print commands in Apple Writer II. If you get no line feed or double-spacing, leave Terminal/Printer mode and adjust Carriage Return on the Print/Program Commands menu to increase or decrease the spacing.

Once you have tried typing to the printer, the procedure can be summarized as follows:

1. Set the Print/Program Commands menu for Print Destination (PD), Single Page (SP), and Carriage Return (CR).
2. Set the printer/modem interface on the ProDOS Commands menu, if you have a serial printer.
3. Turn on the printer.
4. Enter Terminal/Printer mode on the Additional Functions menu.
5. Press RETURN at the end of a line.
6. Leave Terminal/Printer mode by pressing ESC-Q.

B

COMPARING VERSIONS OF APPLE WRITER II: DOS 3.3 VS. PRODOS

The DOS 3.3 and ProDOS versions of Apple Writer II are much more alike than they are different. All of the commands you give in Apple Writer II and in WPL are the same in both versions. The main difference is that the ProDOS version offers several features not available in the DOS 3.3 version.

Unlike Apple Writer II DOS 3.3, the ProDOS version allows you to operate a modem inside the program. Also there are more printers that can communicate with Apple Writer II ProDOS. A serial printer/modem interface and a new Terminal/Printer mode enable you to tell Apple Writer II ProDOS about your printer and modem.

Another feature introduced in the ProDOS version is the ability to create a subdirectory. Only volumes and files are used in Apple Writer II DOS 3.3.

Three commands not available in the DOS 3.3 version are useful additions in the ProDOS version. One is [A], the Adjust Screen Display command, which matches the length of the line of text on the screen to the left and right margins set on the Print/Program Commands menu. The second is [_], the Page/Line Count command, which provides the page number and line number at the position of the cursor. The third is a new tab function: using the SOLID APPLE key together with either the LEFT ARROW or RIGHT ARROW key allows you to tab over text without inserting spaces.

Apple Writer II DOS 3.3 has a feature the ProDOS version does not have: the WPL Program MOVER on the Master disk, which copies a file from one data disk to another. Instead, with Apple Writer II ProDOS you copy a file using the ProDOS User's Disk for the Apple IIe and the Systems Utilities Disk for the Apple IIc.

Other differences can be categorized as differences in the menus, differences in syntax, and differences in default settings. These are covered in the following sections.

COMPARING MENUS

The menu from which you select operating system features is, understandably, different for each version. Figure B-1 shows the DOS Commands menu for Apple Writer II DOS 3.3, and Figure B-2 shows the ProDOS Commands menu for Apple Writer II ProDOS. Note that the ProDOS Commands menu lists four selections

```
   DOS COMMANDS

A. Catalog
B. Rename File
C. Verify File
D. Lock    File
E. Unlock File
F. Delete File
G. Initialize disk

   Press RETURN to Exit

   Enter your selection (A - G) :
```

Figure B-1.   *DOS Commands menu for Apple Writer II DOS 3.3*

```
  ProDOS COMMANDS

A.  Catalog
B.  Rename File
C.  Lock    File
D.  Unlock File
E.  Delete File
F.  List Volumes On-Line
G.  Create Subdirectory
H.  Set Prefix Volume
I.  Format Volume
J.  Set Printer/Modem Interface

    Press RETURN to Exit

    Enter Your Selection (A - J) :
```

Figure B-2. *ProDOS Commands menu for Apple Writer II ProDOS*

that do not appear on the DOS Commands menu: F, List Volumes On-Line; G, Create Subdirectory; H, Set Prefix Volume; and J, Set Printer/Modem/Interface. Selection I, Format Volume, achieves the same result as G, Initialize Disk, on the DOS Commands menu. Also note that C, Verify File, appears on the DOS Commands menu but not on the ProDOS Commands menu.

The Additional Functions menu in Apple Writer II DOS 3.3 is shown in Figure B-3. Figure B-4 shows the comparable menu in Apple Writer II ProDOS. Notice that selection I is slightly different: the ProDOS version can connect the keyboard to a modem as well as to a printer. In Apple Writer II ProDOS, you cannot convert Apple Writer 1.1 files as you can in Apple Writer II DOS 3.3. You can, however, convert Apple Writer II DOS 3.3 files to Apple Writer II ProDOS with the ProDOS User's Disk (IIe) and the Systems Utilities Disk (IIc).

The Print/Program Commands menu contains the identical commands in both versions. The same commands can also be embedded in documents. However, Apple Writer II DOS 3.3 cannot print past column 79, and in Apple Writer II ProDOS, you cannot print to a file, that is, set Print Destination (PD) to 8.

Both versions have a Help menu; these menus differ according to the differences in the two versions.

```
      ADDITIONAL FUNCTIONS MENU

A. Load Tab File
B. Save Tab File
C. Load Print/Program Value File
D. Save Print/Program Value File
E. Load [G]lossary File
F. Save [G]lossary File
G. Toggle Carriage Return Display
H. Toggle Data Line Display
I. Connect Keyboard to Printer
J. Convert Apple Writer 1.1 Files
K. Quit Apple Writer

      Press RETURN to Exit

      Enter your selection (A - K) :
```

Figure B-3.   *Additional Functions Menu in Apple Writer II DOS 3.3*

COMPARING DEFAULT SETTINGS

Three of the default settings on the Apple Writer II DOS 3.3 Print/
Program Commands menu are different from their counterparts on
the menu in Apple Writer II ProDOS. In Apple Writer II DOS 3.3,

```
      ADDITIONAL FUNCTIONS MENU

A. Load Tab File
B. Save Tab File
C. Load Print/Program Value File
D. Save Print/Program Value File
E. Load [G]lossary File
F. Save [G]lossary File
G. Toggle Carriage Return Display
H. Toggle Data Line Display
I. Connect Keyboard to Printer/Modem
J. Quit Apple Writer

      Press RETURN to Exit

      Enter your selection (A - J) :
```

Figure B-4.   *Additional Functions Menu in Apple Writer II ProDOS*

the default for Left Margin (LM) is 9, for Right Margin (RM) it is 79, and for Carriage Return (CR) it is 0. In the Apple Writer II ProDOS the default settings are LM0, RM78, and CR1.

The default tab settings are also different. In Apple Writer II DOS 3.3, the ruler is automatically set with tabs every eight spaces, ending at column 72. The default tabs on the ruler in Apple Writer II ProDOS are set every tenth space, up to column 69.

The files on the Apple Writer II DOS 3.3 Master disk that contain the default print values and tab settings are named PRT.SYS and TAB.SYS; on the Apple Writer II ProDOS Master disk, these files are named SYS.PRT and SYS.TAB.

COMPARING SYNTAX

The rules for naming volumes, subdirectories, and files in Apple Writer II ProDOS are more limiting than in Apple Writer II DOS 3.3. (There are no subdirectory names in Apple Writer II DOS 3.3, because there are no subdirectories.)

Topic	Covered In
List Volumes On-Line	Getting Started
Naming volumes, subdirectories, and files	Getting Started, Chapters 2 and 5
Help menu	Chapter 1
Set Prefix	Chapter 3
Adjust Screen Display command	Chapter 4
Default print values	Chapters 4 and 7 Appendix C
Create Subdirectory	Chapter 5
Tabbing over text and spaces	Chapter 8
Printing more than 80 columns	Chapter 8
Default tab settings	Chapter 8, Appendix C
Page and Line Count command	Chapter 9
Delimiters	Chapters 9 and 11
Modems	Appendix A
Set Printer/Modem Interface	Appendix A
Connect Keyboard to Printer	Appendix A

Table B-1.   *Summary of Distinctions Between Apple Writer II Versions*

The way Apple Writer II DOS 3.3 determines which disk drive contains which disk is not the same as in Apple Writer II ProDOS. Instead, the ProDOS version uses delimiters (slashes) to separate volume, subdirectory, and file names. The prefix determines which disk the files are loaded from and saved to.

In effect, designating the disk and slot drive in Apple Writer II DOS 3.3 is comparable to setting the prefix in Apple Writer II ProDOS; however, the procedures differ significantly.

Table B-1 summarizes these differences and indicates where in this book you can find explanations pertaining to Apple Writer II ProDOS.

C

CUSTOMIZING FILES ON THE MASTER DISK

Apple Writer II automatically loads the default values on the Print/Program Commands menu and the default tab settings on the ruler when you start the program. You can customize your working copy of the Master disk so that your defaults are automatically loaded instead. You should not, of course, alter the original Master disk; if you ever need to make another copy, you'll want the original to be intact.

Figure C-1 shows the two files listed on the AW2MASTER catalog that Apple Writer II loads at startup. The SYS.PRT file contains the defaults for the Print/Program Commands menu. The SYS.TAB file contains the default tab settings.

Do not confuse the SYS.PRT or the SYS.TAB file with any other files on the Master disk. Notice that under the column headed "Type", there are several files categorized as "System" files; these files are essential for the program's proper operation. *Do not try to modify System files.* As you can see, the asterisk in front of them indicates that such files are locked; they should remain locked.

```
AW2MASTER (05/10/84 16:01) V000

Type     Blocks  Name           Created  Time   Modified  Time   Length
*System    30    PRODOS         09/28/83 00:00  09/18/84  00:00  14848
*System     1    AW.SYSTEM      05/15/84 12:28  01/11/84  17:51    461
 Binary     1    SYS.PRT        05/15/84 12:28  05/15/84  12:14    368
 Binary     1    SYS.TAB        05/15/84 12:28  04/20/84  14:08    128
*System    33    AWC.SYS        12/12/84 00:00  12/12/84  00:00  16009
*System    34    AWD.SYS        12/12/84 00:00  12/12/84  00:00  16395
*System    33    AWB.SYS        12/12/84 00:00  12/12/84  00:00  15967
*Binary     9    FORMATTER      05/15/84 12:29  03/15/84  15:13   4096
*Text       1    ADDRESSES      05/15/84 12:29  04/20/84  14:11    159
*Text       3    FORMLET        05/15/84 12:29  04/20/84  14:11    590
*Text       3    CLAUSES        05/15/84 12:30  04/20/84  14:11    651
*Text       1    ADDRS          05/15/84 12:30  04/20/84  14:11    263
*Text       1    CONTRACTEND    05/15/84 12:30  04/20/84  14:12    508
*Text       1    CONTPRINT      05/15/84 12:30  04/20/84  14:12    420
*Text       1    FORMLETTER     05/15/84 12:30  04/20/84  14:13    453
```

Figure C-1.   *Files listed on AW2MASTER catalog*

CREATING A DEFAULT PRINT VALUES FILE

Some of the current defaults on the Print/Program Commands menu may be unsuitable for most of your work. For example, if the print destination (PD) for your printer is not 1, you must change PD every time you print; or if you generally use single sheets instead of fanfold paper, you must frequently change the default for SP. There may be left and right margin settings you use most of the time that would be more convenient than the current defaults.

To have Apple Writer II automatically load your defaults on the Print/Program Commands menu, you replace the defaults in the SYS.PRT file with your own print values. Here's how:

1. Rename the SYS.PRT file on the ProDOS Commands menu if you want to keep these print values on your working copy of the Master disk.

2. Put the Print/Program Commands menu on the screen and set the values you want to have loaded automatically each time you load the program.

3. Save your values as a print value file named SYS.PRT on the Additional Functions menu.

Unless you have occasional use for the defaults Apple Writer II sets, you might as well delete the SYS.PRT file by giving the file containing your defaults the same name. (The file still exists on the original Master disk.) But if you prefer to have both files on your working copy, you must rename SYS.PRT before you can give your file the same name.

If you are using a serial printer or a modem, you can also save your serial settings in the SYS.PRT file and they, too, will be loaded automatically when you start Apple Writer II. Set the serial interface (as explained in Appendix A) before you save the values you set on the Print/Program Commands menu.

CREATING A DEFAULT TAB FILE

To have Apple Writer II automatically load your default tab settings, you follow a similar procedure:

1. Rename the SYS.TAB file on the ProDOS Commands menu if you prefer to keep these tab settings on your copy of the Master disk.

2. With the ruler on the screen of the editing display, purge all the tabs at once or clear any tabs you don't want. Set the ones you do want.

3. Save your default tabs in a tab file named SYS.TAB on the Additional Functions menu.

D

COMMAND SUMMARY

This Appendix summarizes the commands in Apple Writer II. Table D-1 lists the CONTROL-character commands as they are given in Apple Writer II and in WPL. Table D-2 lists commands that only appear in WPL programs. Table D-3 shows all the ways to move the cursor, and Table D-4 indicates the methods for deleting and retrieving text.

Tables D-5 and D-6 list all the commands for printing and formatting. Tables D-7, D-8, and D-9 list the variations on the Load, Save, and Find commands, respectively.

In Apple Writer II	In WPL	Meaning
[A]	A	Adjust screen display
[B]	B	Move cursor to beginning of document
[C]	C	Enter Case Change mode
[D]	D	Set direction arrow
[E]	E	Move cursor to end of document
[F]	F	Search for text in document
[G]	G	Display Glossary buffer contents
[L]	L	Load file
[N]	N	Clear screen of editing display
[O]	O	Display ProDOS Commands menu
[P]	P	Give a Print command or a Program command
[Q]	Q	Display Additional Functions menu
[R]		Enter Replace mode
[S]	S	Save file
[T]	T	Give a Tab command
[V]		Enter Control-Character Insertion mode
[W]	W	Delete or retrieve word
[X]	X	Delete or retrieve paragraph
[Y]	Y	Split screen
[Z]	Z	Toggle word wraparound
[—]	—	Display page and line count

Table D-1.   *Control-Character Commands*

Command Name		Meaning
PAS	Assign String	Assign value on one side of = to string variable
PCS	Compare String	Compare one string (or string variable) to another string (or string variable)
PGO	Go	Execute next labeled command
PIN	Input	Display program message; wait for RETURN
PLS	Load String	Load text string from file
PND	No Display	Turn off screen display of document in memory
PPR	Print	Display program message
PQT	Quit	End program
PRT	Return	Return from subroutine
PSR	Subroutine	Execute subroutine
PSX	Set X	Set value of numeric variable X
PSY	Set Y	Set value of numeric variable Y
PSZ	Set Z	Set value of numeric variable Z
PYD	Yes Display	Turn on screen display of document in memory

Table D-2.   *WPL Commands*

Press		To Move Cursor
↑	UP ARROW	Up one line
↓	DOWN ARROW	Down one line
←	LEFT ARROW	Left one character
→	RIGHT ARROW	Right one character
⌘ - ↑	SOLID APPLE- UP ARROW	Up 22 lines
⌘ - ↓	SOLID APPLE- DOWN ARROW	Down 22 lines
⌘ - ←	SOLID APPLE- LEFT ARROW	Left one word
⌘ - →	SOLID APPLE- RIGHT ARROW	Right one word
⌘ - TAB	SOLID APPLE- TAB	Over text and spaces
[B]	CONTROL-B	Beginning of document
[E]	CONTROL-E	End of document

Table D-3.   *Cursor Movement Commands*

Keys		Function
DELETE		Deletes a character permanently
⌂ - ←	OPEN APPLE- LEFT ARROW	Deletes a character temporarily
⌂ - →	OPEN APPLE- RIGHT ARROW	Retrieves a character
[W] (<)	CONTROL-W	Deletes a word temporarily
[W] (>)	CONTROL-W	Retrieves a word
[X] (<)	CONTROL-X	Deletes a paragraph temporarily
[X] (>)	CONTROL-X	Retrieves a paragraph

Table D-4.   *Delete and Retrieve Commands*

	Keys	Meaning
	[P]?	Display Print/Program Commands menu
	[P]NP	Print document
	[P]CP	Print subsequent document
	[P]DO	Start WPL program

Table D-5. *Print Commands*

	With [P]	Command	Default	Meaning
	SP	Single Page	0	Sets printer for fanfold paper
	PD	Print Destination	1	Printer connected to card in slot 1 or to port 1
	CR	Carriage Return	1	Apple Writer II issues a line feed
	LM	Left Margin	0	Sets left margin
	PM	Paragraph Margin	0	Indents first line of paragraph
	RM	Right Margin	78	Sets right margin
	TM	Top Margin	1	Sets blank line(s) between header and first line of text
	BM	Bottom Margin	1	Sets blank line(s) between last line of page text and footer
	PN	Page Number	1	Sets number of first page for counting
	PL	Printed Lines	58	Sets total number of printed lines on a page
	PI	Page Interval	66	Sets number of lines per page from top to bottom edge of paper
	LI	Line Interval	0	Sets line spacing
	UT	Underline Token	\	Marks text to be underlined
		Print Mode	LJ	Sets how text is distributed between left and right margins
	LJ			
	FJ			
	CJ			
	RJ			
	TL	Top Line	(blank)	Formats a header or page number
	BL	Bottom Line	(blank)	Formats a footer or page number

Table D-6. *Printing Commands and Formatting Commands*

Keys	Meaning
[L] file name	Load file named
[L]?	Display catalog
[L]=	Load file named on data line
[L]#!beginning!end!	Copy text between delimiters
[L]file name \	Peek at file named
[L]file name!beginning!end!	Load part of file named
[L]file name!beginning!end!N	Load part of file named without markers
[L]file name!beginning!end!A	Load all occurrences of text between delimiters from file named
[L]file name!beginning!end!NA	Load all occurrences of text between file named without markers

Table D-7.   *Load Commands*

Keys	Meaning
[S]file name	Save document in memory to disk
[S]?	Display catalog
[S]=	Save in file named on data line
[S]file name!end!	Save part of document on screen in separate file
[S]file name!end!+	Save part of document on screen onto end of named file

Table D-8.   *Save Commands*

Keys	Meaning
[F]/text/	Find first occurrence of text in document
[F]/text/text/	Find and replace text
[F]/text/text/A	Find and replace all occurrences
[F]/text//	Find text and replace with nothing

Table D-9.   *Find Commands*

INDEX